Leigh
Adams
THE BOOK

Leigh
Adams
THE BOOK

BRIAN BURFORD & LEIGH ADAMS

The
History
Press

First published 2010

The History Press
The Mill, Brimscombe Port
Stroud, Gloucestershire, GL5 2QG
www.thehistorypress.co.uk

British Library Cataloguing in Publication Data.
A catalogue record for this book is available from the British Library.

ISBN 978 0 7524 5673 7

Typesetting and origination by The History Press
Printed in Great Britain

Contents

Acknowledgements

Brian Burford

No matter how versed you might be in the subject matter, a project of this size is rarely completed without valuable assistance and co-operation of many people. Therefore I'd like to thank the following people for their help and giving up their valuable time: Pete Ansell, Richard Clark, Rod Colquhoun, Gordon Day, James Easter, Irek Igielski, Tony Jackson, Mark Loram, Jason Lyons, Tim Osmond, Randy Owen, Shane Parker, Mike Patrick, Mick Smith, Alan Whale, and thanks to the staff at The History Press.

A special thank you, of course, to Leigh for his generosity and his time, Kylie for her unwavering and dedicated help, and his parents for taking time out during their visit to contribute their memories of their son's glittering career.

This book is dedicated to my little friend Tiger (may your spirit always roam free) and to my hero and very special friend, Kelly Moran – you were an inspiration. Travel well.

Leigh Adams

A big thanks to Brian for doing such a great job with this project. Thanks to Rocket for writing the foreword and Clarkie for the unique introduction, plus many great years of friendship. Of course, I must express my thanks to my family, who have sacrificed so much for my career, and Kylie for helping manage it all. Without the help of my parents I probably wouldn't have had this career to write about. My gratitude also goes to Broady for his unfailing years of support, Tim Osmond and my various other mechanics/support team over the years. Finally thanks to Mike Patrick, *Speedway Star*, my sponsors and supporters, plus Randy Owen and all the crew from Owen Bros for 18 great years.

Foreword

Well, finally a book about Leigh Adams, the rider, the career and most importantly the man that gave new meaning to the term 'control'. I first became aware of Leigh in the late '80s when I went along to a knockabout speedway track an hour south of Sydney called Appin.

It was run by former Australian Champion Bob Sharpe, who had somehow coerced the one and only Phil Crump to take part in one of his Sunday afternoon meetings. Crump's arrival in a two-tone Nissan Patrol four-wheel-drive was met with much enthusiasm by the locals, as was their fascination for the skinny little kid he had with him – some 'gun' kid from down south.

The stars of the Appin shows were Craig Boyce, Todd Wiltshire and, on occasion, Mick Poole. The 'Adams' kid was unique in a number of ways when compared to his New South Wales adversaries, many of whom he was seeing for the first time. Firstly, he was very young, something that was rare for a speedway rider in NSW, as we didn't have junior speedway like they did down south. Secondly, he wore JT Racing USA motocross body armour over his leathers – a bit weird, but interesting just the same. Thirdly, his bike was immaculate! It was as if he'd spent all week polishing it! Surely he didn't go as well as he looked – he must be just another cocky Victorian from the town that was perceived by the Mildura locals to 'own the sport'!

I can't remember who won that day, but I remember everyone asking 'who the hell is this Leigh Adams kid?' He simply did not make mistakes and looked almost as if he wasn't trying – I remember being at least a little envious of his technique.

My meetings with Leigh in the following couple of years were literally zero. I was a half-assed dirt tracker trying to ride speedway on a brand new bike that I only had because my mum won the lottery, while Leigh was on the crest of a wave and taking the Poole Pirates and the National League (now the Premier League) by storm.

Several years later, Leigh gave 15 competitors a free riding lesson in the 1992 Australian Championship at the now-defunct North Arm circuit in

Adelaide, and I was unfortunate enough to be one of the students that night, as were some riders with far better credentials than me. He annihilated the field and the writing was on the wall that we were watching someone out of the ordinary.

I got to know Leigh much better in the years that followed and while I don't claim to have all the answers, I think I know him better than most. Away from the track I believe Leigh is quite complex. We have been friends for the best part of 20 years and while I always get the feeling Leigh would bail me out if I were in some sort of trouble, we certainly aren't 'close' in the way you might be with a best mate.

I don't think I'm the Lone Ranger there – Leigh has some good friends and he treats them well, but he's not typical in a 'mate' sense. He's not a loner either – he is generally drawn to extroverts and I've long believed this is a side-effect of his utter professionalism over such a long period, which simply does not allow for outlandish behaviour. What I'm saying is that Leigh gets his kicks from other people telling stories about their experiences. He giggles uncontrollably at any high-quality story told in the right manner and he'll often request to hear the same story twice, such is his fascination for the stupidity of others.

One of the things that played a huge part in Leigh and I striking up a strong and enduring friendship, came in the early '90s when he and I toured Poland as part of a young Australia team. I think two things became clear to Leigh that week (apart from the fact that I couldn't ride). The first was that my bikes were absolute garbage and really weren't fit to be used as doorstops, let alone for league racing; and second, was the fact that I came to life after the racing was done.

I was happier telling jokes and chasing chicks in the bar than lining up in a speedway race! This, I believe, was the catalyst for Leigh taking a shine to me – he's always looking for a laugh and doesn't want to have to generate the humour himself. I was the exact opposite of him and that made him laugh – everyone wants to laugh don't they?

It was around the time Jason Crump hit the UK scene for the first time (1992) that Leigh and I had started to hang out and I also found Jason to be good company. He was a superb kid and a credit to his parents, Phil and Carole. We shared a love of music and he often came over to hear the latest stuff I had – much of which I'd received from *Speedway Star*'s Richard Clark, a great bloke and talented musician in his own right.

Interestingly, I actually find a musical bond with someone to be a huge step toward long-term friendship, but despite Leigh liking music that I found repulsive, we got on like a house on fire, as did young Jason and I.

I'm not sure that I was ever prompted to choose between Jason and Leigh as far as which of the two I would support in their endeavours to become the world's best, and I have since learned that despite trying to convince myself otherwise, it is not until a race is in motion that I actually know who I'm cheering for – that is, I can't hide it!

During the 1995 Australian Title at Gosford, NSW, a terrible off-camber 280-metre track an hour north of Sydney, Jason and Leigh went head-to-head for the then prestigious National Championship. When they clashed I cheered for Leigh and my path was set – I was a Leigh Adams fan and my loyalty has never wavered despite always maintaining a healthy respect and admiration for Jason and what he has achieved.

Back in the UK, I remember a set of identical twins who rode for Arena-Essex in the early '90s and one of them was riding reserve for Arena when Leigh was the number 1. Adams was in a league of his own around that place, a track that requires the utmost skill, and on this particular night he was sublime.

One of the twins (the Ledwith brothers) said to Leigh, 'Man, that was insane, I'd cut off my arm to be able to do that.' The combination of the accent and that statement made me laugh aloud, but he was quick to pull me up. 'Hey, I'm serious mate,' he said.

It made me appreciate very early just what an effect Adams was having on the UK scene and later I understood where the person in question was coming from. It is tough for a reserve or 'struggling' rider to watch the ease with which Adams rides and then go out and struggle themselves – this became more apparent and relevant to me as time went on.

Has there ever been a more successful rider than Leigh Adams? Definitely. Has there ever been a better speedway rider than Leigh Adams? That is something that could fuel a debate between speedway fans for days on end. Leigh has suffered very few injuries during his career; in fact I would suggest that most footballers would have a worse medical record than Adams – incredible when you consider the nature of the sport. This, again, is all down to control.

I have been fortunate enough to contribute to a couple of books before now and I think the words contained within the covers of a book need to be an honest assessment of the subject, not a chance to unleash unlimited praise on it – that is something I find extremely boring. I consider books to be a slightly risky forum simply because the words cannot be taken back, so let's hope that won't be necessary!

What sort of person is Leigh Adams? I was almost going to say I don't really know, but I'd rather take a shot at it.

Leigh is a fiercely loyal family man and really I think he won his own personal World Championship the day he met Kylie. She's smart, attractive, loyal, a great mum and focused. Winning Kylie may well be Leigh's greatest victory to date. She treats his many house guests well, though I'm sure deep down, at least in my case, she must be thinking – 'not this big-mouthed dickhead again!'

Leigh is a businessman. Sure, speedway is a fragmented sport that demands a gypsy lifestyle, but the Adams clan knows where every penny comes from and where every penny goes. He has been a mainstay of the British scene for twenty years and in my opinion the backbone of it for the last five. If not the backbone, certainly the key vertebrae! To be able to roll up at a local track and see a rider like Leigh Adams perform is a luxury – one that will soon be just a memory.

In my experience I have found that Leigh is not a good listener, but he has improved in this department over the past few years. He looks at you while you're talking and politely nods his head, but I have often found there is no-one home. Perhaps he's busy? Perhaps he's distracted? Hard to say, but I'm enjoying speaking to him these days far more than I did five years ago.

He loves motor sport and has a 'special place' in his house where he gets away and watches anything that involves engines and wheels. He is very knowledgeable when it comes to this sort of thing and is a big fan of many drivers and riders, who unbeknown to him probably share mutual admiration.

So, with Leigh's career now drawing to a close and no senior World Championship in the cabinet, how does that make me, his number one fan and more importantly, a friend, feel? Not as bad as I thought to be honest. I used to have sleepless nights in Australia waiting for the results of each Grand Prix and on reflection there was certainly more bad news than good. But the highs were high and the lows were okay.

I consider myself very fortunate to have spent a considerable amount of time with Leigh over the past eighteen years and ride the waves of emotion that those years have brought. When he missed out on becoming world number three by the narrowest of margins in 2004 in Norway, I was trackside and I burst into tears. It might have looked stupid, but it's how I felt and was an accurate measure of how passionately I wanted Leigh to succeed. The train and plane trip early the next morning would be easily the lowest points of my involvement in speedway, possibly my life. At that level everyone wants to win and how could I begrudge Greg Hancock taking Leigh's number three? He is a great bloke himself.

I hope you get as much pleasure from reading this book as I have from being part of the Adams set-up for the last fifteen years. It's been a blast and I wouldn't change it for the world.

ROD COLQUHOUN
Long-time Leigh Adams media liaison and former rider

Introduction

It's no good. You just can't avoid it. Hide all the mirrors you want, it still won't prevent that fleeting glance of an old(-ish!) geezer you catch as you pass HMV, Waterstone's or a pub, i.e. places of interest in your high street. 'Who the hell is that shabby, decrepit-looking bloke? Oh hell, it's me!'

Time just doesn't wait for any man. It stomps all over him, gives him a good kicking against the wall, drags him into the gutter before sprinting off gleefully, leaving him pathetically panting long, long in its wake. In short, time passes while you stand there getting old. The skin wrinkled. The hair grey. The pace more leisurely.

And it really doesn't help matters when somebody you first met as a scrawny, curly-headed, wide-eyed Aussie youngster some 21 years ago (oh, lor!) turns to you and says 'Mate, I've got to start thinking about retirement.' Thanks. Thanks a bunch. Thanks for reminding me time has just done all of the above and a bit more. Yes, 21 years ago.

Leigh was with that well-known manager/mechanic and bearer of grudges, Norrie Allan. 'Norm', as he's affectionately known, was looking after Leigh on his first visit to our shores. He even had a little hair in those days. That's Norm I'm talking about.

My addled brain says it was Belle Vue and a washed-out meeting, but I wouldn't even bet your last dollar on all of that. But I do know we went for a bite to eat somewhere, and that's when I first talked with Leigh.

From the get-go he was friendly, approachable, intelligent, ever-curious and, as we all knew already, absolute dynamite on a speedway bike. I can't even begin to count the number of times our paths have crossed since (and I know he wouldn't want to!), but it's up there in the hundreds. And I can't even begin to count the number of laps I've watched this master at work. You're talking thousands. And I can't even begin to count the number of words I've written about the man. You're talking tens of thousands. But I do know you're going to struggle to find one bad word among that little lot. Come to think of it, you're shovelling snow uphill in a heat-wave to try and find that many bad times or laps either!

Hell, I can even remember this friendly, approachable, intelligent, ever-curious, piece of dynamite on two wheels introducing me, a few months later, to a drop-dead gorgeous girl who just happened to be his girlfriend. And who just happened to end up marrying him. Life? Unfair? Don't get me started. . . .

What do you give the man who's got nearly everything? Oh all right, Kylie. (And that was despite a best effort on day two of Leigh's 'Bucks' Do', as Aussies prefer to call their stag parties, serenading her down the 'phone from Swindon. Don't bother, it didn't work.)

Come to think of it, how come that time geezer has got it in for me but has left her completely alone? So, so unfair.

But, boy, have we had us some times in those 21 years and counting! You're right, I did say 'day two' a few sentences earlier, and that was just two of those times!

We've travelled the length and breadth of Britain's green and pleasant, Scotland, Wales and the home bit, to and fro to Poland, Sweden, Denmark, Czecho, Italy, Germany, Slovenia, Australia and Swindon. We've even thrown Dublin into the mix.

And where speedway bikes are ridden, he has done so, usually brilliantly. He in search of much fame, and much good fortune. Me happy to string along for the ride, and occasionally attempt to make some sense from such chaos. That I succeeded, if I ever did, would be down to the man himself, as ever, freely giving of his time, patiently answering often inane questions through the best of times and sometimes the worst.

But, always, always willing to sit down and talk about the latest 15-pointer, the new track record, the ones that got away, the many, many highs, the few lows, the wins, the Grand Prix golds, the wins, the World Cup victories, the wins, the odd, extremely odd, mechanical mishap, and the wins. Thinking back now, the man has the patience of an absolute saint!

Mind you, maybe he just can't face going through much more of that, and that's why the word 'retirement' has popped into his head! Perhaps that patience has finally been worn down.

'If he asks me that just one more time. . .'.

We've sat in the van and chewed the fat over life, the universe, the after-life (if any), world affairs, television, music (that tends to be one of the shorter conversations with the old boy, different tastes are one thing but you'd struggle to call his 'taste'), hopes, ambitions, and back to life again.

And speedway. Where all human life can be observed anyway. Edinburgh to Swindon. Workington to Swindon. Swindon to Stockholm. Stockholm to Wroclaw. Swindon to Swindon. Chewing up the miles like so much gum.

But in between all those miles, those wins, highs and lows, he's always been the same old Leigh. Generous, gentlemanly, gregarious (look it up, Leigh). Before practice. After practice. Pre-meeting. Post-meeting. If he's got the time, he has never ceased to share it (or his beer, come to that!).

'Gentlemanly, there you go, that's his downfall!'

Knew you'd leap on that one.

One word to all you doubters. Codswallop. (I can come up with much worse, but there's a family audience out there.) Haven't you been paying attention these past 21 years? The man's been an absolute legend.

And if you don't believe me, try taking a casual stroll through the streets of Leszno one morning in his company. It's like trying to take David Beckham for a cookery lesson in Salford. Beatlemania? This is Adamsmania! The doubters have it down that he'll be the one remembered for never achieving what he should have done. Balderdash! (Again, a softened term for family viewing.)

If you honestly think the Leigh Adams we're talking about was an under-achiever, remove yourself from my company forthwith and never again darken my door. Perspective does seem to be one thing missing among some of those so eager to pounce upon a keyboard and share their every opinion and thought with the oh-so-lucky rest of us.

From that humble beginning those 20-odd years ago, Leigh Adams has gone on to become one of the greatest riders the sport has ever known. 'Yes, but if he'd been a bit more aggressive. . .'. Oh, give it a rest. Ask Hans Andersen about Saturday 16 August 2008. He'll readily, if not happily, recall leading the final of the Scandinavian Grand Prix at Malilla that day. And he'll also remember Mr Adams roaring up the inside of him on the last lap, prisoners unacceptable. That was Leigh's second GP win of that particular season, not bad for somebody some once said would never win one. Idiots! There's that door again, darken it not!

And yet, through all this attainment of legendary status, titles, race wins, trophies, medals, etc., the Leigh Adams I know remains exactly the same as the one I first met. In today's relentless (and tedious) haste by nobodies ridiculously anxious to pretend they're somebodies, Leigh's modest, unassuming and generous nature is a huge talent of itself. And I haven't even got to his wonderful sense of humour. Tell 'em about the duck, Leigh!

I'm proud to know Leigh and Kylie. I guess, summing up, what I'm trying to say is I'm as a big a fan of Leigh (and Kylie) as anyone out there (and now, probably one of his oldest!). And, believe me, when you're a Leigh Adams fan, it's for life, not just Christmas. Twinkle, twinkle, little star. . . .

RICHARD CLARK
Editor, *Speedway Star*

1

A Family Affair

Christmas Day, 1976

John Adams was thankful that he was a fit man because pushing his then five-year-old son Leigh around the family's 25-acre spread on a Honda MR50 was tiring. Up and down and in and out the orange trees they would go as his excited boy was trying to get to grips with this little motorcycle. While trying to teach him how to ride his new bike, he claims that he ran a mini marathon that day.

Anyone looking on at this scene wouldn't have believed that Leigh would grow up to be one of the world's greatest speedway riders. The smooth style that would characterise this racer certainly wasn't on show yet, and neither was any sense of balance.

'He couldn't balance on the thing,' his father recalls. 'I think I must have run up and down the orange rows, backwards and forwards, ten times. I'd be pushing him and pushing him and then I'd let him go and he'd just crash straight into the orange tree! He couldn't get the hang of using the handlebars to get his balance, but once he got that, he was okay. I was fit because I used to do a lot of training and running for the trials riding. I used to run three nights a week with Jason Lyons' dad, Rodney. He was an umpire for Aussie Rules football, so he had to be fit.'

Unsurprisingly, having regular impacts with the trunk of an orange tree left a memorable impression with Leigh because this was his earliest recollection of riding a motorcycle. He says that he can 'vaguely' remember getting the MR50, which is a machine that has launched the careers of many future Aussie motorcycle stars, including multi-World Champion Mick Doohan and the tough-as-teak AMA Superbike Champion Mat Mladin.

Leigh Adams was born in Mildura, Victoria, on 28 April 1971. He was two years younger than his brother, Andrew, and they were born into a family that were enthusiastic about motorcycle riding. Their father estimated that, over the years, between them, they've had around thirty-five motorcycles

A young Leigh in 1975. (Adams Family Archive)

in the family, including a trike that Andrew used to ride with a very young Leigh as a passenger.

Their mother, Joan, remembers, 'It had three wheels and there was a little seat in the back, and Leigh used to sit up in this seat and he used to make out that he was in the sidecar. In Australia, sidecar speedway is very big, so they used to pretend that they were a sidecar team. Andrew was good enough that he could ride this three-wheeler bike on two wheels, with Leigh in the back.'

'They used to ride all round the yard, out the front, down the footpath, just on two wheels, with Leigh hanging out of the back,' John adds. 'If they did it on three wheels it would have been a lot easier, but no, it had to be on two.'

With John riding competitively as a trials rider – he was runner-up in the Victorian Championship – this meant that the whole family would pack up and go off riding during the weekends. This took them to New South Wales as well as all over their native state of Victoria.

'We used to cruise around with dad,' says Leigh. 'To be honest, in Mildura, everyone rode bikes. Where we came from was a farming area, and motocross and trials riding were really popular – motorbikes are a huge part of Mildura and it's quite famous.'

Therefore, surrounded by motorcycles and all things associated with motorcycle racing, it seems likely that the boys, Leigh in particular, gained their enthusiasm for bikes from the many sources that encircled them.

'That was the start,' Joan agrees, 'with John riding trials there would be other kids there with their motorbikes. And Andrew and Leigh thought, yes, we want to go into motorbikes.'

This vibrant scene was enhanced by the presence of Mildura's Olympic Park Speedway. Formed in 1947, the Mildura and District Motorcycle Club were given permission for their club's site to officially be called Olympic Park by the 1956 Melbourne Olympic Games committee after the club was selected to stage a 500cc Grand Prix on a road circuit close to where the Mildura Airport currently stands.

The venue has remained steadfast while other famous places like the Exhibition Ground in Brisbane and the Sydney Showground closed their doors following the fall in popularity of motorcycle speedway. Therefore, Mildura is to Australian Speedway what Belle Vue is to England, Costa Mesa is to the USA and Pardubice is to the Czech Republic, established venues that have survived the various peaks and troughs that modern-day speedway racing suffers from.

Mildura's healthy motorcycle club also catered for junior as well as senior competitors. Excited by the speed, the thrill of riding and inspired by their father's competitive racing, both Leigh and Andrew took up motocross. To start with Leigh rode a Honda CR80, but that proved a bit problematic and it was replaced by a Yamaha YZ80.

'The motorbike club was flourishing and it was so popular. When we used to do motocross there were grids of thirty kids, it was unbelievable,' says Leigh.

It's not surprising that motorcycles were all the rage in Mildura because the city is located in the Sunraysia region of the country. On a map, the area sits in the chest of the Murray Valley and spreads across the state border into south-western New South Wales.

The area is known for its above average sunshine hours with 122 clear days per year and with a yearly average temperature of 23.6°C, it's an agreeable climate for riding bikes.

'We're pretty lucky in Mildura because about 21ks away there is what we call the Sunset Country where you can ride all day – actually it's called the Murray Sunset National Park. That's where these guys go now when Leigh comes home,' John reveals.

Jason Lyons, son of former rider Rod Lyons, was another talented rider to emerge from Mildura at the same time as Leigh. With both families being friends, combined with their common interest in motorcycles, Jason would spend time with Leigh and his brother riding their bikes. He agrees that the region offered plenty of opportunities for bikers of all ages to go off, practice and have fun.

'When we were learning to ride we used to go out and ride on the Nowingi Salt Flats where there was no fence and you could build your own track. We used to practice out there, weekend after weekend, and the family would have a barbecue. You could go out there any day of the week if you wanted to because there was nothing out there. Back in those days it was a lot easier if we wanted to have a practice and try something, you just throw the bike into the trailer, go down to the bush and burn some litres.'

The small city of Mildura is located in north-western Victoria in southern Australia and is approximately 337 miles (543km) from Melbourne. It's positioned alongside the nation's biggest river, the Murray, which forms a border between the states of Victoria and New South Wales. A census taken in 2006 recorded its population at just over 30,000 people.

With the Murray and Darling Rivers providing an irrigation corridor, Mildura is considered to be at the centre of what is often referred to as 'Victoria's Food Bowl'. Over 80 per cent of Victoria's grape production comes from Mildura, but it's also known as a major producer of citrus fruit, in particular oranges, which is the Adams' family business.

Sited on the edge of the settlement, they have two properties that cover 40 acres and they have a shop on the road to Melbourne from which they sell their oranges.

John Adams says: 'Citrus was and still is our business, but the majority now happens to be grapes. We'd pack all our own oranges, we've got a big machine that washes and waxes them, grades them into their sizes, then we put them into boxes, forklift them out to the back of the shop, bag them all, and sell them. We also sell things that are in season and are locally grown, like honey, jam, pistachio nuts, watermelons, pumpkins and so on.'

Unfortunately, as much as they liked riding their motorcycles, there was also the small matter of obtaining an education. Leigh began his school years at Irymple South Primary before moving to Mildura High School – now called Chaffey Secondary College. His final years of education were spent at Irymple Technical School – now called Irymple Secondary College. He describes his academic talents as 'never a scholar, I just cruised through it.'

'He wasn't interested in that type of thing, he was more of a hands-on type of guy,' says his father. 'We never had any behavioural problems with him or anything like that.'

His mother recalls that his reading material mainly consisted of bike magazines. And while that might not be in the league of the classic works of Charles Dickens or Jane Austen, Joan does believe that her sons' involvement in the motorcycle club in Mildura was a positive influence on their upbringing.

'They always had friends around, and friends within motorcycling . . . all the families went and we went along as a family, so the kids didn't go off as much in those days as they do now.'

The saying goes: the Devil makes work for idle hands. But not, it seems, if you're a keen motorcyclist. Jason Lyons would join Leigh riding around and would eventually progress to be a Grand Prix rider himself and he remembers, 'When we were messing around or something it was always on motorbikes, riding round the block. So we never really got up to mischief because we were occupied with riding.'

Speedway has a worthy reputation as a family sport. Not only because the whole family can attend a race meeting and not feel intimidated or threatened, but also because everyone involved in the business side, riders, mechanics, team managers, promoters, etc., treat it, for the most part, like a family – including all the ups and downs that families experience.

Having already competed in trials, the Adams family had established a close-knit group of friends and their home was so busy with all aspects of motorcycling that at times Joan felt as though they were running the

Irymple South Motorcycle Club from their house. The Adams and the Lyons families were very close; in fact, to this day Joan remains close friends with Christine Lyons.

'We're only a mile or two miles away from each other,' says Jason. 'As boys we all grew up together with motorbikes and Leigh's older brother used to race as well. We'd all go out over the weekends, even when we weren't racing the families would be going out for tea or having a barbecue or something. But most of our time was spent at speedway and stuff like that.'

The Adams' business and that acreage would provide the boys with plenty of opportunities to combine their chores with honing their motorbike skills by riding around their property. At the end of their school day, they would drop their bags of learning material, get changed, and kick-start their motorcycles. Their father had set them a task of picking oranges for an hour after school, but their enthusiasm for riding their machines often overrode their duty.

'Of course, I could hear them coming,' their father remembers. 'They'd get off the school bus, drop all their gear, and away they'd go, wam, wam! They'd come here and they'd say, "Hey dad, how ya going?". "How's it going Leigh, how's it going Andrew – where's your bags?" I'd reply. "Oh we forgot our bags!" And then off they'd go all the way back, wam! wam!, all the way back to the shed, and then come roaring back again with their bags of picked oranges. We used to say, "Here they come, with no bags!"'

Joan smiles at the memory and says, 'I always knew that my children were home because I could hear them.'

'I'd be riding my motorcycle every night,' Leigh recalls. 'It probably wasn't *every* night, but as often as I could I'd be riding my bike.'

Although Andrew and Leigh both shared an interest in motorcycles, they were quite different. Sometimes there is a fierce rivalry between siblings, especially when both of them are engaged in something competitive. However, while there is always some form of competition between brothers, there wasn't the spirited rivalry that was shown by some.

While Leigh displayed some of his smooth approach to racing early in motocross, his brother Andrew was the opposite.

'Andrew's very different,' says John. 'He rode motocross very aggressively. He was a good starter and a hard rider, he'd push and shove. But he just liked the social side of things more than Leigh. He never set his mind to it and he never really wanted to be a professional rider. He's only just stopped riding motorbikes, but now he's got back into it because he's got three boys and he's doing the same now, they're all into riding and playing footie. He's in the business with us, he runs it basically.'

'He was a motocrosser,' Leigh assesses. 'He didn't have much style and he was a bit bigger and older than me.'

Australia was accepted as the birthplace of speedway racing when Johnnie Hoskins staged the first speedway meeting at West Maitland in 1923. While Leigh was taking his first shaky rides on a Honda MR50, Australian Speedway had been given a boost when Mildura local Phil Crump finished third in the 1976 World Individual Speedway Championships. Along with Aub Lawson's third place in 1958, it was the closest that an Aussie had come to claiming the individual crown since Jack Young's back-to-back title triumphs in 1951 and 1952.

Furthermore, that same year, Australia won their first World Team Cup title and fulfilled the potential that this new generation of Aussie racers had displayed when they first headed for Europe. Billy Sanders, Phil Herne, Gary Middleton and John Boulger joined Crumpie in the victorious side that defeated Poland, Sweden and the Soviet Union at London's White City stadium.

Therefore, Australian Speedway was enjoying an upswing in popularity both at home and on the world's stage – and Phil Crump was hailed as a hero in Mildura. On the back of Crumpie's success, speedway racing in Mildura grew in both stature and popularity.

'Crumpie was the benchmark for speedway in Mildura,' John Adams says. 'He was one of the pioneers of that time, him and John Boulger, they were the first ones that I recognised that went over there (to the British League) and did well. When they came home, they went faster than anyone else – that's how we saw what speedway was all about.'

During those days it was common that the sport's top stars would 'winter' in Australia. In fact, England used to send a Test side to race against the Australians. It was a handy way of taking a break from the pressure of racing in Europe, while at the same time they could keep themselves sharp and race fit by competing in a few meetings as well.

Although his international commitments prevented him from getting directly involved with the club, they were able to call on Crump's contacts in order to bring over some of the big names to Mildura.

By now John Adams was heavily involved in the motorcycle club in Mildura (he was the President in 1979) and the success of Crumpie, Billy Sanders and others proved to be an inspiration for many.

John Adams says, 'We decided that we'd promote it pretty well. We had the one speedway co-ordinator, Sy Nunan, and he actually organised the programmes. He used to call Crumpie and ask him to see if he could get a couple of English guys to come over here and ride speedway. He worked for

Telecom Australia and used to spend hours on the phone organising all these riders and he lifted the standard. So we brought over Bruce Penhall, Ivan Mauger, the whole lot, we'd run big meetings with big-name riders. They went up the Gold Coast, did a few meetings there, and then to Adelaide. Then my brother, Brian, coordinated the speedway for a while. Back in those days there wasn't the (European racing) activity going on like it is now.'

Meanwhile, over the state border into South Australia, Adelaide pointed the way forward with their Sidewinders junior project. News spread fast.

'We heard about this Sidewinders speedway and Mildura Speedway was quite strong,' recalls John. 'So one afternoon a few of us decided – those that were interested – to hop on a bus and go and see this Sidewinders.'

Formed in 1976 by a group of fathers and their sons, Sidewinders began with a track behind the gas works. As a place to ride it was fine, but was quite unpopular with the spectators. Via a Mini Bike Club another site was found at Wingfield. A team of volunteers began the process of building a 112-metre dolomite track, erecting a safety fence, installing lights and all the other facilities needed to run junior speedway meetings.

All the effort and hard work that the volunteers had put into Sidewinders paid off when Steve Baker became the first Australian to win the 1983 European Junior Championship – the forerunner to the World Under-21 Championship.

Mildura may have been put on the speedway map by the success of Phil Crump, but when the Mildura Motorcycle Club travelled to Adelaide to see the Sidewinders set-up, they were inspired to put in place a similar junior programme that would set in motion a conveyor belt of talent that is still producing young stars today.

Sy Nunan had long harboured a dream to produce a motorcycle that was suitable for juniors, and seeing the Sidewinders project was the last piece of inspiration he required to get to work. Although it was modelled on a Jawa, he designed a junior speedway bike from scratch. He scaled all the dimensions down to 85 per cent and all the features were made with safety uppermost in his mind. Made from solid aluminium, the rear wheel hub in particular was difficult to make and it took Nunan four hours of work on his lathe to complete. The frame itself cost in the region of $350, but the Honda motor, a 125cc four-stroke to begin with, was extra. Sy's brother Tim made the fibreglass tanks and mudguards, and then the prototype was finished.

Children often want to be like the grown-ups, and do grown-up things. Unfortunately, as they're usually smaller than the average adult, this means that most of these things are too big for them. Therefore, a mini version of something that your parents use is bound to attract interest. The junior speedway bike was a stunning piece of engineering that looked, and was, a smaller version of a conventional speedway machine.

Nunan took the bike to the club and a syndicate was formed that included Nunan, Fred Hancock, Royce Fawdry, Rupert Wheatland, Rod Brighton, Jim O'Brian, Mick Storer, Mrs Jean Duncan and John Adams. Eventually a junior motorcycle club followed.

John sums up the events that led to the construction of the bikes and the formation of the syndicate, 'We had a look at the Sidewinder set-up there, and we measured all the bikes, track size and what have you. Then we decided we'd form a syndicate of about ten or twelve of us, and we would build some junior speedway bikes. What they had was old Jawa bikes that had been cut down, different sizes and shapes, different wheels and that sort of thing. So we set this syndicate up. Sy Nunan designed the bike, and Joan and Fred Hancock co-ordinated it all, which was pretty hard to do. But we ended up with, all together, ten bikes. I did all the wheels, laced all the wheels, we got all these bikes going, and in the meantime we built the track in the centre of Mildura. It sort of went from there.'

The track was built on the inside of the existing speedway track and measured 118 metres (130 yards) and the straights approximately measured 29 metres (32 yards). Meanwhile, every member of the syndicate contributed something to the construction of the machines. Their talents and enthusiasm for the project were put to use on the premises belonging to Sy Nunan, Fred Hancock or Rupert Wheatland, whether that was some practical expertise with a lathe, making a jig for the frames, welding, filing down parts to fit, or just painting.

When Kim Hancock took the prototype out onto the track at Mildura for a demonstration, local journalist Bob Fox reported that 'inquiries poured in regarding the machines and the proposed new club.'

John Adams recalls, 'The kids were still racing motocross, but then they got a bit interested in speedway. We got to a stage where we started travelling away with the speedway and Leigh basically branched off into that. Andrew also fell into juniors for a while, but then he went junior water skiing with some people – so we bought a boat.'

Encouraged by the performances of Phil Crump and seeing some of the world's top stars, Leigh and Andrew were keen on the sport. However, the hot climate also had a say in giving junior speedway a go as their mother reveals: 'When you're in Australia, summer is really too hot for motocross – you don't do any really. They weren't active in the summer, so we used to go to the speedway. When it was suggested that they build these junior

Left to right: Leigh, brother Andrew Adams, Kim Hancock and David O'Brian admire the junior bike that was financed and built by members of the Mildura Motorcycle Club syndicate. (Adams Family Archive)

speedway bikes, we thought we'd start them in junior speedway. That's the way it all started.'

'Traditionally, speedway was staged on a Sunday in Mildura – always Sunday night,' Leigh says. 'The syndicate was where it all started. I was nine and my brother was eleven. We built the bikes and we did speedway. It got more popular, but we continued with motocross and enduros as well for a bit of fun, so yeah, bikes were a huge part of our lives.'

2

Kids Today, Stars Tomorrow

'Leigh was just so happy to wait at the line and let the others take off. He'd go, "Mmm," then he'd catch them up, but he wouldn't pass,' recalls Joan Adams.

Although it was obvious that he had the speed and the ability, it became a talking point among the other parents that Leigh Adams appeared to be happy to follow his rivals rather than blast by them.

'Leigh was only ready to go racing when he wanted to race, which was fair enough, I was never going to force him,' says his father. 'He just enjoyed riding; and people used to say to me, "Why don't you get him to start racing?" Then all of a sudden he just started racing, and in that year I don't think he lost one race. He just decided that he was going to go for it. I reckon that's how he learned. He was prepared to learn how to do it before he went racing.'

The calculated and thinking side of Leigh's character came to the fore during the early days of junior racing. Although he was obviously used to riding bikes and racing motorcycles in competition, he didn't rush headlong into racing a speedway bike until he was comfortable with the machine he was riding and the different aspects of racing speedway.

Meanwhile his brother, Andrew, brought his motocross skills to the sport and felt no compunction at all to hold back.

'He was the gater. He wasn't like a speedway rider as such. He would push and shove and would cause chaos on the first corner, no doubt about that,' their father smiles. 'If he wanted to win, he would win. He wasn't the best slider or anything, but if someone was beside him, look out!'

'When they first started, Andrew was probably better than Leigh,' Joan adds. 'But then Leigh became the better rider, more spectacular to watch. Ever since he got on that little bike he always looked like he was in control, except at the start when he was just happy to trail along behind the others.'

Not for long, though. Eventually, that competitive spirit that would carry him to the sport's ultimate competition took over, and he never looked back. So what was it that turned the happy, laid-back Leigh, into the smooth racer Leigh? With so many kids, and mainly boys, all together in a competitive environment, it seems inevitable that there would be some ribbing among them. However, while that was sure to have taken place, Leigh says that wasn't one of the reasons why he began racing.

He shakes his head: 'Not at all. I just enjoyed it and I was always fast. All of a sudden, bang! I just started getting involved and made some starts. You just mature don't you; you're a kid and then you're a teenager.'

While Leigh began to get to grips with riding speedway and also began showing the style that would thrill millions across the globe, Andrew's interest would eventually take an altogether different direction, swapping terra firma for water skiing.

Mildura's success for nurturing young talent was due to the enthusiasm of the syndicate, whose own credentials were helped by having former rider Rod Lyons in the organisation. He was Jason's father and was among the first successful riders when Mildura's Olympic Park began staging solo speedway in 1960. Therefore his experience was a valuable asset when it came to coaching the young riders.

Meanwhile, in Adelaide, Lenny Bowes, Shane Bowes' father, was instrumental in the running of the Sidewinders club and Shane Parker's dad used to prepare the track. Riders from both venues would travel between the two every weekend to practice and race.

'We used to do some miles,' Leigh recalls. 'We'd go over in the morning and then come back that night. It was a four-hour drive (eight-hour round trip). It was popular, the Normans, the Parkers, Craig Hodgson, and all those kids were there. They were good times.

'We're talking twenty-five kids or more, there were A-grade and B-grade riders and that's where we all came from. Pretty much all the Aussies who came over to the UK came from those two junior clubs. Craig Boyce and Todd Wiltshire were an exception, they came from flat track, the short circuit, it's a bit different, like a speedway track but you've got a right-hand loop in it and they run motocross bikes on that.'

'The best part of it was that between all the juniors and the two clubs, there was a good relationship and we both grew because of it,' John Adams believes. 'There was no hate between the Mildura kids and the Sidewinder kids, they all raced like crazy on the track, but after they were all good mates. Even on the management side of it, they were only too happy to have us over there, and we were only too happy to have their kids at our club.'

However, Adelaide is a big city, especially when compared with sleepy little Mildura. The South Australian city is the fifth largest in the country with over one million inhabitants, and the boys from that area brought a little bit of that decadent city lifestyle with them, as Leigh recalls. 'The South Australian boys were pretty wild lads, they didn't mind a party. When I walked out the back of the changing rooms once, I found some of them were smoking a big fat joint!'

John Adams adds: 'We went to a twenty-five year reunion and Shane Parker was saying "Do you remember that big hill where we all used to go over there after the meeting and puff away!"'

These were interesting times for the young riders, a time that was filled with new experiences as they juggled their lives between racing junior speedway, schooling and, of course, all the other things that are part of growing up when you're a teenager. However, the family atmosphere of the club ensured that nothing really progressed much beyond boys trying out new things and testing the boundaries.

Understandably, because the Sidewinders club had been operating longer than Mildura's junior programme, they were a bit further down the road than their Victoria counterparts in terms of machine developments. At this stage Leigh was riding the machines that had been built by the syndicate, but now that he had shaken off his cautious side he wanted to win races and was eager to improve his bike to be on the pace.

'We were running these bikes that dad built for many years,' Leigh explains. 'In Adelaide they had the Jawa frames cut down, and they were always a little bit better. They played with the dimensions on them and had them pretty much dialled in. So we went and bought this bike in Adelaide. When we got that machine, off we went and we kept it until the end.'

'They were a little bit bigger and they had done a lot of work, they had played with them and shortened the back end,' John describes. 'Leigh rode it once and he said that it handled beautifully.'

All racing is competitive, but when it comes to junior racing there is often the added dimension of competitive parents. Many good junior programmes have been damaged by the attitude of some parents who can place too much pressure on their children to succeed – often trying to live their dreams through their kids.

> **'they all raced like crazy on the track, but after they were all good mates.'**
>
> **John Adams**

Furthermore, their desire to see little Johnny at the front often brings them into conflict with the organisers of the club itself by making demands that are designed to favour their child. This causes resentment among the other parents and young riders, and also confrontation with the organisers. At the very least such conflicts can cause good people, with a valuable contribution, to walk away; and at worst it can be responsible for the end of the junior programme. Pretty quickly they've forgotten why they were there in the first place and it's the kids who suffer and, of course, the sport as a whole.

Happily, this didn't happen in Mildura. The family atmosphere was maintained and, in fact, a unique bond was formed between everyone that was involved, as John Adams points out. 'Everywhere you go you run into somebody who benefited from the junior days. A lot of people that are racing in the UK would say that they used to come to our house for a barbecue during their junior racing days. We were all close and we tried to keep a family atmosphere.

'I remember one time we went to Perth, and the Lyons and the Aldertons came with us. Christine Lyons, Jason's mum, is really good friends with Joan. I was good friends with Rodney Lyons and Nigel Alderton's dad, Brian and I, are best mates, to this day. If we went anywhere, all three of us would go together. Even now, we've got wonderful relationships with all the parents that we had in those younger days.

'When we were racing I guess it was an unwritten rule that when we went to speedway we were all in our own camp,' John continues. 'But afterwards it didn't matter if Jason beat Leigh, or Leigh beat Jason, or Leigh beat Nigel, or whatever, it was all finished and we were friends. It never got nasty and that was terrific, because it can. People have lost friends through speedway because of stupidity, through the parents being ridiculous. We never really spoke about it, after the meeting it was "good ride Jase" or whatever.'

However, one of the main reasons for how they managed to curb the parents' excitement over the success, or otherwise, of their children was actually written in the rules. Evidently, there was no messing about.

'Any involvement from a parent and they'd penalise the kid – most probably they wouldn't be able to ride the next week. Or they'd get the parent, take him out of the pits and tell him to stay out there,' John reveals.

And although there was obviously some rivalry between the boys from Sidewinders and their Victoria counterparts, it never escalated to anything other than the friendly kind, as Jason Lyons recalls. 'It was pretty tough competition back then. We all started about the same time and we used to go to Adelaide quite a lot and they used to come to Mildura. We used to be quite busy on the weekends. There was Shane Parker, Scott Norman, Ryan Sullivan, Mark Lemon, Billy Lellman, all those boys grew up together and we're all good friends now. I don't think there was rivalry as such, but as Australians, we're all very competitive and we all want to win. Back then we were all aggressive, just as we are now, but we all had that winning bug and we all wanted to be first. 90 per cent of the time Leigh was first!' he laughs.

'Some of these junior races were full-on,' says Leigh. 'Even now I will go and watch the juniors and the racing is very competitive. It can put the senior racing to shame.'

With a new bike acquired from Adelaide, Leigh began to stamp his authority on the racing. He was showing tremendous potential, speed and natural ability, and he was even refining his trademark smooth-as-silk style.

Like many things in life, when you're at the beginning of something new, a pastime that could become a future career, it's important that you iron out any bad habits as early as you can before they get ingrained into your technique. Former world number two Eric Langton once said that England's double World Champion Peter Craven had a 'flat spot' in the middle of the turns. By the time Craven had signed for Belle Vue and could benefit from Langton's tuition, he'd gone too far down the road in his career for Langton to cure him of that habit.

Therefore, having training schools run by respected and professional riders are a vital part of the learning process. Ivan Mauger, the New Zealander who went on to win the world title six times, still runs training schools all over the world. Like many others, Leigh also attended one of these schools run by the Kiwi, but he names another, less-well known international for having a major influence on his early development – John Boulger.

Boulger qualified for two World Finals in 1973 and 1977, and was a member of Australia's first successful World Team Cup team and also a double Australian Champion. He raced in the British League for thirteen consecutive seasons, mainly for Leicester, and retired from international competition at the end of the '79 season. His tutoring skills had been used for some time at Sidewinders, and he would use drawings to illustrate how the rider's bodyweight should be distributed through the bike and onto the back wheel. With Mildura now having a thriving junior club of their own, Boulger travelled to Victoria to coach their boys.

'More than anybody else, I probably learnt the most from John Boulger,' Leigh admits. 'I did go to Ivan's schools, but John Boulger came to Mildura and did some coaching and he was brilliant. Football's the same isn't it? Not the best footballers make the best coaches. It was just the way he went about telling you how to ride a bike properly, it just all made sense. The way he got through to you was very good. Ivan was probably more technical, but John went back to the basics, which is like anything, if you don't know the basics, the technical stuff is out the door. You've got to get your basics right. So I definitely learnt the most from John Boulger.'

As a coach, Boulger's interest didn't begin and end at the training sessions because he would take the time to watch his pupils putting what they learned to the test when they were racing later. If he needed to, he'd offer further advice when the time was right.

'I've always had a pretty nice style, on the seat and go,' Leigh says. 'It's weird, whatever style the juniors had, it would be the same at seniors – they very rarely changed. So that's why it's so important when they're juniors to get the basics right. Even now, I find that you can teach them when they're young, but as soon as they get any bad habits later on, you can't get rid of them. So with John Boulger and what he taught me, I really went back and thought about it. That helped me, and it still helps me now.'

Your nation's National Championship is one of the most important competitions for a racer to win. Every rider wants to be their country's number one rider. The prestige and reputation that comes with that status also has other benefits when it comes to negotiating a better deal overseas, or making yourself more attractive to prospective sponsors.

In 1981/82, it was decided to stage an Australian Under-16 Championship, so the young riders could have their own National Championship. As the scene grew its level of professionalism increased, so staging its own Aussie National seemed a natural progression.

Held in Adelaide, Paul Snadden, from South Australia, won the first ever Under-16 Championship with 13 points. Second place went to Michael Carter and Dave Cheshire, who would go on to carve out a moderately successful career in the British League, was third.

The following season Mildura staged the new Under-16 National Championship. Leigh was 11 years old when he took to the track to ride in this meeting, and when you consider that the eventual winner, Craig Hodgson was 14, and how a child's body can develop between the ages of 12 and 16, it's quite astonishing that Adams finished third overall behind runner-up Jeff Meyer and Hodgson. Not only did he finish third, but he had to face his brother and Michael Carter in a three-rider run-off for the final podium place. Undoubtedly, this victory banished any memories people may have had of a Leigh Adams who was content to sit back when he first began sliding a speedway bike.

That season also saw the Olympic Park stage the Under-16 Australian Pairs Championship. Hodgson and Meyer paired up to win this competition, but

Leigh Adams leads Michael Carter, c. 1983. (Adams Family Archive)

Andrew Adams could take some consolation from losing a run-off to his little brother when he finished in second place with his partner David Harding.

However, Leigh's third place in the Under-16s alerted the world to his emerging talent. A short, but prominent report of the meeting was published in the British magazine *Speedway Star.* Interestingly, his first appearance in the world's longest-running and most famous speedway publication followed directly underneath the report of Phil Crump's victory in the Mildura Masters that took place the day after the Under-16s.

Adams would finish second in the competition in 1986 (85/86 season), losing a run-off to Shane Parker. But in the 1986/87 season, he repeated Craig Hodgson's double success by winning the National with a perfect score of 15 points, and then teamed up with Jason Lyons to win the Pairs Championship.

Adams and Lyons tied with the Adelaide duo of Shane Parker and Scott Norman on 27 points, and a run-off was required to decide first place. Leigh exacted some revenge for his defeat at the hands of Parker the previous season and clinched top spot with his long-time friend Jason.

Lyons has fond memories of winning that Pairs event, but believes that they could have won more than one.

'Back in those days, with Leigh being a little bit better than me, we probably could have won it a few more times, but I was crashing a lot more and learning the hard way. We used to do a bit of team riding, and back then we used to do a lot of practising together.'

Leigh (left) and Jason Lyons, the 1986 Australian Junior Best Pairs Champions.
(Adams Family Archive)

Junior meetings were run before the senior events. Therefore, these young riders were catching the attention of the public and the seasoned, seen-it-all-before motorcycle journalists. After reporting on Leigh's Under-16 success and his Pairs victory with Lyons, journalist Peter White recognised the potential of Scott Norman and Shane Parker as well as the Mildura duo, and wrote, 'Note the names. They might be kids today, but they could be stars tomorrow.'

The junior programme in Mildura had proven to be a good breeding ground for junior riders in Victoria. The following season Leigh lost the Under-16 title to fellow Victorian rider Jason Hawkes. A year later, the top three riders all hailed from Victoria. Hawkes retained the title by beating Phil Crump's son, Jason, in a run-off and in third place was Mark Lemon. The days of the boys from Adelaide holding any advantage over their southern rivals was well and truly at an end.

'Look at the amount of riders that went over to England, just from Mildura, not all of them made it, but they're all kids that have come through the juniors,' John Adams says proudly. 'A lot of people don't realise that speedway is a big apprenticeship, a very big apprenticeship.'

His son agrees, and with so many experienced riders still racing at the sharp end on the world's stage and at other levels, it's clear that having the knowledge is a major asset over youthful enthusiasm and bravery.

'You can't come in and take it on now like Michael Lee did all those years ago,' believes Leigh. 'It's the bikes, the equipment, your fitness, your mental preparation and the bar has been lifted so much you can't do it. It's a big mental game, it really is.'

The junior clubs in Mildura and Adelaide had ushered in a new era of Australian racers. Unwittingly, this era, of which Leigh was one of the most influential riders, would be one of the most successful international periods in the history of Australian Speedway.

There is a sporting culture in Australia that definitely lends itself to encouraging and developing young talent. Whether that individual wants to become a professional or remain a happy amateur, they seem to be able to provide the facilities for that person to practice and train. This certainly isn't the case in other countries where they are lacking in some services due to insufficient finance or just too many limitations placed on them by nanny laws. Although Australia continues to nurture and develop an impressive number of young riders, restrictions such as insurance and health and safety have made it more difficult for youngsters to get the track time when they want it, as Jason Lyons points out. 'The club side of things have changed now, you've got to book practices and things in advance because of health and safety; you've got to have ambulances and numbers to call people and that sort of stuff. It's still a club effort, but you don't go down on your own anymore and have a practice after work or something like that. It's got to be an organised practice event. Back in those days it was a lot easier and accessible for everyone.'

In April 1987, Leigh was 16 years old and could now race with the seniors. For any young rider moving up to the next level is quite an exciting prospect. However, being successful in the juniors doesn't always mean that you're going to hit similar heights when you turn professional. There is little doubt, though, that racing 125cc bikes as a teenager does give you a solid platform from which to make the move to competing on a 500cc machine. As far as Leigh Adams was concerned, he didn't give it that much thought and was quite relaxed about it. He viewed racing against riders of the calibre of Phil Crump as merely the next phase.

'It was a natural progression, when you turned 15, you would buy a senior bike and you'd practice on it. I had a really good start on a junior bike and that helped me. I could ride a senior bike and be pretty safe. A lot of these kids who didn't have a good style on juniors, it would really stand out at senior level.

'They were happy days,' he says of his junior racing. 'All the kids got on, all the parents got along – it was really good. The problem now is that there are bigger stakes at the end, everyone can see what everybody's got and all that. That's why there's more pressure involved. Towards the end of my time it was starting to get bitchy with the parents.

'Back when I started riding 500s they didn't have the laydown engines either, it was uprights, and they were pretty fragile and they'd put you in the fence as soon as look at you. So there were a lot of kids crashing.'

3

The Master & the Apprentice

There was a belief that emerged in England about speedway racing in Australia; and that was that all racing took place on big tracks measuring at least 360 metres or more. This was probably because speedway took place at venues that would also run car racing. A night out at the speedway could include solo and sidecar speedway, and midget and sprint cars. Therefore, tracks at Brisbane, Claremont, Parramatta, Liverpool – where the 1982 World Pairs Final was staged – and the Sydney Showground, were large tracks that could accommodate all types of oval racing.

In contrast, tracks that held just bike racing were less numerous, but Mildura was one of them. Following a suggestion from Jerry Cornell, solo speedway was first staged there in 1960 and its early stars were the aforementioned Rod Lyons and Phil Sedgmen. It was Phil Crump who put the 310-metre track on the map through his success at all levels of racing and, as a result, Mildura has become an iconic name in the sport.

However, despite its glowing reputation, the Mildura circuit is not the easiest of tracks to conquer and is something of a puzzle for the inexperienced. Over the years it has caught out many top names who have struggled to master its complexities.

Leigh says: 'It's a really tough track, really hard, and we have sidecars there that are involved in the meeting. So it gets quite rough and rutty and stuff like that. It's a really hard track to master – if you can master Mildura, you can master anywhere in the world. It's got everything that will try to bring you unstuck. It's got long straights and tight corners, quite grippy, rutty coming off the corners where the sidecars run, so it's got a lot of aspects to it. And to go good, to run fast, is really hard. I know guys now, like I'd talk to Boycey (Craig Boyce) and they hate it, absolutely hate it. Billy Sanders absolutely hated the place, he could never get around it and he looked like a junior round there. It's hard to explain, but it's a tough track. I really love it. I went through a phase, I don't know why, when I couldn't get on with it and then something clicked and off I went and I have a ball there now.'

Sidecar racing is very popular in Australia and Jason Lyons believes that because they race in the opposite direction to speedway – clockwise as opposed to anti-clockwise – this also makes the surface even more demanding for the bike racers. 'They're digging ruts coming out of the corner just where we're going into the corners, so it can be difficult to ride. Mildura is a hard one and most of the Aussie ones are quite difficult because of the ruts made by sidecars, so we had to learn to turn the bikes on those surfaces – which definitely helped our riding styles for the slicker tracks.'

Given that speedway racing is quite vulnerable to rain, it seems that Australia, and in particular the sunshine region of Mildura and Victoria, would be ideal for the sport. Unfortunately, this isn't always the case and the bright sunshine has been an issue with Olympic Park for some years, as Leigh reveals. 'They'd start the meeting quite late, say 8.30 p.m., because they had trouble with the sun and heat – nine times out of ten it's too hot. As the sun goes down, it shines right in on the first corner and they've always had this theory that it was dangerous. They've only just realised now that it's not that dangerous and they run a little earlier. It's the same thing at Swindon, it shines straight down the back straight. I've been trying to tell them for ages that in England the sun's only at a bad point for a very short time. But in Mildura they've always had that theory so they'd start when the sun goes down. Sometimes we wouldn't start racing until quarter to nine or something and it would drag on. But the juniors would start at six o'clock normally, run for an hour, then they'd have practice, and go on from there.'

Junior racing plays an important role in preparing you for riding the bigger 500cc machine at senior level. However, the transition is not necessarily a smooth one.

'I always had a pretty good style, but it is a big jump going up to the seniors. A 500 is a lethal thing, and back then they were the old upright engines and with Mildura being a difficult track, there were some huge crashes. I was included in all of that and I had my fair share of crashes in my first year! It's a big step, probably a little bit too much. At the end of the day the juniors teach you the basics, the fundamentals of speedway and how to ride a bike. It's just a matter of harnessing a 500; it's tough and it's hard work.'

Leigh's friend and Under-16 Pairs partner Jason Lyons experienced some difficulties when trying to adapt his style to a 500cc machine, and it wasn't just the extra speed and power that he had to contend with.

'For a little fella like me it was difficult because I was quite short at the time. It was just a learning process, but it was definitely faster.'

Jason Hawkes was one talented rider from the Mildura junior programme who found it very hard. Every generation seems to have a junior rider with bags of ability who doesn't quite make the grade. Hawkes, a double Under-16 National Champion, was one of them and it was a crash while trying to tame the power of a 500cc machine that, by and large, brought his promising career to a stop.

'He was really good on a junior bike, really smooth and always had good equipment. He travelled to Perth with us in 86/87 and that was the year when he won the Under-16 National,' Leigh says. 'I went over there as the reigning champ and he knocked me off my pedestal. It just shows his ability because he won it again the following year.

'He was showing a little bit of promise on the big bikes, but then he crashed at Shepparton and broke his leg really badly. It didn't heal properly and he had a lot of complications with it. He still has trouble now, and he's busted it again a couple of times on motocross bikes. A really good talent, he rode a bike beautifully, put everything into it, but never made it.

'Jason never really got the right opening and the leg-break put him back a year and he never recovered from it. He rode for Belle Vue for a year and I think John Perrin ruined him . . . that finished his speedway career! He was small, and that's what helped him in junior speedway because once you get to 15 or 16 you get too tall and too heavy for a junior speedway bike, and that's when you really struggle. Unfortunately this break set him way back.'

Leigh's first season as a professional coincided with Phil Crump's retirement from racing in England. Suffering from a niggling scaphoid injury, the often damp British summers were not helping Crump's aching wrist, and at 35 years old he decided that it was time to soothe his aching bones by spending the rest of his racing career under the warmth of Victoria's sun.

Although Phil Crump is now bewildered and amazed at how quickly the passage of time flashes by, he was not surprised by the speed of his young rival. If Leigh was having any issues adapting to a 500, it wasn't visible to the Mildura legend.

'It only seems like yesterday when, of course, it was probably 20-odd years ago. He was just starting out, whereas I was almost at the end of my career. But as soon as Leigh was on a 500 he was fast. In fact, right the way back to the days when they would all go riding in the bush, Leigh was the best of that group – he was a bit special.'

Speedway racing in Australia is predominately individual competitions. There is some team racing and England used to send a Test team Down Under to race against the Australians. On some occasions, however, the Australians ran team events and Leigh rode for the Mildura Marauders during his first year as a senior racer.

Needless to say, with so many individual competitions, the promoters needed big names to draw the public; subsequently Crump received a lot of bookings. And as they both hailed from the same town, he would ask the promoters if there was a spot for a young up-and-coming rider in the meeting. As a result, Adams found himself travelling around with Phil and learning the circuits in Oz.

'I've known the Adams family from day one in the Mildura Motorcycle Club,' says Crump. 'When I go home, after I've been to visit my parents, my next stop is nearly always the Adams' place. I've always got along good with them, John, Joan, Andrew and Leigh and their uncle; I'd guess you'd say we're pretty close.

'I was sponsored by Trevor Harding and he was running a lot of meetings then, so it was relatively easy to get Leigh a ride. We had a lot of fun too, we'd go water skiing together and things like that. We spent a fair bit of time in the car travelling to Alice Springs and Brisbane.'

'He'd been doing it for fifteen, twenty years, so he knew everything,' says Adams. 'So when I stepped into seniors he helped me out a hell of a lot by taking me around. And he was still at the top in Australia. I'd travel with him to a lot of meetings, Brisbane, Alice Springs, Perth, I went to New Zealand once with him. He didn't let on much, bike wise, the technical side of things, he was trying to keep on top of things and didn't want to give too much away. And that's what I'm like now. I've got these young kids coming through and I could probably tell them everything, but why do that when they could turn round and beat me? Phil was the same.'

'They were known as "The Master and the Apprentice", and he was very good to Leigh in getting him rides,' adds Joan Adams.

Travelling is part and parcel of a speedway rider's life. At this time the Polish and Swedish Leagues had yet to open their doors to foreign riders like they have now. During this modern era, at the height of the season, a successful rider can find himself riding in as many as four different countries within a week. As his career progressed, Leigh would grow into that heavy schedule.

However, the travelling experience with Phil Crump would become invaluable as it provided him with ability to take long journeys and flights in his stride. During one occasion though, Leigh encountered a mammoth trip that, to this day, ranks up there as one of the longest journeys he has ever undertaken in order to slide a speedway machine in competition.

First senior season in Australia, 87/88. (Adams Family Archive)

'One time we were racing at Sydney on a Friday night, so we left Thursday afternoon, went up to Hay, stayed there, then went to Sydney, raced there at Parramatta, then got in the car and drove overnight to Brisbane, which is another ten hours north. We raced at Brisbane on the Saturday night, turned around and did Mildura on the Sunday night, which is another eighteen hours' drive – unbelievable.

'But, the most unbelievable thing is, when we took off down the road from Mildura, I think Craig Hodgson was with us and Crumpie had one of his mates with him, we got going down the road and Crumpie goes, "Oh no." He'd realised that his insurance wasn't any good for us because we were under 21 so we couldn't drive. Phil and his mate drove the whole way and he was riding in between. He had an eighteen-hour drive back to Mildura, he slept a little bit, but not much, while Craig and I were sparko'd in the back thinking, this is cool we don't have to drive, and there was Phil racing and driving! That was probably the heaviest schedule I've ever done. By the time we got back to Mildura, I just went home, had a shower, and just drove straight to the track. We didn't have time to do anything. We just pulled the bikes off the back of the trailer and off we went!'

Being able to drive is a must for a young rider who has designs on racing overseas. Leigh got his licence at the age of 17, but he had to bend the rules a bit in order to get a driving licence at that age. In the nearby states of New South Wales and South Australia you could get a licence at 17, but in Victoria you had to be 18 years old.

'Mildura is an hour away from the South Australian border and over the river is New South Wales. Everyone tries to find people over in South Australia or New South Wales to use their address so that they can have their test at 17. Luckily, our best friends lived in New South Wales, so I used their address. They had to take me to the police station to get my Ps and everything. It was a small town and the police station was just a little wooden house. You'd walk in and they probably had three policemen on patrol!'

Even back then, though, the requirements in Oz to qualify for a driving licence were less stringent than they were in Europe.

'We just went for a drive,' he laughs. 'It was pretty casual, nothing like it is nowadays – it was so easy. So I had my licence when I was 17 and that set me up for when I went over to England. It's easier than it is in England, although in Australia you can get on a road and know that you're on it for 300km (187 miles). You'll see a truck every now and again and maybe a few cars, but that's it. I enjoy driving in Australia because it's not stressful, it's pretty relaxing and the speed limit is 110kmh (68mph) and they're pretty strict with it. So you don't speed and you cruise along. It's a little bit too slow because it can make you tired!'

Leigh's reputation as one of Australia's most promising young speedway riders could have made the less-than-stringent testing for motorcycles licences even easier.

'There was a big concrete reservoir where they stored the water for the town. There was a big road running around it and the policeman couldn't see anything because a hedge was in front of the station. He came out, and he knew who I was, and he said: "Okay, get on your bike and ride around there." It was just like a triangle, and I came back and he said: "Yep, no worries, that was good," and wrote out my motorbike licence!'

Ability and talent may influence how quickly you adapt to riding a 500cc speedway bike, but that was only part of the process. In order to be competitive against the more experienced riders, one also had to get used to riding on bigger tracks, which meant higher speeds, the cunning of experienced riders and some quite intimidating venues.

'We were brought up on clay tracks, concrete walls, tyre walls, all that sort of stuff. The surface on the tracks, which would also run car racing, could bring up ball bearings and all sorts of things. When we went over to England everyone was going on about the Exeter fence, they were all talking about this steel fence, but that was a soft fence for us! I'd go along and think, "what's the big deal?" because we had a solid concrete fence with dirt behind it that did not give at all. 60 per cent of the tracks were car tracks, big fast ones, prepared grippy and a bit rough, and that helped us because when we went over to England we weren't fazed by anything.

'I do remember going to Broken Hill for the first time, looking at it, and thinking, shit . . . what am I doing here? I saw (Shane) Parker go out and practice – in Australia we always have practice – and he just attacked it, and I thought, fair enough.

'Crumpie, Sedgie, me and Lyonsie did a trip together because we were in the same meetings, and we went to Newcastle Speedway and then Appin on the way back. Newcastle was this big car track and I shit myself. I was only 16, my first year in seniors, it was terrible and I only got 5 points or something. Appin was a small slick one and I won that meeting. It was just experience and we were still pretty green with senior bikes, we bought this thing and we didn't know much at all, we were just going racing, basically. I soon adapted to it, though.'

The 'thing' that they had bought was a bike that used to belong to none other than multi-World Champion, Hans Nielsen.

'This guy had bought it from Hans Nielsen and it was the only one of these bikes that had a Hans Nielsen seat on it, and he was my hero. I think it had his mudguards on it as well. In those days all those riders like Hans and

Sam (Ermolenko) would do these meetings in Australia and then they'd flog their bikes off at the end of it. This one was the Hans Nielsen replica. I bought that and I was running just the one bike,' he recalls.

Leigh may have taken racing on the big tracks and with experienced riders all in his stride, but for his parents, especially his mother, it was a slightly different story.

'He did his first year following Crumpie and then the next year he was beating him,' she says. 'The first year he went into seniors, he wasn't that big, had a small frame if you like, I used to think: Oh dear, my little boy with these big bikes. The first meeting in Mildura they put him into B-grade and he won those races. They used to have meetings every week in Mildura, so the

Leading the way at Appin in 1987. Note the tyre wall safety fence. (Adams Family Archive)

next week they put him into the A-grade. I looked at the programme, saw the line-up and thought: Oh golly, gee. But it was the best thing that ever happened because all those A-grade riders were good riders; they didn't do the crashing and the bumping, so Leigh was able to pick things up. Some of the other tracks were scary; they had great big tractor tyres for a safety fence.'

His mother was right to be concerned because it was at Renmark, a track used extensively for car racing, where Danish star Tommy Knudsen crashed and broke his back.

Just like in the juniors, there were a lot of meetings to race in if you were keen – and Leigh was most certainly keen. However, as much as he was a promising young star on the rise, making a living from the sport in Australia wasn't possible for the youngster at that time. Therefore, Adams needed a career – or at least a job to earn his keep – and he got an apprenticeship as a diesel mechanic at G.E.M.B. Trucks. His father had been a mechanic for sixteen years, and Leigh soon discovered that being a mechanic was one of the dirtiest of working experiences.

'I was a pretty good worker and I used to enjoy it. I used to come home with lumps of grease in my hair and my hands would never be clean. I worked really hard. I never stood around, I was always working non-stop from the time I arrived to the time that I went home. Like my dad always said, "Don't sit around, sweep the floors, clean your tools." I did enjoy it, but I used to come home covered in shit. It was interesting and there was always something different coming in and I used to drive the trucks in and out.'

'These guys knew that Leigh was racing speedway and we used to pick him up at five o'clock and blast off to Broken Hill and places like that,' Leigh's father remembers. 'We'd drive into the track just as they were warming their bikes up. Then we'd race and come back.'

During his first season riding with the seniors he made history by becoming the youngest national finalist. He finished runner-up to Phil Crump in the Victorian Championship and so qualified for his first Australian Championship – which also doubled-up as a World Championship qualifying round – by defeating Nigel Tremelling in a run-off.

Staged at Murray Bridge, Crumpie won the meeting with an unbeaten score. However, Leigh wasn't intimidated by the field that also included the experienced Steve Regeling, Troy Butler and Steve Baker as he raced to equal eighth by scoring 8 points. While he may not recall the meeting for anything other than it being his first Aussie final, the venue's first staging of this prestigious meeting is often remembered for the chilly weather and heavy rain in the area that delayed the start of the meeting. Torrential rain caused flooding, and a teenager died in the storm.

Nonetheless, Leigh finished his first season on a 500 by winning the Australian Under-21 Championship at North Arm with an unbeaten display. Second went to Scott Norman and third to Craig Boyce.

Speedway Star's report described Adams' performance as 'sizzling . . . the toast of Aussie Speedway' and continued, 'Best race of the night was Heat 6 when Adams clashed with Boyce. The lead swapped continually until the last lap when Adams blasted round the outside and floored his rival with sheer speed.'

Using what he had learned during his first season, his second campaign was characterised by a more professional approach to racing.

The first Australian Under-21 title, 1988. Leigh is seen here flanked by Scott Norman (left) and Craig Boyce (right) with fourth-placed Billy Lellman. (Adams Family Archive)

John Adams recalls, 'When Leigh started in senior speedway, my brother, Brian, who was a school teacher and was also in the motorcycle club – he did a lot of the promotion for the speedway – he got on board with Leigh and basically managed him, got him going as far as sponsors were concerned. He got sponsors for clothing, a sponsored bike, and he's a good talker. He taught Leigh how to go and see the sponsors, talk to them, tell them what he's been doing, and to communicate with them. He did do a lot and he'd travel with us to Perth and some of the big trips like that.'

Brian Adams' influence lived long with his nephew, and that professionalism grew with him as he climbed up the ladder.

'He was very clever, had a lot of contacts and I've still got some of those sponsors now,' says Leigh. 'We got Castrol oils, Adrian Kidd Solicitors and I got cash money, $10,000, from Chem-mart – who are a chemist company – which was a lot of money back then so I went and got a brand new bike, which was about $8,500, a brand new bike from front to back. That was unheard of back then because everybody had second-hand stuff. I bought a new Godden because Hans Nielsen was on them and that was the bike to have.

'Up to that point I had one bike, a second-hand bike, but it was a bit old and things were starting to break on it. So to have this $10,000 and a brand new bike, that was huge for me, and the start of my career. That's when it all got professional, we weren't amateur anymore – we were looking after sponsors.'

Interest in Australia's emerging talent was gathering pace. Following Crump's retirement from international racing and the death of Billy Sanders, Australian Speedway was looking for the next generation of racers to take on the world. Consequently the scene in Australia was not only youthful, but also vibrant and competitive. Neil Street was Phil Crump's father-in-law and, as well as being an accomplished international rider in his own right, he also made one of the first four-valve engines, the Street Conversion, in the early '70s. In 1988, Streetie was the team manager of the Poole Pirates on the south coast of England and always kept an eye on developing talent in Australia. Therefore, with Leigh Adams showing rapid progress while racing in the shadows of Crumpie, Street had insider knowledge about the young Mildurian.

However, Street had already spoken to John Adams about Leigh possibly having a trial in England with Poole.

'Neil said to us quietly, "Has Leigh ever thought about coming over to England?" He was just in his first year and Streetie saw some potential in him. If you thought you were good enough to go to England, you'd go to Streetie and he would say: "Nah, not yet, you're not ready yet." He approached us and, because he was with Poole, he must have spoken to the promoters, and basically he said that he was ready to go to England if he wanted to. And we talked about it, but he had an apprenticeship as a diesel mechanic.

'I didn't even know how they worked the points system in the UK; Carole Crump (Phil's wife at the time) had to explain all that to me. Carole would say, "Oh Phil got 12 last night," and I'd go, "What's this 12?"'

Having already signed Gary Allan, Craig Boyce and Steve and Tony Landgon for Poole, he was also keen to get Adams over.

'Streetie rang us and said, "Come over, they're prepared to give you an air fare to come over and just have a look", Leigh recalls. 'It was the normal deal, as soon as you're in the seniors you want to go to England to race. Sure enough, they weren't stupid, they saw a bit of potential, and "come over and have a look" meant that I had to sign for them. In those days I didn't twig those things, you sign a document and that's it. I didn't know any of that at the time. I didn't think too much about the whole thing. It just happened. I had the opportunity to go over and just ride.'

But Poole weren't the only club interested in bringing him over for a trial because their rivals Wimbledon were also keen. They had signed Todd Wiltshire that year and he had made an immediate impact, and it was Todd who recommended him to the club's management.

'Sitting back in Australia, I thought of Wimbledon and being in London, Todd (Wiltshire) was there, while Boycey and the Langdons were down at Poole. I thought of London and the bright lights of the capital city and thought, nah, it would be all partying and that it could be bad. But as it turned out it was the opposite, the guys were partying pretty hard down at Poole. I didn't realise that until I turned up. I always thought, well it was Poole and Streetie would have them all clean-cut, which was totally the opposite really.'

Taking a few weeks' holiday to look into a possible career overseas when you're in the early stages of an apprenticeship, doesn't display the sort of dedication that your employer might have expected. Luckily for Leigh, his bosses were more obliging than one may have anticipated.

'These guys that Leigh worked for, Graham Elder and Mick Bayer, were very good; says John Adams. 'Leigh went to them and said, "Look I've been offered to go over to England and have a ride," and they said, "Yeah do it." For a young bloke like Leigh it was pretty exciting because Crumpie had set the standard in Australia, or Mildura, and every time that he came back he was just better and better.'

Taking some holiday from his work at G.E.M.B. Trucks, Adams flew to England and stayed with Neil Street for a month to get a feel for what it was like to race in Britain. Once again he was able to travel part of the way with Phil Crump because he'd been invited to ride in a Rest of the World side against the USA at Ascot. Therefore, Crump stopped off in California, while Adams, accompanied by Carole Crump, carried on to England.

Barely twenty-four hours after touching down, Leigh made his first appearance at Poole on Tuesday 16 August 1988, and was introduced to the crowd shortly before their National League match with Middlesbrough – which they won 65–31. After the match he took his first spin around the track.

In those days the National League also ran a small junior league (500cc amateur league) match in the second half of the meeting, and Poole were at the top of the league with a 100 per cent record. Having done enough in his after-meeting practice to impress the onlookers, it was decided to put him into the junior side the following Saturday for their trip to Arena-Essex.

Finding fellow Aussie youngsters and brothers, Steve and Tony Langdon and Gary Allan as team-mates, he appeared in two races and won both of them as the Poole junior side won the encounter 23–6.

> **'Leigh looked the business . . . every inch the thoroughbred.'**
>
> **Richard Comben**

Richard Comben was the *Speedway Star* correspondent for Poole and he enthused, 'Leigh looked the business and looks every inch a thoroughbred.'

Shown around by Neil Street, he went on to ride in further junior meetings, scoring 6 at Exeter and in the return match at Poole, and then gathered 8 points at Rye House. For the most part, the opposition were not a match for the young Australian whose natural ability was sufficient to get the best out of a bike that was loaned to him in order to put him through his paces.

In an interview he gave to *Speedway Star*'s Bob Radford shortly before catching his flight home, he said, 'I've enjoyed riding in the junior league during the month I've been here, but I would have liked to see how I'd done in the team.' And then showed his ambition when he added, 'My aim with Poole next year will be an 8 or 9-point average. I'd like 10 of course, but that wouldn't be a sensible target when all the tracks are new.'

Adams impressed the Poole bosses during his short stay and Pete Ansell confidently told *Speedway Mail International*, 'Leigh came here for some experience, he has done very well and visited several tracks. We do expect to have him in the Poole line-up next year.'

Leigh's introduction and the beginning of his education in the wider world of speedway racing weren't over just yet: 'My plan was to fly straight back, but Phil wasn't originally going to come to England. There was a week gap or something in America, so he decided to fly in – Ivan (Mauger) got cheap fares through Continental Airways – it was a bit of a surprise because no-one expected him. So he flew in, and we decided then that I would go back to America with them and watch the World Cup in Long Beach. I had to go to London to get a visa, because I didn't have one originally because I was transiting through. I went to London, got a visa, and flew to Long Beach and then flew back to Melbourne.'

The World Team Cup Final in California featured the four leading speedway nations, the eventual winners Denmark, England, Sweden and the hosts. Among the world's elite who had assembled in the US were Erik Gundersen, his arch-rival Hans Nielsen, Jan O. Pedersen, Sam Ermolenko and the mercurial Moran brothers, Kelly and Shawn, Kelvin Tatum, Simon Wigg, Per Jonsson and Leigh's future team-mate, Jimmy Nilsen.

'The Danes were dominant and the driving force. I was just a young kid, and Crumpie took me under his wing and off we went to America. He hired a van and took me around. We watched the racing at Long Beach and Ascot, which had a big sprint car track, flat track, a little speedway track in the middle, and go karts beside it.

'After the World Cup everybody went back to this party at the go kart track, and I remember going in there because all the guys were there, the Danes, the Yanks . . . it was such a huge eye-opener. I shall never forget it, they had like bins full of Budweisers on ice, and I was only 17 and I couldn't drink, especially in America because you can't drink until you're 21. At that age you take it all in your stride, but it was cool. It was fantastic to see Erik Gundersen ride, he was the World Champion at the time and it was the only time I saw him race. I went with the flow basically.

'I've been past Ascot a couple of times since, it's right on the motorway or highway, and there is nothing there. The Agajanian family owned it and sold it off, but what a place. If I was able to go back there now, as it was then, it would be huge to me, but at the time it was just, fair enough, here I was in the big smoke, LA. I was lucky because I had Crumpie and two of his mates with him and they took me under their wing and I just tagged along – I didn't have to think about too much, which I couldn't back then, I must have been so green, I was so wet behind the ears you wouldn't believe it!'

While Leigh may have been a little naïve to the ways of British Speedway and the unwritten laws, he was wily enough to realise that he shouldn't get carried away with all the praise being heaped upon him. Perhaps it was the gentlemanly thing to do to sign up for the team after they had paid your airfare and given you a chance to show what you could do. But he was also mature enough to realise that it could all go wrong and he could be back after a month or two, flat broke and wondering what to do next.

Craig Boyce and Todd Wiltshire had made quite an impression riding in the National League for Poole and Wimbledon respectively, while Craig Hodgson had also more than held his own at Peterborough. But there was also the other side. Fellow Victoria rider Nigel Tremelling, who had also benefited from Crump's experience, had won the Australian Under-18 Championship ahead of Hodgson and Shane Bowes in 1986, but failed to make the grade at Poole.

As the season came to a close in Europe, Leigh began his second year of senior racing pondering whether or not he was ready to race in Britain. In mid-November, Crump and Adams – the Master and the Apprentice – were booked to ride at Speedway Park in Adelaide. A series of scratch races saw Crump and Adams trade race wins and position as they fought their way to the final.

Crumpie missed the gate in the final, but rocketed through from the back to lead the race – game over, so the packed stands thought. But no-one reckoned on the tenacious teenager, Adams, who slipped underneath his mentor on the final lap, taking Ashley Norton with him, and pulled away on the run-in to the chequered flag to thunderous applause. Everyone in Adelaide thought that his speedway apprenticeship was over after they had witnessed that race.

Due to the varying lengths of the tracks in Australia, the races on the big tracks were quite often run over three laps (usually venues that stage car racing) as opposed to the traditional four. Therefore, you could ride at Mildura one night and run in races over four laps, then a few evenings later you could be at somewhere like Archerfield and race over three laps.

In the midst of alternating between the two lengths and combine that with inexperience, it's not surprising that one could get confused. Besides, the distance of some of these tracks is such that you feel like you've completed four laps when you've only done three! During a trip to Renmark, when Leigh Adams was 17, it was looking likely that he was going to smash Simon Wigg's track record. He had the speed, but so long was the distance that he miscounted and pulled up after three laps!

He soon redeemed himself, however, with a mature and methodical performance that belied his tender years. Leigh appeared in an indoor meeting at the Brigadoon Equestrian Centre in Perth. On a tiny 120-metre circuit, he headed the qualifiers for the final with an unbeaten 12 points. In the six-lap final, with a stunning display of track craft, Adams picked off the more experienced English duo of Neil Evitts and Andy Smith to take victory. It was a performance that reporter Ken Brown would never forget as he said: 'That 63 seconds of brilliance will live for a long time in the memories of all who witnessed it.'

Shortly after, reports filtered back to the UK that Adams may not ride in the British League after all in 1989. He wanted to feel confident that he was

Multi-World Champion Ivan Mauger poses in front of his pupils at a training school at North Arm over the weekend of 3/4 December 1988. There are many famous faces here; Leigh is standing, second from the right (no. 11). (Dave Schooling)

ready for such an undertaking and didn't want to jeopardise a very good apprenticeship as a mechanic until he was sure. Such news didn't go down too well in Dorset as the Pirates promotion had already begun making team plans that included the Australian.

'That 63 seconds of brilliance will live for a long time in the memories of all who witnessed it.'

Ken Brown (Reporter)

Faced with a big decision, like most young men, Leigh sought advice from his parents, in particular his father's wisdom.

'At that age, if it didn't work out he could come back and get on with his life. Leigh said to me, "What do you think about education and all that sort of thing?" and I said, "Go over there, see how you go, if you don't go good, you can always come back after, it doesn't matter if you're 40 years old, you can always go to college, retrain yourself and do something."'

From 1972 to 1989, Phil Crump had won the Victoria Championship thirteen times. Only Danny Kennedy, John McNeil, Rod Hunter and Bill Barrett had managed to wrestle the state title away from his grasp. The man who was called 'The Mildura Marvel' in Britain was made to race hard for the crown by the young pretender Adams in the 1987/88 season, and that performance was the prequel to a stunning display that he would provide a year later.

Leigh won his first Victorian Championship with a 15-point maximum in 88/89. His victory marked the end of Crump's reign and the beginning of a new era. It could have also gone some way to convincing himself that his apprenticeship in Australia was at an end, and he was ready to take on the rigours of racing in the British League.

Now all he had to do was find a way of telling his employers at the truck company, who were providing him with a valuable mechanic's apprenticeship, that he was going overseas to race speedway professionally.

Meanwhile, Pete Ansell tucked a contract into his briefcase and clicked it shut, as he and fellow Poole promoter Mervyn Stewksbury made their final preparations to travel Down Under to take in the Aussie title race at Newcastle – and to finalise an agreement that would make Leigh Adams a Poole Pirates rider.

4

Pints, Points & Prizes

When Leigh had decided that he would definitely go and try his luck in England, it took him three weeks to pluck up the courage and tell G.E.M.B. Trucks. He was mindful of how important an apprenticeship was to a young man who wasn't academically-minded, and they had already allowed him to take a month off in order to see what it would be like to race in England. Therefore, Leigh didn't want to be seen as taking advantage of their good nature and then letting them down. He needn't have worried, though, because they were more than understanding and compliant, as John Adams reveals:

'They said, "Well, Leigh, we know that you're interested in bikes and you're going okay. I'll tell you what we'll do, we'll hold your apprenticeship for twelve months, and if you don't like speedway, you can come back and pick up your apprenticeship," which was terrific of them to do that. He was a good worker, but he'd come home covered in muck.'

The apprenticeship was one dilemma, but the other was a matter of the heart because Leigh also had a girlfriend to leave behind. He had met his future wife, Kylie, three years earlier through his schoolfriends.

'They (his friends) lived down where Kylie was from – which was about half an hour from where I was – and they were involved with motorbikes too. Where they come from was complete bush. It was Easter time and they always used to go camping by the river, it was traditional for all the kids from that area. I got invited down there to go motorbike riding with my mates along the river bank. I met them at one of the houses and we went to the camp, and Kylie was there with her brother and sister, they all used to go together. And that was it, it was pretty much love at first sight. I know it sounds pretty silly, but as soon as we clocked eyes on each other that was it. I said to my mate, "Who's that girl?" and I got her number and it went from there.

'Since we met, we had been going out with each other the whole time. We were pretty young, but we didn't know what was going to happen, or how it would work out, so we put it (the relationship) on hold for a year while I went to England to race for Poole.'

However, the teenage years are not always the best time of a person's life to make decisions with regard to affairs of the heart. Kylie remembers the situation being a little different, and it wasn't quite so much clear-cut as it was coded. He did what a lot of young lads do at that age, he avoided telling her what was happening and gave her the cold shoulder instead!

While he was getting his affairs in order, Pete Ansell and Mervyn Stewksbury had left England for Australia on 9 January 1989 to finalise their contracts with their riders for the forthcoming season in Britain. Having already done the groundwork with Adams by bringing him over to Poole for a month, they were confident that they would secure his signature on a 1989 contract. Having qualified for his second Australian National Championship in Newcastle, New South Wales, it was arranged that they'd meet in the city to finalise the deal.

Unsurprisingly, teenager Leigh took his father along with him and also his uncle, Brian, who had begun to play quite an important role in his nephew's career. However, Leigh's uncle was keen to try and get better financial terms from the Pirates management as Pete Ansell recalls, 'His uncle did most of the negotiations because being young, Leigh didn't understand too much and his uncle was trying to get the best possible deal, which is understandable because he was looking after his interests. Everybody is going to try to get a bit more, but at the end of the day you know what your limits are and how the business runs. We always knew that Leigh was very professional, very dedicated in what he was going to do and where he was going. Neil Street was the biggest factor for us because he recommended him and he knew the family very well.'

It would appear that Ansell and Stewksbury brought more with them from England than just contracts for their riders – some disagreeable English weather! Loads of the wet stuff had been falling in the area all afternoon, but amazingly it had missed the stadium. Unfortunately, the stadium couldn't avoid the rain forever and it interrupted the Australian Final and eventually forced it to be abandoned – Mick Poole had an unbeaten score at the time of the call-off. It was decided to rearrange the prestigious meeting the next day, which meant that the Australian Pairs Championship – that was originally scheduled for the following day – had to be held over.

Glenn Doyle won the restaging while Leigh had a disappointing evening and scored 6 points. He had better luck in the Pairs though. Partnered with Phil Crump, the Mildura duo grabbed the runners-up place with a combined total of 23 points (Leigh scored 10), behind the victorious New South Wales pairing of Stephen Davies (18) and Chris Watson (10) on 28. It was after this meeting that Adams confirmed that he had signed an agreement to ride for Poole.

He didn't have long to test his mettle against some of the world's elite either. About a fortnight after that meeting Adams found himself rubbing shoulders with Tommy Knudsen, Sam Ermolenko, Shawn Moran and Bobby Schwartz at Mildura in the International Masters. A traditional twenty-heat, sixteen-rider format was used, except the top six would face each other in a winner-takes-all final.

Leigh qualified second behind Crump with 12 points, and met Ermolenko, Knudsen, David Walsh and Bobby Schwartz in the final. However, Adams' race didn't last long as he tangled with an uncompromising Schwartz and was excluded. It was left to Crumpie to uphold local pride and with a tough race he won the meeting after another coming together with an American, this time Ermolenko who was sent over the fence. Sam was excluded, the race declared, and Crumpie was the winner.

A few weeks later Leigh had another chance to lock horns with some of the top names of the sport in the West End Solo International at Wayville, Adelaide. In addition to the above riders Simon Wigg, Kai Niemi, Einar Kyllingstad and Phil Collins were among the impressive field that attracted an appreciative 14,000 audience.

This time the event was run along the lines of the World Longtrack meetings, with eighteen riders contesting three heats each, with six riders in a race. There were two semi-finals and then a sudden death final. After the qualifying races had been completed, Adams found himself joint leader with Ermolenko on 14 points.

Having drawn – on paper – the easier of the two semi-finals, he showed his lack of experience as he finished fourth behind Mick Poole, Craig Hodgson and Kai Niemi. The meeting was won by Shawn Moran.

While Leigh possesses a tremendous amount of natural ability, he is also a thinker. Having dipped out of that semi-final, the new Poole Pirate learned from that experience and put it right at the Red Centre, Alice Springs. At the time, the meeting was reported to be one of the richest motorcycle events of the season with an overall prize fund believed to have been $10,000. No travelling expenses were paid to the riders, but they did earn $20 per point and the sudden death final was worth $2,500 – with $1,000 going to the overall winner. Such prize money was exceptionally good at that time, especially as the Arunga Park stadium was regarded as almost off the radar as far as Australian Speedway was concerned.

From his base in Mildura, Leigh undertook the 3,000-mile, two-and-a-half day drive to the venue with Crumpie and Neil Street. The journey was indeed an arduous one, even for experienced men like his companions. Located in the Northern Territory, as they headed deep into the outback, cruising across the unforgiving land, their journey would have been accompanied by red dust and the heat that characterises the centre of Australia.

Remote and with a population today of not more than 28,000, the party from Mildura were pleasantly surprised when they arrived. Neil Street summed up what they were anticipating when he said, 'I was expecting a country cowboy turn-out. Instead it's one of the best tracks in the country!'

Phil Crump echoed that praise and added, 'It was smooth, fast, with lots of different lines for passing. It's a very good racing track.'

It was certainly one of the hottest meetings that Leigh had raced in. During the day the mercury had topped 40°C before dropping away to a still-sweltering 30°C. The riders were peeling their leathers off between races as if the material was stuck to them with treacle.

The Red Centre 1000 was a mammoth fifty-two-heat programme that was split between solo and sidecar racing, and the Grand Final for the solos didn't come to the tapes until 12.15 a.m. Furthermore, the promoters gave their biggest crowd of the year value for money because the admission cost was $7, compared with the $18 charged a fortnight earlier at the Sydney Showground; the Alice Springs public were indeed treated to a very reasonable evening's worth of racing.

Admittedly most of the crowd had come to see Crump, but it was Adams who stole the show. A taster of what was to come saw Leigh pass his Victorian rival for a race win as he 'gracefully' raced to an unbeaten score. However, Crumpie returned the compliment in the semi-final with a smooth and convincing pass of his own, but second was good enough to transfer to the big-money final.

As is often the case with speedway racing, the choice of starting positions was vital. Adams was drawn off the outside gate, right next to the concrete wall, while Crumpie was handily placed in gate three. The rest of the grid was filled by Nathan Simpson, Darryl Simpson and local boys Glen Baxter and Dave Jackson. Opinion at the time was that drawing the outside gate had as good as finished the youngster's chances of pocketing the cash.

However, in a scene that would become familiar all over the world, Leigh made a lightning start from the unfavoured gate, and kept the throttle wide open as he cleared the pack and was reported to have, 'screamed into the lead before they'd done half a lap.' Even though Northern Territory Champion Baxter was on his tail all the way, there was nothing he could do about him. Crump finished third, and was heard to utter afterwards, 'I think I've taught the boy too much!' Leigh was ready for England.

Watching your teenage son head approximately 10,000 miles away to a foreign land is not an easy thing to do. Even more so when you realise that he's going to race a motorcycle in one of the hardest speedway leagues in the world; a league that contained experienced riders who had performed at the very highest level, but also rough, raw and untried youngsters who could be roaring off into the lead one minute, and then tearing down several sections of the safety fence the next. Then there were the hard nuts that had no respect for reputations and were infamous for their willingness to take a rider out to the fence and leave him high and dry – or worse – rather than let him pass. If Leigh Adams was going to make it as an international speedway rider, he'd have to conquer all of that and more.

'I think I've taught the boy too much!'

Phil Crump

His original departure may have been over twenty years ago, and he's come back and returned again regularly ever since, but Joan Adams' memory of that first farewell to her youngest son still carries an emotional resonance that only a mother can convey, 'I didn't want my little boy going away,' she recalls.

'This was the turning point for us,' John Adams acknowledges. 'We were quite happy because Streetie promised me one thing, he said, "John, I can remember when I came over from Australia, started riding speedway, a family took me in for twelve months and got me on my feet." He said, "I will promise you that Leigh will get looked after by us, he won't go without anything. He'll get fed, he'll get looked after like he's our son," and that was exactly what he did. When somebody says that, what do you do? Especially a bloke like Streetie: he's not a drinker, he's a decent living sort of a guy, so we were quite happy for him to take that twelve-months challenge.'

Even though John Adams said that he didn't like to look too far back into the family's history, his English connections proved very helpful when it came to acquiring a permit to race in England.

'My dad was born on the Isle of Wight and he came out to Australia when he was two years old, so Leigh was able to get patriality, which was good, it made it a lot easier for him.'

'That really helped me, and it still does now,' says Leigh. 'I don't need work permits, I can come in and out of England when I want. It's getting harder and harder to get permits, and it helps me getting into the country all the time, travelling backwards and forwards from aboard, I can slip through the quick lanes, so that's been a big help.'

The Streets, Neil and his wife Mary, became Leigh's surrogate parents during his first full season racing in England. He stayed with them in Exeter, which was considered to be a bit of an outpost on British Speedway's map. But it was home from home for the teenager Adams, and just the sort of grounding he required at that stage of his career and life.

'I didn't realise how far out of the way it was; I didn't even think about it – it was just a dot on the map of where you live,' Leigh reflects. 'It's not until now you realise it was a long way out. It was a pain sometimes when you had to get off the boat from Dover and it was a fair old drive down to Exeter. But it was no worse than guys who were living in Scotland then like Bowesy (Shane Bowes), Parker (Shane) and Lyons (Jason). It was no worse, maybe a bit better, but it was remote. Exeter was strong then too, the speedway was strong and there were a lot of speedway people down there. I got linked up with a few, so it wasn't like I was down there on my lonesome.

'Living my life there was brilliant. I had a family environment, Mary was like my mum and it was a great set-up. If the truth was known it probably wasn't a bad thing that I was out of the way a little bit. I would go up and stay with Boycey (Craig Boyce) and Lango (Tony Langdon) sometimes, and we'd have a few parties and that, but I could always get away from that scene and do my own thing in Exeter – it was a blessing.'

Adams recalls an early introduction to one English pastime in particular, courtesy of Tony Langdon.

'I didn't drink; I never had a drink until I went to England. I can remember that first night in Poole, Lango came into the bar – I must have gone out with the boys. Lango came up to me with a pint of beer in his hand and said: "Welcome to England, you've got to have a pint when you're in England." I hated beer, and I said: "Lango I hate the stuff." I didn't drink at all. Steve and Tony Langdon were top guys though, but I'd just come over, it was a big step.'

Located at Neil Street's home meant that not only was he based with a family who were well-versed in all things speedway, but he also had access to a workshop as well as Streetie's extensive knowledge of engines. This wasn't a clean and clinical looking environment, though, it was disorganised and untidy; but its appearance gave it a homely atmosphere, and with it, a reassuring confidence.

'I had a little workshop at Streetie's house. But about a twenty-five-minute drive from his house, he had a shed where his workshop was and you hadn't seen anything like it. There was this shack and there was stuff everywhere, old bikes, old engines and it was damp, but there was a lot of money's worth of equipment and this was where he built the four-valve conversion. It was unique to see it pretty much as it was when he built the four-valve. It hadn't changed; it was this wooden shed out in this little village.

'At the time you don't think about all that, you're just happy to have what you've got. For a while that year we had hosepipe bans because of the hot weather, a heat wave, and I couldn't use a pressure washer or anything, only a bucket and it was pretty hard going. But you didn't think about it, you just did it, it was all part of it. These days the kids wouldn't think about washing their bikes without a pressure washer.'

Leigh may have been thousands of miles from home, in a strange country where rain seemed more plentiful than sunshine, but being surrounded by so many Aussies in the Pirates side helped him to settle in. Craig Boyce, Tony Langdon and Gary Allan added a very distinctive Antipodean flavour to the south coast, so much so that the team was referred to as 'the Wimborne Outback'. Alun Rossiter was signed from Swindon and was made captain and he was joined by Alastair Stevens and Kevin Smart, with Steve Leigh, Jon Surman, and Mike Lewthwaite filling in at different points during what was a memorable campaign.

There was little doubt that the Pirates management were convinced that in Leigh Adams they had signed a marvellous prospect, not least because he came in on an assessed 2-point average which meant that he was a statistical bargain. Anyone with the slightest knowledge of speedway knew full well that Adams would easily surpass that figure.

In fact, during his very first meeting for Poole on Friday 24 March, he scorched to an impressive paid maximum from five rides (14+1) as the Pirates demolished Exeter, 62–34. A tapes exclusion got him off to a disappointing start in the return match at the famous County Ground, but he still raced to 10 points as they defeated Exeter to win the Easter Challenge Trophy.

If that wasn't enough to convince any critics that he was something special, then another a four-ride maximum against Danish touring side, Slangerup (Kulsvierne) was sweetened by the fact that he also established a new track record of 62.4 seconds. However, due to a starting gate malfunction, the races were begun on the green light and because of that, referee, Mick Barnes, deemed that the new record couldn't stand. Barnes' decision was overruled by the BSPA and the new time was entered into the record books. In fact, it remains a track record at Wimborne Road because the track was altered the following July because the football team – who the Pirates shared the stadium with – were promoted and they required a wider pitch.

Leigh certainly cut a distinctive figure as he roared around Britain's National League tracks because he wore motocross-style shoulder pads.

Lance King wore something similar but his were more discreet. Given how well Adams was racing, some of his rivals may have thought, to paraphrase a well-known energy drink, that they gave him wings.

'I had snapped my collar bone twice in Australia and I just wore them to try and protect my collar bones a bit,' Leigh explains. 'It was the thing I wore in England because I think I broke my collar bone twice in one year. I didn't even think about it, but people would say: "Oh yeah, you're the kid who used to wear the shoulder pads," because no-one wore them in speedway much. In motocross it was the known thing and it probably made me stand out from the others. I'm surprised it didn't take off!' he laughs.

When the Pirates inflicted an early season defeat over the highly-fancied Ipswich at Foxhall Heath – Adams scored a paid 14 from six rides – Leigh confidently predicted that Poole would 'take some stopping'. And he couldn't have been more accurate for the Dorset team completed twelve undefeated matches until they lost an inter-league challenge fixture at Swindon – Leigh scored 8 points during his first appearance at the venue where he would eventually establish himself as one of the club's greatest ever riders.

Leigh outside Nigel Crabtree (Stoke), Kevin Smart and Ian Stead. Note Leigh's shoulder pads. (Gordon Day Archive)

It would be a season of new experiences for him, such as how to read his opponents by reputation and on the track, the traditional northern tours when a southern-based club like Poole would race at Berwick and Glasgow on successive days and, of course, just learning the business of being a full-time professional rider.

'You always knew of your hard nuts and that sort of thing, and Andy Galvin was the hard rider of that league. I just went and raced. I wasn't the best of starters back then, but Poole was a good track for me because I could pass there. I didn't have anything flash, just a standard Godden.

'Even those Scottish tours and all that, you just get in and drive from Exeter to Glasgow, you didn't think about it. Luckily I had Streetie and he would always drive there and I'd drive home or whatever. His son, Andy, he helped as a mechanic for quite a bit. But I never got involved with engines, I just washed my bikes and I'd give them to Streetie. I still don't know much about engines, in the fact of tuning them. I know how to ride one, what's good and what's bad and what needs changing, but to actually prepare an engine, no I couldn't do that now. Which I think has been a good thing for me because a lot of people get screwed up by being too technical, putting in this cam for that track and that cam for this track and all that sort of stuff. I've never been like that and I'm not a person who blames engines; I've always blamed myself when I had a bad meeting, and just get on with the next one.'

Nonetheless he was setting a hot pace and he also got to represent Australia in a five-match Test series against a National League Select. Unfortunately, Australia lost the series, 3–1, with one Test drawn. Leigh found the going a little hard and he only scored double figures once at Poole (12), but Australian team manager James Easter was well aware that the teenager was one for the future and intended to give him a taste of World Team Cup action later in the season.

'I thought he was incredibly mature for his age,' says Easter. 'He was 18 with a 35-year-old head on his shoulders. He was totally different to any speedway rider I had seen before. I had seven years of bringing over green-eyed Aussies who were pretty wild individuals – they couldn't spell Europe, never mind know what it was like! His attitude, even in the younger days, was totally different from the high-living, party boys that I was used to.

'We took him to Newcastle one time with the Aussie team and he rode like somebody who had been racing for twenty years – you've never seen anything so composed in all your life.

'I actually met Leigh when he was 14 years old, I don't think he would have remembered it,' Easter says. 'I went to Mildura in 1986 and he was there

Action from the National League v Australia Test at Poole, 7 June 1989. Craig Boyce and Leigh Adams fend off an inside challenge from Neville Tatum. Tatum would later crash and gift the Aussies a 5–1. (Gordon Day Archive)

with his dad. His dad said this is James, and he said, "Nice to meet you Mr Easter." And from that day forward we always called each other Mr Adams and Mr Easter, and we got on very, very well. When he came over he was going to be the great white hope and he was amazing. And he developed into a very decent human being as well as an incredibly good speedway rider.

'What I always believed in, if you were going to make something decent of these boys you had to try and blood them in gradually, there was no use chucking them in at the deep end because it just wouldn't work. So what we did, at the latter part of the season, wherever we could, we used to take a young, green Aussie team up to places like Newcastle and Edinburgh, call them the Wallabies, so that we could have a look at what the youngsters were like, bleed them in like that. We also used to use the World Cup, because in those days it was a different system, and we used take the youngsters with us and Leigh was one of them.'

Adams made his World Cup debut in a qualifying round at Rzeszow in Poland, where they faced the hosts, Italy and Hungary. Australia was in Group B and they had won the first match in Hungary. Over two matches, they had to win on aggregate in order to qualify for another two-match contest in Group A, where the top two aggregate scoring teams would qualify for the final itself.

Holding a 4-point advantage over Hungary, Leigh joined Troy Butler, Stephen Davies, Craig Boyce and Mick Poole for his first trip behind the Iron Curtain. Easter says, 'What I would say to these boys is, "Look, we're going to take you there, show you what it's like, you're going to learn by it, it's a learning experience not a money-making experience, you've got to learn what the culture is like, you've got to learn how to deal with it, you've got to learn how to grow up in difficult circumstances, but I'll guarantee you two rides. Whatever happens, you're still going to get two rides." And that's what we did.'

Australia won the meeting with Poland second, while Hungary and Italy finished far behind. Adams got his two rides and made an immediate impression.

'I was reserve, and we were leading by so much they just put me in and I won my two races. That was pretty amazing because it was all Communist, Berlin and East Germany all that sort of stuff,' Leigh says.

Easter has a more detailed memory to share, 'He did Armando Castagna up like a kipper! We put him in, he had a rough old Pole, and rough old Hungarian, and he went inside the Pole, where there wasn't a gap, and then rounded Castagna all on the same turn. And we all went, "Oh my God, that's quality!", and from that minute we knew he was going to make it.

'We came back, and whatever we won, we'd split it between the five riders and he couldn't believe that he had just done two rides, had a learning experience and got paid what people like Troy Butler, Stephen Davies and Micky Poole had been paid and I said, "Look, that's part and parcel of knowing what a team is like, and you'll learn by it." He didn't want it first of all; I've never known a speedway rider in my life turn it down. He said that he didn't want it because he said that he didn't deserve it, and I said, "No, no, without you, we can't operate." So that's what we did.'

While the meeting might have been a significant event in the career of the Australian, he remembers it more now for the experience of the Berlin Wall and the Communist regime.

'James was also a travel agent so he organised all our trips, and back then it was a big deal going to Poland. I guess you could have gone straight through, but James would split the trip up. So we'd drive right in, go in through the wall, spend the night in Berlin, and go back out again.

1. Motorcycles were always a part of the family: proud father John Adams with his two boys Leigh (nearest camera) on his Honda MR50, and Andrew. (Adams Family Archive)

2. The obligatory school photo – aged 9. (Adams Family Archive)

3. An early study of Leigh racing a junior bike at Mildura in 1981. (Adams Family Archive)

4. Leigh practising at Mildura, 1983. (Adams Family Archive)

5. An unusual ground-level picture of Leigh leading a junior race in 1985. The 'armchair' style is already visible. (Adams Family Archive)

6. The first of many trophies after third place in the 1983 Australian Junior Championship. (Adams Family Archive)

7. Australian Junior Champion, 1986. Left to right: Scott Norman (2nd), Shane Parker (3rd), Jason Lyons (2nd) and first-placed Leigh. (Adams Family Archive)

8. The 1989 Poole Pirates team which won the National League title. Standing, left to right: Kevin Smart, Gary Allan, Neil Street (team manager), Tony Langdon and Alastair Stevens. Front: Leigh, Alun Rossiter, Justin Elkins (mascot, who would later join Leigh at Swindon in 1992) and Craig Boyce. (Gordon Day Archive)

9. A Poole Pirate in 1989. (Gordon Day Archive)

10. First season for Swindon, 1990. (Adams Family Archive)

11. The 1990 World Pairs Final, Landshut, Germany. Hans Nielsen goes down with Todd Wiltshire (partially hidden) and is about to collect Gerd Riss. Leigh is ready to take evasive action to the left. This was a pivotal moment because Nielsen's exclusion from this race, and Riss being unable to continue, put the young Aussie pair of Adams and Wiltshire in the driving seat. (www.mike-patrick.com)

12. Concentration at the start line for Swindon. He would have to refine his starting technique to consistently challenge at world level. (Adams Family Archive)

13. In action for Swindon during his first season as a Robin in 1990. (Adams Family Archive)

14. Team riding with Paul Dugard for the Robins in 1991. (Adams Family Archive)

15. *About to tuck in to the cake at his belated 21st birthday celebrations, since he was away riding in England on his real birthday. (Adams Family Archive)*

16. *His first Australian National Championship, 1992. (Adams Family Archive)*

17. History in the making: Leigh with his 1992 Australian Under-21 title, thus creating a unique Grand Slam of Aussie titles: state, pairs, U-21 and senior crown. Joining him in the picture are, from left to right: his father John, brother Andrew, tuner and mechanic Tim Osmond and Steve Baker. (Adams Family Archive)

18. Hiding from immigration on the trip to Pfaffenhofen. Mick Day, who was a mechanic for Simon Wigg, is turned to the camera. (Adams Family Archive)

19. Leading Mark Loram in the run-off for the World Under-21 Championship. (www.mike-patrick.com)

20. 1992 World Under-21 Champion. He also held the Australian Under-21 title at the time. (www.mike-patrick.com)

21. On his way to his first World Final, winner of the Commonwealth Championship at King's Lynn in 1993. (Adams Family Archive)

22. In action for Polish club Lublin. Leigh gates alongside Hans Nielsen. (Adams Family Archive)

23. Together with Kylie before the 1994 World Championship semi-final at Bradford. Note Leigh's broken finger which is taped up. (www.mike-patrick.com)

24. Disappointment at Bradford in the opening race when a mechanical failure meant that he didn't get off the start line and would eventually be eliminated from the 1994 World Championship race. The body language says it all. (www.mike-patrick.com)

25. 1995 Grand Prix Challenge
Champion and a guaranteed
place in the 1996 World
Championship.
(www.mike-patrick.com)

26. Pictured with David Tapp,
1995. Leigh's left shoulder is
strapped up 'Aussie Rules
Football style'.
(www.mike-patrick.com)

27. The happy couple, 30 November 1996. (Adams Family Archive)

28. The Australian International Masters Series was always fun, but also very competitive. Here Craig Boyce (left) tries to resist Leigh's challenge at Townsville. (Adams Family Archive)

29. With Steve Johnston (right) as a team in the Aussie Masters Series. 'There was never a dull moment,' Leigh recalls. (Adams Family Archive)

30. Australian International Masters Series Champion, 1997. He won the championship four times in total. (Tony Jackson)

31. Team Owen Bros Racing. Left to right: Norrie Allan, Terry Broadbank, Mark Loram, Randy Owen, Leigh, John 'Dude' McLachlan and Paul Honeyman. An interesting indication as to how this team was put together, Broadbank moved over to Mark's side to even up the team element, while Honeyman, who wasn't a mechanic, just an occasional helper, was added to the line-up for the picture. (Adams Family Archive)

32. Displaying his disappointment at British Speedway's first attempt at a race suit in 1998 for Swindon. (Adams Family Archive)

33. 1999 World Team Cup Champions with Australia. Jason Lyons, Todd Wiltshire, Ryan Sullivan, Leigh and team manager Neil Street. (www.mike-patrick.com)

34. Leigh with the rider that he regards as a big influence, a good friend and the best of all-time, Tony Rickardsson at Masarna. (Roland Bärtilsson)

35. Checking out track conditions at Masarna. (Roland Bärtilsson)

36. The King's Lynn Knights 'Dream Team' – a thoughtful Leigh contemplates the content of the team talk at King's Lynn in 2000. Craig Boyce (standing, centre) listens to the views from the hidden Steve Masters. The others in the picture are Travis McGowan (2), Jason Crump (1), John Cook (4), Brian Griffin and Tom Madsen is standing next to Boyce. (www.mike-patrick.com)

37. There was always rivalry with Todd Wiltshire. This photograph was taken after the 2000/01 Australian Final when Todd's exuberant riding may have clinched him the title, but his tactics angered Leigh. This confrontation took place on the centre green in full view of the public. (James Baker)

The west side was just incredible, there would be BMWs, Mercedes, and all that stuff, and it was just like Australia, discos, pubs, the place was just rocking. But then you'd drive five minutes out, get to the border, the wall, look over, and it was dingy, you couldn't imagine it was so close. Those people in the east were able to smell it, it was bad really.

'Literally you'd look over the wall and it was just doom and gloom. They had a platform there where you could walk up and look over. They had soldiers and dogs walking up and down, and a museum. It was special to see that, and then to go to Poland and see how that was because they were all Communist then, and we needed visas and we're talking about four days to drive in and out of the place.

'The queues just to get into Berlin . . .' he wistfully recalls, 'they'd search your cars, have mirrors under your vehicles to make sure there were no bodies; you'd have to have all the bikes out and all that. Then, we'd come back out, and you'd do the same again, another four-hour queue to get out of Poland. You just put up with it.'

James Easter would be pleased to hear Leigh speak appreciatively of the experience, because he would go out of his way to educate his young riders about the history and the different culture of Berlin and Europe. 'We used to go through Berlin, park up and I'd take them around and give them a history lesson for the day. We'd show them what the wall was like, what Germany was like during the war and just show them a bit of Europe and how people would do things. I think it stuck with them for many years. They used to call them "My little holidays". Whenever I see them now, they always remember that little bit of it. I can clearly remember going round Berlin, when the wall was up, and seeing Leigh sat in the back seat of the van with his mouth open, especially when we went through the wall. He was an 18-year-old, raw Aussie and pretty green.'

This early learning experience was also critical in building the team spirit within the Australian camp, not only for that era, but for the successful period that followed.

Leigh Adams remembers, 'Being with a bunch of Aussies there was always something going on, someone would be strumming a guitar or something while we waited. We were crammed into a couple of vans, but they were good times and good experiences. There aren't too many people who have good stories like that and it was an eye-opener for me.'

Once behind the Iron Curtain the Aussies were treated to a very different world to the one that they had experienced in the West and at home.

'It was proper Communist; driving through, all their cars were Ladas and Trabants and we'd come bombing along in vans. Before I left I was warned,

Leigh pictured with Joe Screen before an inter-league match race in 1989. These were the two sensations of British speedway that year with Screen riding in the top flight. This was taken before Poole's match with Milton Keynes on 26 September. Adams was using borrowed equipment because his was still in transit from the World Under-21 final in Italy and he went on to lose all three races to Screen. (Gordon Day Archive)

"Take all your old stuff, carbies and all that," so we were cutting deals for our equipment left, right and centre.

'We didn't go out, it was unheard of, you didn't go out to eat or anything like that. It was a known thing that if you ate their food you would get sick. So James was very well-organised and he would always have these eskies made up with food. We felt like we were being watched, and we stuck out in the crowd because of our clothes alone. It was a great experience. The kids these days just lob into Poland and it's just like being in England with pubs, restaurants, and all that, but I've seen it, lived it and experienced it.'

As the season progressed, Adams qualified for the World Under-21 Final – he won the first qualifying round in Frederiksborg, Denmark – and finished seventh with 9 points. His sensational season was grabbing the headlines everywhere and he acquired sponsors because of it. It was a busy year for the Australian, with plenty to do and experience. However, as the autumn months arrived and the climate became cooler, his thoughts began to think of home.

'He used to call every week,' his mother says. 'I think he might have been a little bit homesick.'

'I think being in that family environment, they were good to him and Streetie got on to those sorts of things,' John adds. 'Mary was so good, she was so friendly and he got attached to her. Streetie kept him busy, and that's what it's all about. He had a terrific grounding of how to be a speedway rider without mixing with what was hanging over the fence.

'We used to say: "If you ever want to phone home, get on the phone, and reverse the charges," and that was about the only thing we ever did for him. Everything he's done, he's done on his own. Not once has he phoned home and said, dad I need $1,000 or something, not once, and that's a credit to him.'

Despite all the care and attention he received from the Streets, and the racing that kept him busy, being 18 years old, thousands of miles from home and away from his family for the longest period of his life so far, he admits that he did get homesick. In fact, as the autumn nights began to draw in, his thoughts turned to home with more regularity.

'Cold, rainy nights in October were the worst,' he says. 'You start to think about your mates at home, and they'll be walking around in shorts and t-shirts and out riding in the evening; while it was dark in England, cold and often wet. For a few years it was always a difficult month, but you acclimatise and you learn to get over it. But you're always looking forward to getting home and some sunshine after a long season in Europe.'

Meanwhile, Poole were having one of their best seasons for many years, helped no end by the performance of Adams and his fellow countrymen. The Pirates were set to win their first league championship for twenty years. If they could follow up a trio of victories on the road by defeating Arena-Essex at home, they would be crowned league champions.

Craig Boyce, Neil Street, Leigh and Tony Langdon celebrate Poole's league championship success in 1989. (www.mike-patrick.com)

The Pirates didn't as much clinch the championship, as ram it home with a convincing 71–24 annihilation of Arena. Leigh scored a paid maximum as Poole's biggest crowd of the season went ballistic with excitement.

Predictably, he did indeed make a complete mockery of the 2-point average, finishing his debut season in Britain with an average of over 9 points – he also represented Poole in the National League Riders' Championship but, plagued my mechanical problems, failed to score. Despite his impressive scores and new experiences, his recollection of the year at Poole isn't as vivid as one might have expected.

'That whole year, I don't know, I can honestly say that I just turned up, I didn't look at records, my average or anything like that. I just wanted to race bikes and race speedway – 100 per cent. I didn't realise all the technicalities of me coming in on a 2-point average and ending up with 9, but the whole season was racing, having fun, and just enjoying it. To win the league, at the time it was good, but when you sit back now and think about it, you realise what a big deal it was.

'I had a really good bunch of guys with me Boycey, Lango, Rosco, he was always full of it, but he had a lean spell there for a while, but as a captain he was really good, I believe there was never a dull moment. So I was locked into a really good environment, especially to be around the Aussies. To do what I did in my first year, I guess it was pretty incredible at the time, but I didn't think about it, I just got on and rode.

'I had good backing that year from Coastal doors and windows – Poole had organised that for me. John Anderson was the guy and he really took me under his wing. He obviously enjoyed the exposure he was getting, but he looked after me with a new bike, bought me a van and leathers and everything like that, so that was a big help.'

Another sponsor was Pete Summers of PJS ignitions, and it was this association that eventually led to Leigh taking the next step up the career ladder. PJS also sponsored Hans Nielsen, who had just won his third world individual title, and because of that link, he got the opportunity to visit 'The Main Dane'.

'Pete used to come to Poole and he did ignition boxes. He linked up with me and helped me out. It was near the end of the season and he said, "I'll ring Hans and we can go up to his house, have lunch and have a look around." I was really excited by that because he was my hero.

'We went up there at 10 o'clock in the morning or something, and had a look around. Hans' wife, Susanne, made lunch for us and he asked, "What are you doing?" I said, "Just riding, you know." And he said, "Do you want to go British League, do you want to get up?" I said, "I hadn't thought about it."

Talking with his hero Hans Nielsen. The Dane was instrumental in Adams' move up to the top flight in 1990. (Adams Family Archive)

And he said: "You've got to get up, you've got to go straightaway, that's most important." I've never thought about it until then. Within an hour, Susanne had drafted letters up for me to send to the BSPA, I signed them and they put them in the envelopes. I'd put in for a transfer because Hans told me that I had to do it.'

To outsiders it probably sounds as though Nielsen bamboozled the young, impressionable Adams. However, Hans Nielsen was one of the greats of the sport who went on to win a fourth world title so, when someone of that standard gives you advice, there would be plenty who would have questioned his sanity if he didn't act upon it.

'It was pretty much because Hans said so,' Leigh admits. 'He put it in black and white and said, "Well you've achieved a 9.5 average, and achieved probably everything you wanted to do in the National League (Second Division), keep going, keep pushing yourself, you're only going to go backwards there, you've gotta step it up and keep going.'"

'In hindsight now, I don't think it would have hurt me if I'd stayed back for another year. I still think I would have achieved everything that I have achieved. It wouldn't have hindered me; I would still be where I am.'

Shortly before Poole's final match against deposed champions Hackney, Leigh stunned the club's management and supporters with a written transfer request. Despite this resolute demand, there were plenty who didn't believe that the 18-year-old Aussie was serious. Even though he had exceeded and fulfilled all expectations, the Poole management would later state in the press that they were waiting for him to make his intentions 'crystal clear'. What was transparent was Leigh's ambition, his dedication and professionalism.

> **'You've gotta step it up and keep going.'**
>
> **Hans Nielsen**

'Whatever I earned I put back into my racing. I think I returned to Australia with £250 in my bank account and thought I was rich – that's true!' he laughs. 'I thought that was cool. I had survived my first year, I didn't have to ring mum or dad or anything like that - that was always the thing with the Aussies, they'd have to ring their parents to bail them out. I've always been pretty proud of that.'

In eight months of racing in Britain and Europe, Leigh's perspective on the world had changed – and the world itself was changing too. Barely a week had passed since he'd left England to return home when the Berlin Wall came tumbling down, and with it Communism began to crack under the pressure as democratic reform came pouring through. Politics and history were about to redefine the boundaries of the speedway world, and Leigh Adams' days as a diesel mechanic were well and truly over.

5

And then it Got Serious

‘I can remember everybody coming up to me in the pits – Ivan Mauger, John Titman, Kevin McDonald (the Godden importer) and they were saying, "You can win this, you're much faster than Doyley (Glenn Doyle)." There was also the fact that I was on a Godden engine and Doyley was on the Italian-made GM. But I was still 18 and I'm thinking, shit, I'm in a run-off for the Aussie title! I wasn't dialled in for the whole thing. In hindsight we were probably faster and should have won, but we didn't.'

That was the 1990 Australian Championship at the Brisbane Exhibition Ground or the 'Ekka'. Leigh had scored 14 points and, interestingly, was the only rider to defeat Doyle, while he dropped his only point to Phil Crump. Joan Adams recalls that Leigh should have chosen the inside gate in the run-off, but he went for the outside and Doyle retained his title.

He was having a productive Aussie season though, having regained the Australian Under-21 title, retained the Victorian Championship and raced for Australia against England at North Arm where he romped to an impressive 18-point maximum. However, Mildura legend Phil Crump was staging a testimonial meeting and a host of top stars from overseas came over including the reigning World Champion, Hans Nielsen.

'That was pretty big because we had Hans Nielsen come to town. That was the era when Crumpie was sponsored by Kwiksnax, Trevor Harding, and he brought a lot of those riders out. Having Hans in Mildura . . . even now it would be big. I raced against him, but I was just in awe the whole time he was here. He just brought a bike, obviously it was a good bike, and a tool box – typical Aussie style, do the season and then sell the bike at the end of it.'

Meanwhile, back in England, it wasn't until shortly before Christmas 1989 that the Poole management finally accepted that Leigh was serious about his move into the top flight, only then after the Australian issued another statement repeating his desire for a move. They responded by slapping a £25,000 transfer fee on the talented racer. It was considered to be an excessive amount at the time, especially when you take into account that Coventry were reported to have paid £18,000 for the more experienced 20-year-old Sean Wilson.

Clubs baulked at the fee and, strangely, the debate continued about whether, after just one NL season – albeit a very impressive one – he should move up. Among the many experts who were in favour of his move was Ivan Mauger who said, 'He has to get out of the National League and into the British League NOW. Not in a year's time, but now.' He gave a lengthy assessment of the Leigh's ability, saying he had the talent to win the world title.

The British League consisted of just nine clubs in 1990. With both the Polish and Swedish Leagues having only just opened up their leagues to foreign riders, those nine teams were crammed with the best riders in the world. At that time it didn't matter what nationality you were, if you were serious about winning a World Championship you simply had to ride in the BL.

Nonetheless, at one stage it seemed a possibility that he could move to Wimbledon who were thinking of joining the top flight. It would have indeed been an exciting prospect to see a team that included Adams and fellow Australian Todd Wiltshire. Unfortunately, Wimbledon decided against moving up and Wiltshire, who also wanted to go up, joined his rival from Mildura on the transfer list for £21,000.

Bradford, Cradley Heath and Wolverhampton were said to be in the race to sign Adams, but it was Swindon who emerged as the favourites to land his signature. The Robins team manager, Ron Byford, said cautiously, 'Obviously we are talking about a very big transfer fee before we even think about Leigh's personal contract.'

After Swindon made two unsuccessful offers to Poole for Adams' services, they finally agreed a deal that saw Gary Chessell move from Swindon to Poole as part of the agreement that included 'a substantial fee'. However, Leigh recalls that the Pirates management were not going to let him go easily.

'It got ugly, Poole didn't want me to go, they wanted to keep me for another season because they had the idea of moving up the following year,' he reveals. 'They said, "Well hang on, why don't you stay for another year and we'll work it out because we maybe going up." I wasn't having any of it; I thought they were trying to do me over, basically. I wanted out, I wanted to go up and I didn't care where it was. I had things pretty nice down there and I could have stayed, but I wanted to go British League, no matter what. It got messy because I was being stubborn and they put a crazy figure on my head, but I sat back and let it all bubble over.'

However, if Poole were a tad disappointed to see their hot shot leave, they must have felt even more disillusioned when a local sponsor, one who had backed Leigh as a Pirate, ended up at Swindon in a far larger role.

'All of a sudden, Coastal Windows became the sponsors of Swindon. I think they put in a little bit of money to help with my transfer, but I got nothing out of it. I guess I thought I was going to sever my ties with Coastal because I was leaving, but they put money into the team sponsorship and it just went from there. They sponsored Swindon for two seasons. Eventually I drifted away from Coastal because they're a Poole-based company and with me riding for Swindon it didn't make good sense for them to back me. I guess it came about because of the link through me and there was a Coastal dealer in Swindon, Ermin Street Windows. It was all linked up through that.'

Setting himself a target of achieving an 8-point average, he joined a young side that included Jimmy Nilsen, Brian Karger, Andrew Silver, the experienced John Davis, Peter Nahlin and David Smart. Therefore, with the addition of Adams, the success-starved Swindon fans were anticipating an exciting season ahead.

Leigh made his debut for Swindon against local rivals Oxford in a Gold Cup fixture on Saturday 24 March 1990, and scored 8 points – he took his first

race win in heat 14. Unfortunately, he couldn't prevent the Robins losing 38–51. It was a very disappointing start for the club, but the team made up for that sluggish beginning by easily defeating King's Lynn – Leigh underlined his ability with 11 points – before racing in a couple of local derbies that played an interesting role in his season.

Swindon pulled off a convincing victory over Oxford at Cowley, during which Adams finished ahead of his hero Hans Nielsen for the first time. Later in the season he would repeat that feat again.

Swindon Robin, 1990.
(Adams Family Archive)

'Well, he was the bench mark, his average was head and shoulders above anyone else,' Leigh reflects. 'I did get to beat him that year and it was just my dream come true. Just like these young kids racing me now, I know what it's like, they're punching the air and carrying on, and I think what are you doing? It's no big deal, it's just one race, but I was the same back then.'

The following Saturday he lined up against Reading, who had signed Todd Wiltshire. Just like Adams, he was in his first season of British League action and impressing the Reading fans with his performances; like Adams he was riding at the reserve berth in the team and he also wanted to establish himself as the Aussie No. 1. During the Robins' narrow 4-point victory they met three times, and Leigh came out on top twice. When the two clubs met, the Adams-Wiltshire clashes added extra spice to a healthy rivalry that already existed between the two sides.

Australian team manager, James Easter, was eagerly watching the progress of these two young chargers in the top flight as he began considering them to represent Australia in the World Pairs Championship. Shortly before the Commonwealth Final of the World Individual Championship, Easter announced Adams and Wiltshire as the country's representatives.

'I got a bit of stick for choosing them because the year before we had done quite well with Troy Butler and Stephen Davies,' Easter says. 'I thought, well they've got to learn so let's try them at the very, very top and see how they go.'

Inexperienced, the duo had their first taste of World Championship racing at Belle Vue in the Commonwealth Final where they both safely qualified. And then they headed for Wiener Neustadt in Austria for the first World Pairs semi-final.

Leigh may have lacked experience at this level, but in his camp he had the very knowledgeable mechanic Norrie Allan. At one time Allan was mechanic to Ivan Mauger and had been helping American Shawn Moran in the long track. However, Moran received a ban for failing an alcohol test so the Scottish-born mechanic took up Adams' request for help.

'Norrie Allan lived in Bristol and Ivan gave me his number and said to give him a ring and he may be able to help me out. At the time he was helping Shawn Moran, just on the long track side of things – that was it, it was pretty casual. So I gave him a ring mid-way through the year and I linked up with him. I had a mechanic from Swindon and Norrie came along and helped us a little bit. He'd do long track meetings, all the continental stuff with Ivan, so he said that he would do the World Pairs with me which we agreed to. That was great because we could go abroad and not get lost! What a bonus!'

The Australian duo was thrust into action during the first race. With six riders in a race, they faced pairings from Italy and New Zealand. Todd finished second to David Bargh, but Leigh was fortunate to pick up fifth place when Armando Castagna retired.

Their professionalism and concentration was tested during their second outing when Poland's Piotr Swist collided with team-mate Ryszard Dolomisiewicz's stricken machine. He was launched with frightening speed toward the wooden safety fence, and such was his bike's impact with the barrier that it tore a gaping hole. Swist, meanwhile, was tossed into the air like a rag doll, cleared a 6ft gap, then his body hideously bounced up six concrete steps before landing on the terracing among astonished spectators. The crash knocked him unconscious and he suffered head injuries, a broken leg and elbow.

The meeting was held up while Swist and Dolomisiewicz received treatment and the fence was repaired. When the event resumed and the race was re-run, the Aussie duo showed their professionalism by finishing first and second ahead of the Swedes, Jimmy Nilsen and Per Jonsson. They were well on their way to qualifying and eventually finished third (Todd 25, Leigh 14) behind England and Sweden to book their place in the World Pairs Final.

'We just thought, mad Poles!' Leigh says of Swist's terrifying crash. 'He went straight through the fence and ended up in the grandstand. There was all this speculation about six riders being in a race and all that was starting up because of safety. Swist's crash highlighted that issue.'

Few tracks in Europe were wide enough to accommodate six riders in a race, but the first turns, where many World Championships were won and lost, were frighteningly over-crowded when six equally determined racers were not prepared to give an inch. It was only the skill and talent of the competitors that prevented more serious crashes.

Swist's accident meant that the FIM finally saw sense and announced that the six-rider format would be dropped in 1991. But not before a dramatic final that would see more injuries. Held at Landshut in Germany, Denmark, represented by Hans Nielsen and Jan O. Pedersen, were the favourites to retain their title. England (Kelvin Tatum/Simon Cross) and Sweden (Nilsen/Jonsson) were expected to challenge the Danes, while few gave the inexperienced young Aussies much chance of grabbing a medal, although Erik Gundersen described them as 'spoilers'.

It was Adams' first World Final of any sort and, naturally, it was all new to him. Thankfully, having the knowledge of Norrie Allan to call upon helped him no end with his preparation for the big event.

'He came along and he knew what it was all about, the FIM machine examining, the hotels, travelling, and that was cool and a really big help.'

Meanwhile, team manager James Easter didn't put any pressure on his young stars.

'We took it really easy. I said to them, "Look, let's do what we can, try hard, but your time will come further on down the road." I told them it was a six-man race, keep out of trouble, gate, look for each other, look for your lines and what you get, you hold.'

However, barely fifteen seconds into the first race and England's challenge was at an end when Simon Cross crashed in the mêlée of the first corner and sustained a back injury. The Aussies met the Danes in the second heat which also included the hosts, Germany, with Gerd Riss and Klaus Lausch. More first-bend carnage followed with this time Nielsen picking up drive and running into Wiltshire causing another crash with five riders in total biting the dust. Riss' meeting was over as he was taken away with what was later diagnosed as a broken ankle, while Nielsen was excluded for unfair riding.

In the re-run Wiltshire, who suffered nothing more than cuts and bruises, streaked away from the start and led, while Leigh disheartened the 10,000-strong German crowd even further by passing Lausch for third. After each pair had raced in three heats, Australia surprisingly led the competition with 21 points, one more than another spoiling nation Hungary (Zoltan Adorjan/Sandor Tihanyi), with Denmark in a chasing third place on 17 points.

When the Aussies finished first and second ahead of Tatum and the American pairing of Ronnie Correy and Kelly Moran in their penultimate outing, they were very much in the driving seat. Meanwhile, Denmark continued to battle on and did enough to meet the Aussies and the Hungarians in the final race. The score line read: Australia 36, Denmark 34, Hungary 32. Unfortunately, experience came to the tapes and reigned supreme as the Danish duo filled the top two places and snatched a last-gasp victory.

'We didn't expect Jan O. to come round like he did ...'

'We decided that I would take the inside gate and, hopefully, run Hans into the corner for Leigh to come underneath,' said Todd. 'It very nearly happened, but we just didn't expect Jan O. to come round like he did.'

Nonetheless, it was a brilliant performance and a silver medal in your first World Final was quite an achievement. Wiltshire scored 25 points and Leigh 15. These days Adams modestly gives most of the credit to his fast-starting partner.

'That was more Todd than me, he was just a trapper back then. You could drop him in and he was just scoring points. Riding with Todd, he was such a good starter, he was gone, he really was, he was out-pacing Hans and Jan O. – it was unbelievable. We were close to winning and everyone was pretty excited, but Norrie was pretty casual about it – he probably knew deep down what was going on and wasn't playing to all the excitement.'

'We nearly won it,' Easter enthuses all these years later. 'We had so many years when we continued to lose top riders like Crumpie (Phil Crump), Billy Sanders, Gary Guglielmi, John Titman, the whole team had gone. But they were absolutely brilliant and a delight to deal with.'

It was around this time that Wiltshire slipped into top gear. A couple of weeks prior to that meeting in Landshut he had qualified from the Overseas Final of the World Individual Championship in second place, while Leigh failed to make the cut with 5 points. When Wiltshire not only went all the way to the World Final but also finished third, Adams admits that he felt envious.

'I remember going to that final and seeing him, and I was so jealous, it was awful and I didn't get close to qualifying. That was hard watching him get everything that year. He and I were the two Aussie kids, and for him to be third in the world was a big shock for me. It probably took me a few years to get to that level and when I qualified for Pocking I wasn't prepared at all. Todd took a different path, but once he went to Reading that year he just progressed in leaps and bounds. We had been duelling in Aussie, but he was the man then. I was jealous, big time, it was gut-wrenching that year, and Reading won everything – they were so dominant.'

'It was awful and I was so jealous and I didn't get close to qualifying.'

The Reading Racers achieved a league and cup double, and their number one, Per Jonsson, also won the World Championship. No such success for Leigh's team who suffered a blow when Brian Karger broke his thigh while riding in his native Denmark. Eventually Swindon found a replacement in the shape of Phil Crump.

Although Crump describes his comeback as a 'mistake', he recognised the improvement made by Leigh since he made the step up to the top flight. In fact, such was Adams' progress that Phil realised that his time at the plate was over.

'Leigh was going good and most of the time he would beat me,' he remembers. 'The only chance I had really was if I made the gate on him, then maybe I could hold on. He was on his way up, and I didn't want to get injured either and that's another reason why it didn't work out for me. I just couldn't compete against these young riders and Leigh, being a Mildura man, watching him race and seeing how he had progressed since those days in Australia, it brought it home to me a bit.'

Adams didn't quite reach his target of an 8-point average during his debut season in the top flight, but he would often top-score for the Robins and recorded his first maximum, a paid 15, against King's Lynn on 27 August.

His international education continued with World Team Championship appearances for Australia. In Group B they faced Hungary, Finland and Poland, and qualified comfortably over two meetings in Szeged, Hungary and Gorzow, Poland – Leigh scored a maximum in Gorzow. Nearly twelve months since his first visit to Gorzow, Adams found that the Berlin Wall had come down, but the ghosts remained and Communism still had a grip on Poland.

'I went back there the next year with my dad and we went for a walk around Checkpoint Charlie and we could see all these buildings where the gunshots had gone off – it was spooky really. It was still the same in Poland; we were still cutting deals with all the guys and trying to get as much out of the trip as we could. If you had cans of Coke, kids were trying to steal them off you. I remember Boycey – he was always lazy, always – he had taken a mechanic, but for two cans of Coke he got this kid out of the crowd to wash his bikes. This kid was just scrubbing away for two cans of Coke, and I thought that was so cool. The hotels, well you've never seen anything like it, they were like hospitals, basically!

'I remember waiting outside of a hotel one time and I could hear this emergency siren coming and we could hear it for ages. In the western world you'd see this ambulance go rushing past at a million miles an hour, not in Poland then, it was a normal Lada that just came idling by!'

However, while Poland was shaking off the restraints of Communism, they had not yet refined the infrastructure and freedom that democracy would promise. Therefore, this made for a volatile economy where some thrived more than others. The mafia, in particular, were able to take advantage of the situation. Speedway, which was finding itself having to deal with the new era of openness and unpredictable financial circumstances due to the weakness of the zloty, were vulnerable to dubious sources of income, as Leigh discovered.

'I think it was at the end of the season at Lublin one year, and I'd flown over to sort out my contract for the following season. I was owed money from the previous year and this guy had stepped in to help the club out.

I think he cleared up the financial problem from that year and I went ahead and signed a contract for that season.

'As I was coming down the stairs from the speedway office, I noticed he had a three-door S-class Mercedes Benz, I think it had a V12 engine which, back in those days, was a pretty flash car. I commented, "Nice car," and he tossed the keys to me and said, "Take it for a drive." So we drove out of town and he kept telling me to "go faster, faster." I said, "No, it's a problem with the police." Next minute he pulled out a magnetic, portable blue light that he used to put on top of the car, so everyone thought he was the police and he could get away with anything! Then I commented on the telephone he had set in the centre console: "Oh, this telephone and the stereo must be a big problem in Poland, with people stealing them?" To which he replied, "No, no problem." and pulled a pistol out of the glove box and handed it to me! So here I was driving along the motorway flat-out, with a pistol in my hand. I thought, what the hell am I doing? and handed it back! Then he took me to his huge house, fronted with big gates, and his own security guard at the gate. The house was being refurbished so there were loads of workers around it. It was like something out of *The Godfather* movie. Later, he turned up at the Grands Prix as a sponsor or something to Robert Dados. I remember saying hello to him. I couldn't say for sure if he was the mafia, but he was definitely dodgy.'

Australia's next trip in the World Cup Team was Olching, Germany, to face the USA, Sweden and the hosts in Group A. Included in the American team was the talented Kelly Moran, but his off-track antics tended to overshadow what a great rider he could be. From the very beginning of his career Leigh was very professional, but the lively Californian was going to give the young Aussie an insight into a racing life on the other side of the track.

'After practice, they had a bar and Craiger (Craig Cummings) had to carry him out over his shoulder because he was that pissed during practice, he was sitting there abusing everybody. I can see it now, Kelly was tiny and Craiger would just lump him over his shoulder – this must have been 5 o'clock. Everyone knew about Kelly, he'd drink, I think Shawn (Moran) was more fun, but Kelly was just abusive. You'd turn up the next day and you'd be thinking, I hope he doesn't get picked for an alcohol test. I was amazed that he could ride.

'Around this time I went to Gdansk for the Solidarity Games, it was athletics, etc, but speedway was involved. Briggo organised the speedway part and it was myself, Mitch Shirra, Kelly Moran and Gary Havelock. It was down to Norrie more than anything because I asked him what he thought and he said, "Yeah do it, you've got a weekend off." We got paid a bit of money and they paid for our flights. We had a direct flight into Warsaw and they took us to a little airport and we waited there for two to three hours for Lech Walesa's (Polish President) private plane, and then they flew us straight into Gdansk.

'Kelly and all of them were completely pissed at Warsaw and they'd bought vodka at the duty free. I remember sitting on that plane going to Gdansk, Mitch was rolling a big fat one, Kelly was drinking vodka, and we were like the kings coming to this meeting, but the boys didn't care, they just went there for a good time. I was thinking, what's Norrie done to me here? We turned up and there were ten or fifteen bikes lined up. We'd pick one out and that's the one you'd ride for the meeting. In the end it poured with rain and they cancelled the meeting half-way through. You couldn't behave like that now, everything is so professional and you can't put your body through that because it's so taxing.'

However, only the winners of Group A qualified for the final and Australia finished third behind the USA and Sweden. America went on to win the World Team Championship, and just to prove what an enigma Kelly Moran was, he was the hero by top scoring with 12 points.

One of the motivations behind Leigh's decision to move up to the British League was to improve his starting. During his year with Poole he came up against BL opposition – interestingly Swindon – in an inter-league challenge, and found that his reflexes at the gate were not as sharp as the oppositions'. He soon realised, however, that while regularly racing against the best could only have a positive affect, he also needed to improve his starting technique.

'Ivan Mauger came over and he tried to help me with my starts.'

'Ivan Mauger came over and he tried to help me with my starts. We went to Swindon and he looked at my technique, but it didn't really help at all! The biggest influence, or help with my starting was through Norrie and the Ace of Aces meeting. Norrie used to do the bar, because he had a pub and a licence, so I went along to help him set-up.

'I was just sitting there and Norrie introduced me to Martin Yeates. I knew of him and heard about him and he was a local boy. Norrie said, "Have a talk with Yeatesy, he was a good starter, he might be able to tell you a few techniques and things." I thought that was pretty cool and he said, "How old are you?" And I said, "20". He replied "Are ya? Well I'm 40 now and I reckon I could beat you out of the start." I just agreed with him and said, "Yeah well, I heard you were a pretty good starter." And he said, "That's your first problem. If you think a 40-year-old is going to beat a 20-year-old out of the start, you're beat already."

'Basically what he was saying was that starting, yeah, you've got to have technique and all that, but it's a confidence game. You've got to think when you get to the tapes you're going to beat the opposition. I never forgot that and it always stuck in my mind. I went into a lot of other ways of trying to be more confident, but I always remember when he said that to me.'

Overall, Adams' second season in England was a success. Swindon were pleased with his performances and he headed Down Under looking forward to showing the locals how much sharper he had become.

He won his third Victorian State Championship and retained the Aussie Under-21 title with an unbeaten score. Meanwhile, national teams from Sweden and the USSR (Soviet Union) were touring Australia. Leigh top-scored with 11 points in Young Australia's narrow 46–43 victory over the Soviets at Mildura and then lined-up in the full national team to face Sweden. They won the first two Tests and Leigh was the top-scorer in the second test at Adelaide with 13 points when he had a confrontation with the safety fence.

'After the match they had a race for the top two scorers from each team, and they put up $500 or something for the winner – that's when I broke my right wrist. I came round the outside of Henka Gustafsson, lifted, bounced off the fence, and went over the handlebars and snap! – landed on my wrist. It snapped off pretty close to the joint, it wasn't compound, but nearly. I spoke to dad at the time and said, "Do we really need to do this race?" we were 50/50, and then okay, we decided, we'll do it. Dad was mechanicing for me and he took me straight to hospital. He was pretty sharp like that and demanded that we go to a specialist.

'They had a Sports Med, a big clinic in Adelaide; a private hospital and I got operated on the next morning by this upper limb surgeon, Dr Andrew Saies. It's weird because this Sports Med has grown and it's in a lot of big cities now. When I did my shoulder in 2007, I got him to check it out and he remembered who I was and asked how my wrist was. He said he'd been watching me on the telly in the Grands Prix and this was fifteen years after that wrist injury. It was nice to meet him again and he was fantastic, but that shut down my Aussie season.

'I missed a meeting or two in England because I was just making sure that it was perfect before I started riding again. To this day, I've still got the plate in there but it has never hindered me and I have full movement. It was a blessing that we really pushed for a specialist because they were pretty pissed off at the hospital, they just wanted to stick the knife in, but dad demanded it!'

Unfortunately, this meant that he couldn't ride in the Australian Championship, and because it doubled as a World Championship qualifying round, Adams' place in the 1991 title hunt was in doubt.

'It was too painful to race,' he says. 'At that stage we had a really good guy, Bill Bates-Brownsword, who was in control of the solo side of things of MA (Motorcycling Australia). He said, "Don't worry, we'll sort something," and he seeded me through to the Commonwealth Final. Fortunately I was in Australia when it happened so I had the sunshine and all that to heal. I was really gutted about the Aussie title, it was a big deal and I wanted to do it!'

Having now got back together with Kylie, young love blossomed again and he decided that he'd like to take her to England with him – not for a holiday, but for the season. It's one thing informing a father that his 18-year-old daughter was going to move out of the family home and live with her boyfriend, but to then add that the accommodation was going to be in a foreign country, he realised that his wish wouldn't be achieved without careful planning.

'I remember asking him if he was sure,' says his mother. 'She did very well with her exams, got very good marks and her father had great ambitions for Kylie, and our boy had to go and tell him what he was going to do. I was for it, but I didn't want Kylie to ruin her career!'

However, to start with he chose the slightly easier option by asking her mother first before tackling her father, who was a different proposition.

'I used to get on with her mum fantastic, I got on fine with her dad, but he was always pretty hard, I knew his reputation – he was quite strict. I thought about it, it didn't come out of the blue. I asked her dad, "I want to take your daughter to England!" When it happened you just get on with it, it was young love really, we survived. You look back and think, bloody hell, it was crazy, but you wouldn't change it for the world. It helped me so much and it gave me a stable lifestyle. I didn't get hooked up with all the boys out partying and all that. That happens to a hell of a lot of them!'

When Leigh returned to England he found that the league structure had changed to include promotion and relegation. Swindon had also made changes to their side, which was now a very young team. Brian Karger was made captain and the Robins management had made two new signings, Australian Rod Colquhoun and the promising Paul Dugard.

The team started well enough and two away victories at reigning champions Reading and Poole saw the Robins topping the southern group

Swindon, 1991. Left to right: Peter Nahlin, Matthew Cross, Rod Colquhoun, Ron Byford (team manager), Brian Karger (on bike), Paul Dugard, Andrew Silver and Leigh. By September only four riders remained from that side and Leigh had emerged as their number one. (Adams Family Archive)

of the Gold Cup. Therefore, confidence was growing within the young side; however, confidence is a fragile thing and it can be easily shattered.

When Poole arrived at Blunsdon on 4 May, Leigh found himself immersed in a hectic opening race with Marvyn Cox. The tussle ended with him making an unwelcome visit into the safety fence that forced him to withdraw from the meeting because he dislocated his shoulder – the Pirates went on to win the encounter.

'He was a hard rider, really hard,' Leigh recalls. 'He came underneath me, knocked me off and I slid into the fence. It didn't dislocate totally, it was more of a lock, it's a semi-dislocation, it pulls up and locks in, and you kind of manipulate it back down. When it's a total dislocation, like I had at Reading, you can put it back in but you've got to know which way to go. This wasn't bad, but it did give me a few hassles and obviously when you do it you can feel it for a long time after. It wasn't really until the next year that I went back to Aussie and had it looked at. I strapped it for the whole of that year. Every meeting I'd kept strapping and plastering it up, just like you'd see in Aussie rules football. It wasn't ideal and any sort of injury is confidence-sapping because you're thinking about that instead of your racing. It got to the stage where I strapped it, it was fine, and I got back to Aussie the next year and it was no problem at all. So I didn't bother strapping it after that. And I didn't have any problems with it for a number of years, but that was the same one that I pulled out at Reading in 2007. To be fair, injury-wise, I've been pretty lucky. I've had a few, but not bad.'

Although he didn't miss any matches through the crash, that incident was pivotal to the Robins' season because they then lost six consecutive matches. Controversially, Karger's loss of form meant that he was released to be replaced by Andy Smith. As the prospect of relegation loomed on the horizon, the management seemed to panic as a succession of injuries and defeats saw a revolving door policy. Karger had the last laugh, though, because he joined Arena-Essex and steered them to promotion, while Swindon were seemingly relegated.

Even though it was a woeful season for the team and a depressing one for the supporters, Adams' form saw him assume the role as the club's number one rider. The figures may have shown the Aussie at the top of the club's averages, but he didn't feel he was racing like a number one rider.

'In 1990 there was no pressure, I was reserve, and whatever came was a bonus really and I think I did pretty good,' he says. 'In 1991 I set my sights pretty high, but the team wasn't doing very good at all. We had a bad year with injuries, but I wasn't built to be number one and I was carrying the team a little bit. By that stage you feel as though you have got a job to do, an average to get, points to score in every meeting, and it was tough because my gating still wasn't that good. I did take into account what my job was, but I was still naïve, just go along and race, score as many points as I could and win as many races. At that stage, I wasn't really a number one rider as such, while Todd was piling the points up for Reading and he had set the world alight.'

He also learnt some other lessons that season too. Bringing Kylie to England and employing a full-time mechanic had soured relations with Norrie Allan.

'I decided I needed a full-time mechanic then. I was living with Norrie in the pub and he was totally against the mechanic thing, he didn't want that.

He was looking at the pennies, and we could have struggled through with Norrie also doing some stuff for me. But Todd had the full-time mechanic and I felt as though that's what I was missing. I brought Justin Thomas in, it seemed to run okay, we lived there a while and then Kylie flew over in May.

'Norrie had a house near the pub that he rented out, so we took that on and I think he had his nose put out of joint. Suddenly I had a full-time mechanic and the girlfriend was over, he thought I was spending too much money.'

Initially, as Kylie remembered, everything was fine.

'I don't remember how or why it went wrong. When I first came over I got on all right with him. When Leigh was away riding I would go over to the pub and have a drink with him and a good old chat. We got on well, but it changed as time went on.'

With mechanic Justin Thomas. (Adams Family Archive)

'The atmosphere was frosty,' Leigh adds. 'I had Justin, and Norrie used to come along. I remember driving to meetings and the atmosphere was terrible. The whole thing probably annoyed Norrie because he wasn't in control. A lot of good things came out of it. He just felt that I was overspending, and he thought that I didn't need what I had all the time with the mechanics and Kylie turning up. He didn't like women around speedway, and we were young then. But at twenty you're bullet-proof and you think whatever you think is the right thing. Kylie had come over, I was going okay, but money-wise I was trying to shuffle everything and he was looking at that point of view.'

The situation couldn't continue. Few people can be really productive when they're surrounded by an unpleasant atmosphere, and Leigh certainly couldn't put all that behind him and concentrate on racing. Therefore, they decided to leave Allan's house in Bristol and seek somewhere else to live.

Malcolm Holloway was a former Swindon rider and he ran the Wheatsheaf public house in the Stratton area of the town. Naturally, because of his presence, it was a magnet for the speedway fraternity, riders, fans and mechanics would all congregate there. It was while Leigh and Kylie were having a drink in the establishment as they scoured the local paper for places to rent, that Neil McCarthy was able to offer them a room. It might not have been ideal, but they had their independence, it was their space, and they were happy.

'We had a little bedroom with a double bed and lived out of suitcases,' Leigh says. 'We couldn't close the door because the bed took up all the room, and we didn't have a wardrobe, only suitcases. It was cool, shoved in this little house, a garage to the rear but we loved it because we had our independence. That was another switch in my career and just going it alone.'

Allan soon formed a successful partnership with Britain's Mark Loram, but his influence did much to set the young Australian on the right path.

'He helped me to do my contracts,' Leigh reveals. 'I think I was on £25 a point at Poole. I didn't do what Darcy Ward did in 2009, but I was high-up in the league's averages, 9.8. I raced for Swindon the next year for pretty much what they offered me. It wasn't until Norrie got hold of me and said that I had to work out my expenditure, the budget, per point, extras here and there, tyres, vehicles and all that sort of thing. During my first season in England I had a guarantee in my contract to get established – I believe they still do that now. But after that you're on your own and deal with your own contracts.

'Norrie helped me a lot with that because I was really green, I didn't know how to structure a contract, how to look for a figure that I wanted to earn and how to go about it, and how you're going to score. Now I always work on 12 points a meeting; average 12 points a meeting, and get a figure at the end. He sat me down and showed me how to do it, and it was pretty simple to him because he had been involved with Ivan (Mauger) and Shawn (Moran); all the bikes, contracts, the whole deal, so there was a lot of good that came from Norrie.

'The mechanic issue at the start, he was right, but I was 20 and I wasn't going to listen to him and thought my way was the only way. As it proved, it was the wrong one, but you don't know these things until you try I guess.'

Adams exited the World Championship at the Overseas Final, and there were no heroics for Australia either as Pardubice became a bogey venue for the Aussies. The magic Adams/Wiltshire pairing of 1990 failed to cast its spell as they failed to make the World Pairs Final, with reserve Glenn Doyle top-scoring with 8 points – Leigh scored 5 of their 18-point total. And then Australia were eliminated at the Czech Republic track by Sweden in the World Team Cup qualifier – Leigh scored 4.

It was a year of consolidation for him as he established himself as Swindon's top rider, and also dipped his steel shoe into Polish League racing for the first time with Lublin. He appeared in nine matches and did really well, top scoring against Gorzow and he got to experience it with Hans Nielsen.

'I always travelled with Hans, met him at the airport and that was really cool. My hero, and suddenly here I am travelling with him, sleeping in hotels, and all that sort of stuff. He'd always have the double bed, always. I'd be on the floor, or on the couch or something, I was definitely the apprentice! But again, it was a great experience to be travelling with him to see how he approached things, bike preparation and things like that. I learned a hell of a lot from him.

'Lublin wasn't a big stadium; some of the ones that we went to were unbelievable. I'd leave a bike there, fly in, and always take an engine. This is something I find funny now, all these kids today have ten engines, an engine for a big track, small track and back then I had three engines. I always took my best engine to Poland, I carried it with me and took it as hand luggage sometimes, or you'd check it in and weight wasn't an issue. I can remember taking a Godden engine with me and I must have had arms like a gorilla! We all did it then: engine was hand luggage, straight through security, and stick it under your seat, but you can't even think about doing that now.

'It wasn't wise to leave engines there because others would ride them when you weren't around. That's the reason I brought it back, and it was my best engine, my favourite engine, I always had to bring it back to England. Then Hans left his there for a while and it was okay, so I began to leave mine.'

Tim Osmond has been Leigh's mechanic and engine-tuner in Australia since the 91/92 season. He revealed how meticulous the Aussie rider is when it comes to preparing bikes for the track.

'Everything has got to be just nice and cleaning the bikes has got to be spot on. All his bikes are exactly the same. He measures everything. When he builds a new bike the seat's got to be in exactly the same spot, handlebars and brackets, so that when he gets off of one and onto another they're exactly the same. He's very fussy with cleaning and maintenance. He's a true professional.'

Adams raced in the Krzysztof Okupski Testimonial meeting at Gorzow and won it with 14 points. In Poland the trophies were usually made of crystal, but the prize this time was a bit unusual.

'I won a really old-fashioned, ugly chair,' Leigh laughs. 'It was a big chair with lions' heads on the end of the arms and things like that. I took it back to Lublin and Hans was riding for them and he said, "Oh that's all right." He liked it, so I swapped it for a heap of tool boxes or something. I didn't even have a house to put it in at that time.'

> **'I won a really old-fashioned, ugly chair.'**

Hans Nielsen's influence, on and off the track, had made an impression on Leigh. So much so that until the middle of 1991 he wore black leathers like his idol. Nevertheless, having made a name for himself as one of the most promising riders to come out of Australia since the 1970s, he decided that it was time to create an identity of his own.

'I had black suits all the time because of Hans. After my first year in England I just realised that I needed my own identity. I went to Bob Radford's one night, he was a reporter and he had all the *Speedway Stars*. I was just flicking through the magazines, looking at pictures, what stood out and tried to get away from the norm – Hans was black and blue, Erik (Gundersen) was white and yellow. Somebody had red bikes and it went from there. It's gone through a lot of variations with added colours and what not, but it's always been red. My hat has always been red and that's probably the more prominent thing, the Owen Bros hat, a red hat. I've always liked red, pretty cool colour, it stands out, and Ferrari are red and they're pretty fast and Ducati, which I have just bought an 1198cc and it's red. Everything I've got now is red, even my speed boat.'

While Nielsen was his hero, Todd Wiltshire had become a rival, much like the friendly rivalry that existed between the Americans, Billy Hamill and Greg Hancock. Having Todd just along the M4 racing for Reading added a further spark to their competition. Eager to improve his starting and recognising his rival's impressive speed from the gate, Leigh decided to try a GM.

'It was probably the Todd factor,' he admits, 'he was the GM man, he was popping out of starts, he never missed many, it was probably then that I tried the GMs. I always rode Godden right from the start; that was my first bike, I never went through the 2-valve, 4-valve, Weslake thing, I missed that era – it was just Godden. The Goddens were always known as powerful engines, and were probably grippier at the start; the GMs were better on slicker starts and slicker tracks. They were a really good engine. I stayed on them for a lot of years and was one of the last riders on Goddens.'

'It was mid-way through '91 that I bought a couple of GMs from Peter Johns. He was doing my stuff then, it must have been through Norrie. I was hopping between the Goddens and the GMs that year.'

When you start to make a name for yourself, it's not long before people want to be associated with you. Famed German engine tuner, Otto Weiss, got in touch with James Easter about helping Leigh in the long track. Weiss had already been linked with another Australian, Steve Baker, but he had made his name using his skills on engines ridden by Jan O. Pedersen and Marvyn Cox.

'Steve had been retired about a year then and James Easter got in touch with me. Otto wanted to help another Aussie, and he approached me and it was right at the end of that year. Jan O. was Otto's top man, he invited me over and I only had a couple of engines at that time. I remember going over at Otto's invitation and he was going to do my engines and we were going to chase the World Longtrack Championship.'

Leigh's father accompanied him, and he was impressed by Weiss' facilities. 'We went there and he had all these engines, cylinder heads, crank cases, all lined up on the benches, he must have had thirty engines, GMs, all ready to have the valves put in them. He had a full-time machine guy just doing all that,' recalls John.

Meanwhile, Leigh was afforded another opportunity to see how the top riders operated on a regular basis. 'I remember being there and Jan O. flew in to pick up some more engines and there was a mass of engines lined up, must have been fifteen and I was drooling – that was like my dream. Otto went to Jan O., "Which one do you want?" And he picked them out, "This one is good, this one is good," he dropped two engines off and took another two – that was it. That's how it all started with Otto. I remember I took a couple of my engines over, he prepared them for me and I took them back to Australia. He was the man then.'

Having Otto Weiss in his corner was a major bonus for him. It brought a positive end to a tough 1991 season. However, he wouldn't have to wait too long before he would see the benefits of joining the German tuner.

6

The Grand Slam

Leigh Adams was both delighted and surprised by the content of the phone call he had received from Otto Weiss. Not only did he illustrate his full support with typical German efficiency, but his actions were unprecedented at the time.

'A week or so before the Australian Championship he called me, and said, "Go to the airport, there is another engine there for you – and this one is special." Back then it was unheard of, but it happens all the time now. I remember going and picking the engine up and that was it. I won everything that year.'

However, along with using Weiss' engines came some provisos that would mean that he would have to end a long-standing agreement, and put some friendships that had developed over the years at risk. This is what he would have to do if he wanted to seriously challenge for the big titles; tough decisions would have to be made and he would have to make them.

'It caused a bit of a problem because Peter Morris was doing my engines and we had become really good friends. Steve (Baker) had been with Otto and there was another tuner in Adelaide, and Otto told me that I must get this certain guy to do the engines, no-one else must look at the engines – that person was Tim Osmond. That was a bit difficult because then I had to go to Peter and say that this man had to do Otto's engines because they were Otto's. It caused a lot of ill-feeling, and the friendship was split up for a long time.'

As the saying goes, as one door closes, another one opens; Leigh's door was left ajar and Tim Osmond was able to step in and form an alliance with the Aussie racer that has remained a constant one ever since.

'Since then, Tim hasn't missed an Aussie final; he's been with me all the way through. That's nearly twenty years and he does all my engines when I go back, and he's been a big link to my success in Australia. It all stemmed around this agreement with Otto Weiss and that's what catapulted my career because suddenly he was in my stable and sending me engines, which was pretty cool.'

Osmond had previously worked with Steve Baker, and due to Baker's tie-up with Weiss, Tim was the German tuner's man in Australia. 'I used to do Steve's stuff before he went overseas,' Osmond explains. 'Around 84/85, Steve went to live with Otto and I went over there and spent three-and-a-half months with them – I got to know them pretty well. The first time I met Leigh was when he was still riding little bikes, he was 14 or 15 then I think. We did an Aussie final at Mildura and I rang up Leigh's dad, John, I knew he used to do trials, so I rang him and asked him if we could come into his place and wash the bikes and do them, and he said we were welcome. I met him there and have known him ever since. When Leigh started using Otto Weiss' engines he said that I was the only one allowed to look at them. He asked me to service his engines and I've been helping him ever since.'

'I don't think he (Morris) looked at the whole picture, and the whole picture was not just in Australia but all over in England and Europe,' adds Leigh's father. 'He had been a good stepping-stone for Leigh, and Tim Osmond was very, very good to him. Better in a way, because Pete was flat-out doing these sprint car engines and he could never dedicate the time to what Leigh could need. Timmy could, he'd drop everything and do his engines.'

This special engine was shipped over especially for the Australian Championship in Adelaide. Having come so close to his first title in 89/90 and then get ruled out of the following season because of injury, the 91/92 Australian Championship was high on his list of priorities. Nonetheless, with his confidence high, Adams began putting everything together like he had never done before. He won the Victorian State Championship and then warmed up for the 'big one' at North Arm by winning the Australian Pairs Championship with long-time friend Jason Lyons.

Then, it was on to Adelaide for the all-important Australian National Championship; a meeting that was marred by the serious pelvic injury sustained by Todd Wiltshire, which forced him into a lengthy, but temporary retirement to recover. For Adams, though, his performance only attracted admiration as he opened his racing with an emphatic victory over the defending champion Craig Boyce and smashed the track record in the process. Cheered on by a large contingent from Mildura, he faltered only briefly when he was headed by Shane Parker in his second outing while on his way to his first Australian crown.

On 8 February 1992, though, he created history by winning the Australian Under-21 Championship with an unbeaten performance to achieve a unique Grand Slam of Aussie crowns: the State, Pairs, National and Under-21 titles. *Speedway Star*'s Australian correspondent Peter White wrote, 'Not many will come along as good as Adams,' while Graeme Frost reported, 'Adams was never challenged and the title was virtually over when the only rider who looked in early heats to have a remote chance of challenging him, fellow Mildurian Mark Lemon, was beaten by yet another Mildura rider, Jason Crump, and it was put beyond doubt in the next race when Lemon's engine blew.

'We won everything, didn't we, I was on fire,' beams Leigh. 'After the disappointment of my injury the season before, it was great to finally get the Aussie title on my resumé.'

Throughout the British close season there was a debate about whether or not Swindon would be relegated to Division Two. After spending thirty-five years in the top league, the club were concerned that their fans wouldn't accept racing in the second division and warned the British Speedway Promoters' Association that they would consider closing down instead of risking financial ruin in Division Two.

'We won everything, didn't we, I was on fire.'

Needless to say, Adams went on record to say that he only wanted to race in the top league and indicated that he would stay in Australia and wait until a chance of a top flight ride became available rather than race in the lower division. Miraculously, the club avoided the drop when Berwick withdrew from the top flight due to financial losses. Therefore, because the rules stated that both leagues had to be of an equal number of teams, the Robins received a lucky reprieve.

Unbelievably, lightning struck the Wiltshire club twice when this time John Davis broke his leg in April and was forced out for the rest of the season. Swindon's depressing tale of misery continued. While the Robins' fans watched the experienced members of the team underperform, they drew immense pleasure from watching Leigh Adams establish himself as the Robins out-and-out number one rider.

Otto Weiss wasn't the only one who Leigh had impressed. It was at the start of this season that a sponsorship emerged that would not only grow into one of the longest personal sponsors in speedway racing, but also a friendship that exists to this day.

'In '91 I got a little van, a Talbot Express, and we ran that all that year. Then I got a letter that came through to Swindon. It was an envelope and it was addressed: 'Leigh Adams, c/o Swindon Speedway.' I opened it up and it was a printed letter from an old dot matrix printer, and it was from Randy

Owen of Owen Brothers Commercials, Hereford. It said that he had helped Paul Fry, been involved with motorbikes, had been to Australia, and had been keeping an eye on me and just wondered if I needed any help or something. I called him and said that I was dead interested, and we went up there, had tea, met him and the rest is history.

'The first two years it was just a sponsorship, but it soon developed into a friendship. We got a van in '92, which was a long wheelbase, blue Talbot Express, all painted up, sign written and done out inside with carpets and everything – that was Hollywood to me. I was on my way then.'

The first Owen Bros-sponsored van. (Adams Family Archive)

Randy Owen had been quite a successful motocross rider. Over the winter of 1968/9, Owen and another British rider, Gordon Adsett took part in the Rothmans International Motocross Series in Australia and cleaned up. But his promising career was curtailed by a nasty cartilage injury and he decided to retire and started his commercial vehicle business in Hereford.

'I had been helping Paul Fry,' Randy Owen recollects, 'and he was racing at King's Lynn at the time when Mark Loram and Henka Gustafsson were in the team. I got a bit of a buzz out of helping Fryer, and I thought it would be pretty good to get involved with a top rider. I asked John Tarr, of JT Commercials, who was in the same business as me and we'd see each other at auctions and he was, and still is, involved in speedway sponsorship. I asked him about Leigh Adams and he said that he was a good rider and going places.

'I wasn't interested in a poser – there are plenty of them around. I'd never seen him, but I liked the idea of helping an Australian because I had been to Australia and enjoyed myself. So I wrote to him and never heard anything for over a month and I thought that he probably had sponsors coming out of his ears. Then he called me, he had been in Germany, and he said that he was very interested. So we met and we hit it off straight away and we had an agreement. There were no contracts, it was just a shake of the hand, and that was it.

'We went to town on his van, kitted it out, two-tone metallic colours, sleeping area, it was really nice. And since then, of course, we've progressed to motor homes. The thing with Leigh is that the van used to come back at the end of the season spotless – it looked the same as when he picked it up. He looked after it and really appreciated the support.

'Leigh and I are similar, and although there is quite an age gap it's never been a problem and we've always got along really well,' Randy says. 'Neither of us are drinkers or anything like that. His parents refer to us as their "English family", it's grown that close over time. My daughter, Caroline, we call her Carrie, she enjoyed the speedway and our involvement with the riders over the years and your children are everything. So when you see that they're getting some enjoyment out of it then you tend to continue with it. But it has developed into a special friendship and the years have flown by. I never thought when I sent that letter that it would turn out the way it has, it's been amazing and very enjoyable.'

Confident, Adams began the season in flying form by recording four full maximums during Swindon's dismal Gold Cup campaign that opened their 1992 season. For the first time since 1989, he had entered the World Under-21 Championship. Previously you couldn't do both the senior and Under-21 world titles, but that was changed for '92. His first qualifying round was at Belle Vue and he finished second behind Joe Screen. Therefore, inspired by the quick engines that Weiss was supplying him with, Leigh travelled to King's Lynn for the Commonwealth Final of the World Championship assured that he could at least finish inside the top eleven and progress to the next stage. Furthermore, aside from his fast engines, he had another reason to feel confident because in the corresponding fixture at Saddlebow Road the previous year he had finished second to the winner Jeremy Doncaster.

'I'm told I'm mixing it more than I used to,' he wrote in his column in *Speedway Star* shortly before the Commonwealth round, 'but I think that is confidence. I'm happier with my starting and am now making three or maybe four starts out of five whereas it used to be one or two if I was lucky. I'm going there with the aim of winning the meeting and if I do, that won't do my confidence any harm at all.'

Unfortunately, his confidence did take a battering; in fact he was stunned. Leigh wasn't at the races at all as he dipped out of the title hunt with just 5 points.

'I was really fast, felt pretty good and felt that I could have got through to the World Final. I should have gone through because my form was good. It was a big shock to me and I bombed out of that one badly, a big disappointment, scary really. I was always looking for one step more and then that happened. It makes you wake up to things doesn't it? I was devastated. So from that time on, I concentrated on the Under-21s – that was all that was left.'

'I was really fast, felt pretty good and felt that I could have gone through to the World Final.'

That disappointment didn't reflect in his form as he continued to stack up double-figure scores for Swindon. He finished third in the World Under-21 semi-final at Tarnow, losing a run-off for second to Mark Loram – Joe Screen won that round as well. He had qualified for the final that was due to be staged at Pfaffenhofen, Germany. Eager to land the title, he left no stone unturned in his preparation and, as luck would have it, Pfaffenhofen was Weiss' local track.

'For that meeting I put in a lot of preparation,' he recalls. 'I flew over throughout the season and he got me a practice at Pfaffenhofen. Otto had rented the track for me, so that I could have a private practice, with Cocker (Marvyn Cox). I had a mechanic in Germany there, Mickey Moster. So yeah, we put in a fair bit of work and we were really prepared for that meeting.

'Obviously at practice we had done dyno sessions, we used to go to Crowzer, they used to make a road-racing sidecar outfit in Munich – Pfaffenhofen is not far from Munich. Back then dynos were pretty much unheard of in speedway, but all the German tuners had them for the long track racing. That year I had done a lot of meetings in Germany, I'd fly in and use his bikes, but that was more to do with the long track but then the speedway took over.'

On form alone Adams was one of the pre-meeting favourites along with the British duo, Joe Screen and Mark Loram. However, in Loram's pit someone arrived who tried to put a spanner in the Aussie's preparations – Norrie Allan.

'We probably saw each other a couple of times in 1992 and he wasn't doing much, just his pub,' Leigh says. 'We spoke and said hello to each other when he came to Swindon, but that was about all. I was just doing my own thing, I had Otto helping me, Owen Bros came on board, Neil (McCarthy) was my mechanic, and Kylie came back too, so it was a good set-up that we had going on at that time. It wasn't until this meeting, the Under-21 final, that he turned up helping Mark. It didn't happen before that, it was just a spur of the moment thing, but he probably wormed his way in there to piss me off!' he laughs.

'We turned up at the Under-21s for practice, and Norrie said to Neil, because he knew he would come to me, that I couldn't use the exhaust that Otto was using and that it was illegal. We went back to Otto's place to wash the bikes, he was on holiday then, so I made some phone calls from his place to check the rule book. I knew it was okay, but he was just trying to stir things up.'

The start of the meeting was delayed for forty-five minutes when a thunderstorm drenched the track. Fortunately, Leigh wasn't out in the first race, but the third. However, nothing was going to disturb his concentration that day.

'That meeting I was totally focussed on winning; I was going to win that meeting whatever,' he says firmly. 'We had that downpour, so it was held up. Now you'd sit there and think, shit, this is going to be off, but I didn't even think that it was going to be off. It was a long break. But they just drained it with sand, graded the slop off and off we went – there were no questions asked, and I didn't even ask the question, just got on with it. It was sandy and rutty, very similar to Mildura, you had to ride with the ruts which probably caught out a few of the guys.

'I knew I had the best equipment, knew I was prepared and my brother had flown in a couple of days before. Brando (Steve Brandon) came and helped me in the pits and did the programme. Everything, the whole jigsaw just fell into place.'

Left to right: Neil McCarthy, Leigh, Andrew Adams and Steve Brandon pictured at the World Under-21 practice. (Adams Family Archive)

Something was definitely trying to test his focus that day though, because his first race, in heat three, also suffered from delays. First of all Robert Johanssen was excluded for a fall, then Viktor Gaidym broke the tapes before Leigh was able to get his meeting off to the best possible start with a race win. After all the riders had completed three rides, the Australian headed the leader board with 9 points, with the British duo of Loram and Screen close behind on 8 each. He lost his fourth race to Screen, but Loram won his, which meant that these three riders were all locked together on 11 points with one race each remaining.

Loram defeated Screen to finish on 14 points, which turned the pressure onto Leigh who had to win his final race to face Loram in a run-off for the world title. He did so with ease.

There was a lot riding on this event for Adams. First of all, having dipped out of the World Championship, the Under-21 was the only major title left for him to win that year; secondly, he was in Germany, Weiss' backyard, and the German tuner had done so much to enable him to lift his game; and thirdly, a new element, Norrie Allan's presence in Loram's pit added an extra incentive for him to ram home his point.

After the rain, the sand used to soak up the moisture had meant that grip was at a premium, so making fast starts was vital. Therefore the choice of gate positions was critical. The omens weren't good when Loram won the toss for starting positions and chose the inside, lining up in gate two as it turned out, while Leigh would start from the outside. However, Adams stormed into the lead on the first turn, and although Loram chased him hard, and got very close on the final lap, the Australian won his first world crown.

'I felt the same as when I won the Aussie title, a relief to get it on my resumé,' he says of his victory. 'I had focussed on it for so long that it was a relief to finally win it.'

'It was my own fault really and, basically, I lacked someone with a bit of experience in my corner,' Mark Loram believes. 'We were both capable of winning it on the day and I'm sure Leigh will agree with that, but at the end of the day he was just one step ahead on the gate. When we had the toss, you could have half and half, you didn't have to go in gate two, you could go between the two. They were very rutty and wet. Me, in my stupidity, didn't think of that, rolled up to the start line, and chose either gate one or two which meant being in a nice deep rut. In hindsight, experience would tell me that if I went between the two I would have a nice bit of fresh ground. At the end of the day that was my mistake and I have to live with it. He deserved to win, even though it was only half a bike's length, it was a good race – I put that one down to bitter experience.'

World Under-21 rostrum: Mark Loram, Leigh and Joe Screen. (Adams Family Archive)

Interestingly, Leigh became the second Australian to win the Under-21 crown, the previous winner was another rider that Weiss worked with, Steve Baker. Such was his progress that year that only an engine failure prevented him from getting at least a rostrum place in the Division One Riders' Championship at Bradford. At that time the meeting included a field that was worthy of a World Final itself – Joe Screen was the winner.

His attention then turned back to the plight of his club, Swindon, who at this stage were fighting a relegation battle with Arena-Essex and Eastbourne. Even though Leigh scored a paid 18-point maximum, he couldn't prevent them losing a pivotal home match against Poole. He followed that up with a similar display at Bradford, but he received scant support from the rest of the team and Swindon were relegated. And this time there would be no escape.

'At the start of the year I thought it was going to be good. We had a lot of experienced guys, but it just didn't happen. We moved to a Thursday race night, and Swindon had raced on a Saturday for many, many years, and that killed it. Crowds were bad, there were more people in the pits! It wasn't nice, but I'm the kind of rider that forgets about all the crap around me and just gets on with my job and do it to the best of my ability – I've always been like that. Back then I didn't get involved with the team, had no input at all, I just went there and did my job. That side of things didn't come into play until later in my career.'

Once again he would finish another season not knowing where his future would lie the following year. Still, having finished fourth in the league's

Kelly Moran (left) and team manager Ron Byford look on as some last-minute adjustments are made to Leigh's machine by a hidden mechanic. (Author's collection)

Pictured wearing the logos of sponsors Chem-mart and tuner Peter Morris. Adams'
rise up the career ladder would be the cause of losing backing from both of them.
(Adams Family Archive)

averages with a 9.55 figure, combined with his world title, it shouldn't be a problem finding a team place for 1993 – or so he thought. The next few months would be a problematic time for him. His climb up the international ladder had already caused a bitter split with tuner Peter Morris, and now he faced another dispute with his sponsor Chem-mart.

'No contracts were drawn up, that's where it got a bit funny,' Leigh begins. 'It was a verbal agreement and it was that they had their name on the right leg of my race suit. I thought it was just for Australia, but they thought it was worldwide. So when I went over to England, I had sponsors there and did what I had to do. I probably ran them on my existing race suit until I got a new one. Once I had new sponsors in England, of course I had to start advertising them. The Chem-mart guys were seeing pictures of me in the local papers with Coastal on my right leg and it happened to be about the time that I got the deal with Owen Brothers and that hurt the relationship as well. It was a little bit of a misunderstanding because they thought that they had my right leg for the rest of my career, but I thought it was just Australia. It was a shame really because they were nice guys and to do that was really cool, but it got a bit frosty at the end.'

Swindon's future was looking bleak and poor attendances didn't give much encouragement to the idea of operating in the Second Division. Meanwhile, Poole had been experiencing some problems of their own when the lease holders, Poole Stadium Development Corporation, went into liquidation and threw speedway and the other sports into doubt.

During one of the BSPA's meetings, Pete Ansell, who was mindful of the fact that Swindon had lost a lot of money, asked Bill Chandler if the stadium owners, British Car Auctions had any thoughts of selling the promotional rights. While discussions began over that possibility, Poole Council ensured the survival of the Pirates by taking over the running of the stadium. A week or so afterwards, Swindon indicated that they would consider renting the venue out for speedway.

On 15 December 1992, it was announced that the Poole promotion were taking control of Swindon Speedway and would be running the team in the Second Division. Therefore, co-promoters Peter Ansell and Mervyn Stewksbury now had a club in the First and Second Division.

While that news was a great relief to Swindon supporters, it certainly wasn't greeted with the same enthusiasm by Leigh Adams. To outsiders, he had the perfect scenario: he didn't want to, and probably couldn't because of the rules, race in the Second Division, but he could ride for the new owners Poole in the First Division without all the hassles normally associated with moving clubs. However, the reality was quite different. True, there was no way that Leigh would have contemplated a season in the Second Division, but the idea of then riding for Poole in the top league after all the difficulties that surrounded his departure from the south coast for Swindon was, to say the least, unappealing.

Meanwhile, as the weeks passed by it became apparent that Poole, having acquired the Robins' assets in the deal, hoped that Adams would ride for the Pirates again. However, many contracts were delayed because of the BSPA's decision to implement a new rigid pay structure that caused outrage among the riders. As the controversy continued in England, Adams retained his Australian title at Brisbane with 14 points, losing only to Scott Norman. Alongside him in the pits was his German tuner, Weiss, and apart from that first race blip, he dominated the meeting, either by leading into the first bend, or passing his rivals seemingly at will.

With his second Aussie title in the bag and qualification for the next round of the World Individual Championship, he returned to England to sort out a team place. He didn't want to ride for Poole and couldn't race for Swindon, so he had no alternative but to seek a transfer.

Marvyn Cox had turned down a return to Poole because of the pay rates, and Leigh's transfer request was particularly disappointing for the Dorset club who saw the Australian as an obvious replacement for Cocker. At the time Leigh said that he didn't like the track at Wimborne Road and said, 'I find the track dangerous; it's too big and fast for the width of the circuit, which leaves you chasing the fence all the time.'

Ansell described Adams' transfer request as 'a complete shock' as the Australian was immediately linked with Coventry. Things got quite heated at one stage when it was reported that the Pirates promotion weren't granting permission for other clubs to talk to the want away World Under-21 Champion.

'They ignored my request for a transfer. They tried to talk me into staying. In hindsight it would have probably have been the best thing ever to go back there because there was always money in Poole, with sponsorship and so forth. But I think I just had a bee in my bonnet, and I didn't like the way they went about things in '89, so I didn't really want to go back there – I was being stubborn,' he acknowledges. 'Here I was World Under-21 Champion and I didn't have a job. I remember thinking, how can that be? I went to the Speedway and Grass Track Show, and went to see Martin Ochiltree (Coventry boss). I sat down with him and I was so close to a deal. That was my only real opportunity, and when that didn't work out I cried. I did the grass track show, and it was all looking good. I went over to Germany to do my bikes at Otto's, and Martin rang me there and told me that they were going to go with Hans (Nielsen). I had my hopes set on Coventry, it was perfect – I was devastated.'

The season was underway and then he was hit with another problem with his Polish League contracts. The PZM (Polish Federation) had to step in to resolve a dispute when his former club, Lublin, claimed that he had agreed a contract with them even though he had arranged to ride for Wroclaw.

'I'd ridden the year before at Lublin, but they owed me money. Hans (Nielsen) had left and I was on my own. I verbally agreed a contract, but I didn't sign anything. They put me down in their squad, but I hadn't given them a proposal, or my terms and they never got back to me. Then Otto Weiss had a link-up with Wroclaw and he said, "Look forget Lublin, come to Wroclaw." But then there was this bind with the two contracts, it got resolved in the end and they let me go to Wroclaw, but I only did two meetings for them!'

Amazingly, after his most successful season so far he had no meetings lined up for 1993 and couldn't get a job!

'I had no meetings anywhere – with a big van from Owen Bros! It was frustrating, awful really,' Leigh says. 'It turned out to be one of the best things ever because we went to Arena-Essex and we loved it there. That's when I first linked up with Terry Russell and of course, Ivan (Henry). I can guarantee you that when I did my deal with Arena I didn't ride for the new pay rates. There were always ways and means through sponsorship and all that. I was on shit money then, and the BSPA rates didn't even match up to that. I wasn't on big money and they wanted to cut it. It was very serious for a lot of the guys.'

There was some irony in Leigh's move to Arena because it was the Hammers who were first promoted to Division One when Swindon were relegated the first time. He was signed on a full transfer for an undisclosed fee. Plenty of people were not very complimentary about the tight little circuit at Arena, but Adams flourished.

'Arena was good. Everyone said, "How do you do it, how do you go there EVERY week?" The track was really flat. I had a good time and really enjoyed it. Ivan was really good because he was helping Bo Petersen and he knew the speedway world and Terry Russell had helped Andy Galvin. It was more like a big family there – they had lived the speedway world. Ivan's place was the Danish capital, there must have been three Danish riders living there. Always a great workshop facility, better than what I had at home, I really enjoyed it.'

Within no time Leigh got into his stride. Taking great delight in contributing to the 71–37 demolition of Poole, and no doubt inspired by the opposition, he scored his first maximum for the Hammers in only his fourth appearance.

Fired up, he laid a ghost from 1992 to rest when he won the Commonwealth Final with 14 points at King's Lynn. In doing so he became the first Australian to win the title and *Speedway Star* journalist Richard Clark wrote of his performance, 'It was hard to believe this same rider mustered only 5 points in last year's Saddlebow slump as you watched him go through increasingly impressive paces . . . he made it look so easy.'

This meeting also marked the end of his association with Otto Weiss and the beginning of a much longer working relationship with Peter Johns.

'I think what happened was, he had been with Jan O. Pedersen for a couple of years and he was always the quickest rider around because of the agreement with Otto. Then he won the World Championship and Otto sent him a big bill for all the engines that he had done for him throughout the whole year. I believe it was that big that he could hardly jump over it! Because they'd fallen out and Jan O. just split with him, I went to him and asked, "Okay, what's going on here?" because there were endless parts, non-stop, he'd be throwing parts at you, try this, try that, take this engine, and when he fell out with Jan O. there was even more, a surplus of engines.

'Luckily, when the fall-out happened I went to Otto and said to him, "Okay let's square this up, what do I pay for what don't I pay for?" The long track was free, I'd come in and ride his bikes, the speedway stuff I'd pay for. That was a bit of a blessing because it could have gotten out of control because here I was with ten to fifteen engines staring at me, probably the best engines around at the time, so it could have got really messy. So that was a bit of a blessing with Jan O. and in the end it just got too expensive, I couldn't afford to stay with him, he got too big and too expensive. Jan O. had won the World Championship in 1991 and I had won the Under-21 in 1992, so I think he realised that suddenly he could make a business out of his speedway, whereas before it was a hobby –he just got too greedy. So I went my own way.'

A mid-meeting blip in the Overseas Final gave Leigh cause for concern but his 7 points were enough to qualify for the World Championship semi-final for the first time. Drawn at Lonigo, Italy, he raced to a confident 11 points and booked his place in his first World Championship.

The 1993 World Final was held at Pocking, Germany, and was supposed to have been the last ever one-off World Final. A Grand Prix system was being introduced for the following year and this meant that this final had an extra incentive for the riders because the top ten would automatically qualify for the new system in 1994. As it was his debut, he wasn't expected to challenge for the world title on this occasion, but a top ten finish wasn't beyond his capabilities. Unfortunately, it wasn't to be a red letter day because he ended the meeting with 3 points.

'I wasn't prepared for it mentally,' he says honestly. 'I think I just wanted to make a World Final, and once I got there, I was in shut-down mode.

I had achieved what I wanted to achieve and that was it. But that was stupid because Chris Louis, who was a year older than me or something, he ran third that year.'

Moreover, he had failed to make the cut for the following year's Grand Prix series; but he was in good company because future World Champions Greg Hancock and Tony Rickardsson also experienced a day to forget. In the final outcome, however, it didn't matter because the Grand Prix didn't come to the tapes in 1994 after all, and it was a case of 'as you were'.

Arena-Essex had battled their way through to the Knockout Cup Final against Bradford – it was the first time since his arrival in Britain in 1989 that Adams had an opportunity to win some silverware at club level. The Hammers, though, were hit by injuries to Brian Karger and Troy Pratt, while Colin White was far from fit. Despite a valiant effort they had to settle for second best to the Yorkshire outfit.

However, the chaotic events that surrounded the second leg when the meeting was held up for forty-minutes while arguments raged over who should, and who shouldn't be included in the respective teams, so angered the promoting duo of Russell and Henry that they made very real threats to close the club and get out of speedway.

Happily, just as Adams thought that he was going to face yet another Australian summer of uncertainty, Arena announced in early December that they would be operating again. He even dared to wonder if he could have finally found some stability for himself in British Speedway.

7

Behind Every Great Man

The Eurythmics' 1985 song, 'Sisters Are Doing it For Themselves', revived and popularised a phrase that has become a cliché – behind every great man is a great woman. That is often true, and it's also true in the case of Leigh Adams. His wife Kylie has been much more than a speedway rider's wife and a mother to their children, she's his best friend, administrator, confidante, and that rare thing, a reassuring presence in the dark recesses that lie between a rock and a hard place.

While marriages and relationships don't suffer the high casualty rate as they do in the entertainment industry, because of the sport's 'here today, gone tomorrow' lifestyle, it's inevitable that many relationships – some of them long-standing – will fall by the wayside.

Kylie Adams has been a rock for her husband and she's kept the home fires burning, but Leigh is quick to acknowledge his wife's significant support. And it was his parents – his mother in particular – who impressed upon me the importance that I speak to Kylie to include her perspective. We did better than that, she wrote it herself, and here it is, in her own words.

• • •

It could quite possibly have been 'April Fool's Day', but it was certainly during the Easter weekend which fell at the end of March/early April 1986 that I first came into contact with Leigh. I can't tell you whether it was the checked flannelette shirt he was wearing, or the skinny jeans! Either way, that day my heart moved like it never had before and little did I know that five years later I would be setting up home with him in England.

So that Easter, on a sandbar on a bank of the Murray River near Mildura, I camped with a big group of friends. We all lived forty-five minutes' drive out of town, so made our own fun by having local parties, motorbike rides and camping trips on weekends and holidays. All the boys in the group had motorbikes and the only reason I was allowed to camp with a mixed gender group at the age of 13 was because my older brother and sister were often there too!

A couple of the guys went off for a motorbike ride one day and on their return to the campsite, they had a mate with them on a Honda CR125. It was Leigh Adams and he was Australian Junior Speedway Champion. Huh? Speedway . . . ? I was just like any young girl at the time – I had no interest in speedway (nor did I really know what it was), but it's fair to say I had a strong interest in boys! I can't remember being formally introduced to Leigh that day but judging from the eye contact between us (we hardly spoke), it wasn't necessary.

We somehow made further contact after that day, probably through the help of those same friends with whom I met him originally, as they went to the same school as Leigh. We had a bit of a 'thing' going for a while, but the next thing I remember he was giving me the 'cold shoulder' on New Year's Eve, 1988, just prior to embarking on his first season in England. The message eventually filtered its way through to me that he couldn't handle having a girlfriend as well as going overseas to race speedway, so this was his way of ending it. An idea that was almost certainly put into his head by others, which annoyed me at the time, but in hindsight, quite a sensible one. I heard through the grapevine of his plans to go to England as, strangely, he hadn't even talked to me about it previously. He broke my heart, but I admired his dedication. I had no choice but to get on with my life thinking I'd never have anything to do with him again.

The end of that season saw Leigh returning to Australia and through a connection with his brother's girlfriend (now wife), things started between us again. Second time around, I figured this time he was serious. The only problem was he would soon be returning to the UK and I was about to start Year 12 – my final year at school, in hopeful preparation for a university degree in Early Childhood Development. I remember while the other girls at school had photos of Bruce Willis or the like inside their lockers, I had photos of Leigh!

So we spent the season of 1990 apart; writing letters and making phone calls to each other. It was probably the best thing as it meant neither of us became distracted from our task in hand. I guess the idea of me going to England drifted into the conversation at some stage, because I remember getting as many shifts as I could from my part-time job at the local village shop, and doing lots of babysitting to save up for my air fare. By this time, I was only half-hearted about going on to university as I just wanted to be with Leigh.

Shortly after his return to Australia that year, I received my VCE (Year 12) results and got accepted into my first choice university in Adelaide. Although I was torn between the two, the inevitable happened and I deferred my place for a year to travel to England with Leigh and attempt to make a decision between life in England and further education. Needless to say, I never did get to university.

Looking back, I can't believe how easily my parents let me do what I did. Not only was I leaving home, but I was moving to the other side of the world and moving in with my boyfriend at 18. I guess at that age they couldn't stop me, but it must have been hard for them to deal with. Luckily, they knew Leigh's family and realised he was a pretty sensible kid. Don't ask me to consider the same when my daughter becomes of age though.

'Not only was I leaving home, but I was moving to the other side of the world.'

Nervous as all hell, there I was sitting on a Continental Airlines aircraft to London in May 1991. Leigh had recommended I fly Continental because they were cheap, and travelling via the USA allowed for plenty of luggage! But the downfall was that it was like a milk run. Adelaide, Sydney, Honolulu, Denver then finally London. I didn't know any different though, so it was all normal to me – but exhausting. Nowadays the most direct route with just one stop in Singapore is much preferred!

My first encounter with speedway in the UK was at Cradley Heath. From that experience (and probably a few others by that time), I knew I hadn't embarked on a glamorous lifestyle. The meeting was a double-header on a Public Holiday with Cradley in the morning and back at Swindon in the evening. I had such a bad cold and combined with the jet-lag, I didn't really feel that great. But there to support Leigh, I was. Still to this day, I have to confess I'm not really a speedway fan, but my passion and enthusiasm lie with Leigh's career. I've grown to love speedway when Leigh is involved and I enthuse about helping him where I can. It gives me great pleasure to see him race and making a living from what he loves.

Contrary to my feelings now, I remember the boredom of going to meetings in England with Leigh in those early years. We'd get there two hours before; I'd sit in the van and try to fill in time, before nervously finding somewhere to sit, quite often alone as I didn't know anyone. But of course the intimidating thing was that a lot of people knew who I was, being his girlfriend.

Once we arrived at the track I was left to my own devices as he concentrated on racing. I really didn't enjoy it and I couldn't wait for the meetings to be over so that I could just be with him again. It wasn't that I worried when Leigh raced, I just didn't enjoy being by myself for the couple of hours. I guess that sounds selfish but alone in a new world is not always fun, and Leigh was the only person I knew really well. Luckily, things are very different now, and through years of experience of visiting different tracks, you meet lots of people, learn how to fill in that down time and best of all get some enjoyment out of the whole deal. On that note I can say during his latter years at Swindon, I have been well looked after with a warm, dry place for myself and the kids to watch the racing every single week.

I can honestly say I have never worried about the safety aspect of his racing and still don't. Possibly because he's luckily escaped many serious injuries and somehow, by chance, I haven't been there watching when he has had bad crashes. But I do get anxious watching him in high-profile meetings like the Grand Prix simply because I want him to do well. Admittedly, as I get older and since the children have been around, I think about things a bit more and the possible dangers. But Leigh is a relatively safe, or more to the point, intelligent rider, so it's only really when other competitors who seem to have no fear and will stop at nothing are racing against him, that I feel any sort of nerves. I don't believe it's any accident that he hasn't had more injuries. You've got to look after yourself to earn a living the next day, simple. But it's his job and one he's performed pretty well over the years and I accepted it as 'normal' a long time ago.

We were living like kings for my first few months in England, but didn't realise it. We rented a four-bedroom house from Norrie Allan just across the road from the pub he ran in Downend near Bristol, where Leigh's speedway workshop was. It was very convenient and we shared it with Leigh's Australian mechanic, Justin. Things were rosy for a while and there is no doubt our time living under Norrie's wing was valuable. But as things progressed, in all honesty it became a bit crowded with the four of us trying to work as a team. Leigh and I decided it was time to move on.

So Justin returned to Australia and Leigh and I went our own way from Norrie. We weren't quite happy with Norrie taking charge and he didn't seem to be too pleased that I still didn't have a job after three months in the country. I remember driving to Swindon one evening, parking in the dark Wheatsheaf pub car park in our van, with the local *Evening Advertiser* newspaper looking for rooms to rent! The feeling was almost like that of being homeless, not that we were, but we knew we had to find alternative digs rather quickly. This was the beginning of a new era of our lives and

Leigh and Kylie in the doorway of Norrie Allan's rented-out house. (Adams Family Archive)

the point where we really bonded as a couple. Simply because every choice we made from here on was our own. At that stage though, I still felt I somehow needed to prove to myself and others that I wasn't a distraction to Leigh's career, which I'm sure was an underlying belief of a few senior onlookers.

The Wheatsheaf was a popular place for speedway people in Swindon to hang out and it was one of the few places we were familiar with. We popped in for a drink and got talking to a few people and it turned out that Neil McCarthy was prepared to rent us a room from his newly-owned two-bedroom house. He also had a garage that Leigh could use as a workshop. In fact, it turned out Neil would also mechanic for Leigh at home meetings at Swindon. So we were as 'happy as Larry' with the way things turned out, even though we were squeezed into the small bedroom of a 'two up, two down', end terrace. The bed took up most of the room and we lived out of suitcases with clothes hanging on the door. I remember the following season when we went to England, we did a 'deal' with Neil to swap bedrooms and have the bigger room!

Living in Swindon was great. I got a job almost straight away and we met lots of people and gained our own independence. My job as a catering assistant at the Castrol Headquarters wasn't glamorous, but it was a paying job. I even got a second job serving breakfast at Blunsdon House Hotel on weekends, which didn't earn us much money but it got me out meeting more people. I was thankful of the social network I had created because by this time Leigh had begun racing in Poland regularly, so independence and the ability to make friends for me was important since most weekends he was away.

It was then I learned this was the beginning of a somewhat lonely lifestyle during much of the speedway season. It didn't bother me too much then, though, and it doesn't now. I enjoy my independence and time to myself sometimes.

During the 91/92 summer in Australia after my first season in England, I was so proud to see Leigh crowned with his first senior Australian Championship, along with the rest of his supportive family. Things were on the up because Leigh's connections had now begun with Otto Weiss. It was all too good to be true when Otto offered Leigh the use of his engines. It was more than that though, it was a taste of Germany and possibly where Leigh's avid love for coffee was established! I think he has an addiction to the stuff. His legs shake when there's a Starbucks in view. I love coffee, but I can't really see what all the fuss about Starbucks is.

The offerings didn't stop there though as early in that 1992 season Leigh received a letter from Randy Owen offering to pledge his support with a van. We couldn't believe that someone was writing to him offering sponsorship! Leigh even asked me at the time if I thought it could be a wind-up. So to put his mind at rest he gave the guy a ring and well, as they say, the rest is history. Randy, his wife Raewyn, their family and the staff at Owen Bros Commercials have become more than sponsors, more like family friends. Leigh has never since had a transporter without Owen Bros written on the side, and he's probably rarely had a photo taken without the Owen Bros logo appearing somewhere on a hat, suit or bike since either.

It felt like the end of the world when Leigh dropped out of the Commonwealth Final at King's Lynn that year. We drove home absolutely gutted and when Leigh rang his parents in Australia to tell them the news,

I remember not wanting to talk on the phone because I was so upset. I guess things were beginning to come together for him and this blow was difficult to handle. Maybe my expectations were too high and when you're young this type of thing seems devastating. Leigh was really gutted, but he was certainly the stronger one out of us and put it behind him more quickly than I did. But it's amazing how circumstances always seem that much better after a good night's sleep and I realised we had to move on.

Exciting things were happening on the personal front though as we managed to purchase our own home that year. We finally had our own space and a wardrobe to hang our clothes! It was one of the best feelings ever. Setting up home also gave me something else to occupy my time while Leigh was away racing which suited me fine. It was right up Leigh's alley too as he's always been fascinated by property. In fact, he was the one who originally spotted the bungalow that we purchased (when it was nearly window-deep with weeds and obviously empty), while riding around on his mountain bike.

Being young, we had no idea about mortgages and purchasing property in our own country, let alone England. So luckily, we had the help of our good friend Pat Bennett who has been bookkeeper and financial adviser to Leigh and I since day one.

Throughout many stages in Leigh's career Pat has not only been on the other end of the phone to answer all sorts of financial queries, but a wonderful friend too. It was a relationship that started via Hans Nielsen and his connection with Pat's brother Peter Summers of PJS Ignitions.

Hans was Leigh's role model from very early on and I still remember Leigh ringing me while I was still in Australia telling me that he had beaten Hans for the first time! Hans and his wife Susanne were the 'Mum and Dad' of speedway when he first started and I think at that stage we all looked up to them. Now Leigh is the 'Daddy' and I guess all these young guys starting out now regard us as the oldies!

So we had a new home and a new trophy to display when Leigh won the World Under-21 Championship in Pfaffenhofen, Germany. Leigh was absolutely pumped with his result. The whole 'career as a speedway rider' concept was becoming real to me with Leigh winning at this level. I can't say it hadn't before, but from this point it started to mean something. We celebrated in true German style at a friend's pub called 'Andy's Pinte'. We were presented with a HUGE brandy glass filled with goodness knows how many shots of Asbach brandy and 10 litres of Coke. We passed it round the table for several hours before finishing it. That was a late night . . . !

Up until around the late 1990s, Australian passport holders needed to obtain visas to visit several European countries including France. This was

Following his World Under-21 triumph, the celebrations begin at Andy's Pinte. Leigh contemplates the big glass of brandy while he's watched by Steve Brandon (left) and Achim 'Becker' Detzel. (Adams Family Archive)

a nuisance for all of the Aussie riders travelling to Europe. It meant sending your passport to the embassy, which could take a week or even two, while at the same time needing your passport to travel elsewhere. It became such a hassle that on a couple of occasions I remember hiding in the back of the van while crossing the French border. In fact, I've never had a French visa in my passport! Leigh actually hid in the van on the trip to Germany for the Under-21s and I have the photo to prove it! Quite a funny sight, but not so funny if we had been searched by immigration.

After such a great year, it seemed ironic that Leigh didn't actually have a team to ride for in England the following season. There was no question of him dropping down a league when Swindon got relegated and taken over by

Poole. He wasn't going to step backwards after all he'd achieved. It would be like growing up and getting used to a new push bike, but then going back to ride the old, smaller one. It wouldn't feel comfortable and you wouldn't make much progress. For some reason he caused great headlines over that decision, but I think that was just the press blowing it out of proportion. Once Leigh has made his mind up about something, he sticks to it. I think they call that stubbornness!

So the move to Arena-Essex was another opening for new friends and acquaintances. We moved into a 'family' of speedway and enjoyed some great years. I can't say the same for the trip around the M25 getting to Arena though. Leigh would normally have to leave Swindon by at least 3 p.m. to miss the Friday afternoon traffic to arrive in good time. I was working flexi-time at the British Telecommunications office in Swindon then and I remember convincing him that I'd work my lunch hour this certain Friday, so he could pick me up at 3.30 p.m. to leave for Arena, just a bit later than usual. The latter part of the trip became tense when we got caught in traffic and I remember Leigh clambering into the back of the van to change into his race suit right there on the motorway! I think we made it to the track by 7.00 p.m. or 7.30 p.m., ready for an 8.00 p.m. start! I wasn't popular, but he managed to get on with it and race, and wasn't annoyed for long which is typical of his nature.

The trips to Hackney in '96 were different. It was like a sightseeing trip every week! We found it best just to drive straight through the centre of London to get there. Big Ben, the Embankment and Tower Bridge became regular sights for us, while most of my friends back in Australia would only see those landmarks on a postcard. I remember once Leigh dropping me at the National Gallery in London while he went to spend the day with Peter Johns at his outer London workshop. I was in awe at seeing this art in the flesh, having studied it at high school. That was the real art appreciation, not just the subject with the same name at school.

Although art was one of my favourite subjects, I soon realised that it wasn't going to benefit me while chasing speedway with Leigh. I never ever wanted to do any secretarial/office work; instead I wanted to go down the creative route. But my career aspiration took a u-turn after being fed up with pushing a tea trolley. I undertook a secretarial and computer course which then allowed me to get various temporary office jobs. After several agency posts I finally ended up working at NatWest bank who were very accommodating with time off for speedway and travelling back and forth to Australia.

Working at the bank is the longest experience I've had in a career besides my current job which has evolved over the years into being a personal assistant for Leigh. Speedway is our joint business interest and it now turns out that I love the office administration work I do and it's something I never get bored with. From selling merchandise to booking a hotel or rearranging a flight after a rained-off meeting at 10 o'clock in the evening, the subject varies and like any business, when you're working for yourself it's all so much more rewarding. But like Leigh, when he retires from the sport, I too will find myself unemployed.

Of course the International Masters Series in Australia was a big part of our life for several years during our summers back home and a lot of fun times were had. It was the sort of school trip experience where you really develop a relationship with your peers. David Tapp put together an awesome concept and we were really like a travelling circus. Leigh seemed to be the common denominator and got involved every year, then each season different international riders would come over to compete and you'd develop a relationship with some new faces. I'm not quite sure how Leigh kept up with the schedule though, after a full season in England. The weird thing was that we'd just get home to Australia after not having seen our families for eight months; then go off on tour for another month straight after Christmas, before heading back to England a few weeks later!

> **'David Tapp put together an awesome concept and we were really like a travelling circus.'**
>
> **Kylie Adams**

After living together for several years, Leigh and I decided it was time to get married. We eventually wanted to start a family and both felt we wanted to be married before. So shortly after our return to Australia in November 1996, we enjoyed one of the best days of our lives and celebrated with friends and family. Of course we had to arrange it around Leigh's racing commitments and most of the organising had been done the previous year while we were home. Afterwards we slipped quietly off to an island for a few days, as that's all the time I could keep Leigh in one place for! My man is by nature a very busy person both physically and mentally. He won't sit still for long and concentrate on one thing before he wants to move on to the next. I have learnt to work with him on that one and see it as a positive characteristic. However, he is very good at sitting still for ages when there's motor sport on the telly . . . hmmm.

Leigh is a great friend who's not easily upset, but push him too far and you'll know about it . . . like I did once. During our early days in England I was young and still learning about life, learning to compromise, learning to live with my boyfriend and generally learning to get on with life with no family around to give immediate support. I was having a young female moment and had pushed Leigh too far one day when he exploded. It's never happened again! From that point I certainly knew where I stood and how far I could go before crossing the line. Undoubtedly without realising, Leigh has helped teach me respect, maturity and to compromise, among many other things.

So having spent more than half of our lives together, thousands of miles away from our families hasn't always been effortless, but during those early years we had no choice but to grow and mature together with little outside involvement. Making our own decisions and choices probably influenced our working relationship as well, because from very early on I was doing all sorts of speedway admin tasks for Leigh, which I enjoyed. He was so easy going and I was eager to please . . . it seemed that we made quite a good team!

Leigh was in Poland when I woke in the night to what felt like mild labour pains. I was close to my pregnancy due date so figured this was 'it', but as I moved around the pains stopped. Thankfully, Leigh arrived home the following afternoon because by the evening I was in full labour. Grateful I was too that we had some good friends visiting that evening, as if it wasn't for them telling Leigh to 'go and have a shower, this is it', I might have still been waiting for him! I think he was in denial that it was actually happening. We arrived at the hospital at 11 p.m. and Declyn was finally born just before daylight the next morning at Swindon's Princess Margaret Hospital.

Our children were both born in England which gives them dual nationalities, but it wasn't something we thought about at the time of conception! The only thing we had to take into consideration was our back-and-forth lifestyle between Australia and England. So we needed to plan being in one country long enough and not needing to fly when I was too far into a pregnancy. We could also have made the choice to leave children until Leigh's speedway career was over, but we always said we wanted to be young parents, so sooner rather than later was what we decided.

The only thing we didn't allow for was the heartache we were to experience every year when we drag our children away from their grandparents and cousins going from Australia to England. Since our plan when Leigh retires from the sport is to live in Australia permanently I know, sadly, we'll experience the same thing one day, but then it will be saying goodbye to friends in England.

During the height of the speedway season Leigh is away an awful lot, maybe three or four days a week, so there are times when I feel like a single parent. The occasions when the kids and I have been to weddings, parties and functions as a single parent family, I have lost count. But it's something I have got used to. Leigh is with us continuously during the off-season so that makes up for it. On the other hand, when he is home, he is quite often able to pick the kids up from school, which is more than a lot of other fathers who work normal hours can do. So it has its good and bad points and we have found ways to deal with them all.

If there is one thing that concerns me about his dangerous career though, it would be all the travelling. Not just the frequent flying but long van trips across the continent. Sometimes he would race in a Grand Prix and then be driven to Poland while sleeping in the back of the van. One morning I got a phone call from him at 7 a.m. during a similar trip, with him telling me his van had been involved in an accident. The van was badly damaged and thankfully he and his mechanic were okay, but it shook us all up. The other thing I have learnt, and probably highlighted by this incident, is how important it is for him to return home to a happy household after his travels and racing. I've flown and travelled a fair bit myself, so I've realised how tough it can be and how nice it is to come home.

Towards myself and our kids, Leigh is the most selfless, generous and considerate person I know for many reasons. One is that he always has time for the kids and is without a question a 'hands-on' father. I run a pretty tight ship within our household as kids thrive on routine and since our routine gets interrupted quite a bit with all the travelling we do, I like to keep it as normal as possible. But sometimes, of course, when Dad comes home, the routine goes out of the window and they see it as a bit of fun! I am of course viewed as the heartless parent then when it's time for homework or bedtime. But that's the way it goes for lots of parents.

On a night when Leigh is home, once the kids are in bed we love nothing better than sitting down with a nice glass of red wine and watching the telly! Quite often it's after a pretty full-on day in the office sorting travel arrangements, replying to emails and general admin stuff. There never seems to be enough hours in the day. But we don't live a rock and roll life and Leigh has never been a person to head down the pub, a choice which some of his mates might find strange, but one I'm probably thankful for. Instead, eating out in a good restaurant is our thing.

Running a speedway business from home, though, brings its issues. With Leigh's busy schedule, we have a mechanic in the workshop constantly, people coming and going and a busy household in general. The lack of privacy can be testing but it's especially the kids I think about. They have got used to the lifestyle, and all of our friends understand it now too, but when the kids' friends first came over I felt a bit awkward until they got to know the situation.

Mechanics do come in handy when they are the only man around the house when Leigh's away . . . to chase down the odd mouse that comes indoors, to witness our children achieve their first crawl, or in Lars Christensen's case, take me to hospital while in labour with Casey.

Leigh was on his way home from Sweden and due to travel to Poole for a meeting that night, when he had to rearrange his commitments and meet me in the labour ward at the hospital. Luckily, he made it all in good time to see Casey born. Obviously he had to continue racing though, and a day or two later he flew back to Sweden for a fixture.

During this time I got bored with being in hospital and rather than wait until the next day for Leigh to come home and collect Casey and I from hospital, I rang Lars and asked him to come and take us home. Who knows what the midwives thought about the whole scenario when Lars was the one who dropped me at the hospital in labour, Leigh was there to share the birth with me, then it was Lars who returned to take Casey and I home from hospital!

So then there were four. Our lifestyle gradually became more involved with children around, which implied that we had to be a bit more organised. Living between houses in Australia and England means having two of almost everything as we literally travel between the two with just a few clothes. For half of my life, twice per year I have had to think between two very different lifestyles and had the upheaval of packing up a family and preparing to leave one house to move to the other. Moving time becomes a slightly stressful period in our household, but after so many years we have actually got it down to a fine art.

The other aspect is our children's education. Since they started school, they have been educated between a school in England and a school in Australia. This hasn't been an easy task, and is in fact one of the biggest concerns of my life. They both do really well coping with the frequent change though, and of course have friends in both countries because of it. They attend most of the year in England, and attend just a few weeks of the year at school in Australia and my theory is what they miss at school, they gain in knowledge from travelling. I don't allow much turn-around time between stepping off the plane and getting back to school, but our biggest task is remembering their teachers' names and the school times in each country!

Declyn and Casey have become great company for me, especially when Leigh is away, and now Declyn has reached the age where he is the man of the house when his Dad's not at home. If I need something vaguely male-orientated to be done, he's my man.

The years since having the children are slightly blurred in my memory (please tell me I'm not alone), but several career moves between Swindon, King's Lynn, Oxford and Poole within his British racing kept Leigh on his toes and broadened his experience with tracks and dealing with promoters.

His Testimonial at Swindon in 2003 is highlighted in my memory because we put a lot of work into it. If something linked to Leigh's career was worth doing, it needed to be done properly. We had a fantastic committee who put in a huge amount of effort and helped draw one of the biggest crowds at Swindon Speedway. It was a memorable occasion for Leigh and earmarked the milestone nicely. I felt it was not only a tribute to him, but paid respect to those who had been instrumental in his career thus far.

The Grand Prix has formed a huge part of his latter career, dominating our plans every season (out goes the family holiday!). It was certainly the aspect which needed the most attention in terms of organisation, and is why the highs are high and the lows are frustrating. But good or bad results, things run on a pretty even keel with him and he's always kept things in perspective. Maybe that's why he's always been so consistent with his racing, but never quite tipped the top of the World Championship. Something which doesn't bother me now, but I couldn't have said that five years ago.

The first time the kids and I witnessed Leigh win a GP was at Eskilstuna in 2007, which is a favourite memory. I couldn't be there for his first ever win since I'd just given birth to Casey, so this was awesome and so exciting for the kids. We all had a great weekend, but unfortunately Scandinavian Airlines were striking at the time, which meant our flight home the next day turned out to be cancelled and we were put on another later that afternoon. Leigh had gone straight to Poland, which left the kids and I to our own devices. Luckily, we were able to take advantage of the late check-out at the Radisson Sky City hotel at Stockholm airport. It was nice to have somewhere to wait other than in an airport terminal and to top things off, the replay of the GP happened to be on TV, so we were able to re-live the excitement of the previous night!

> **'The first time the kids and I witnessed Leigh win a GP was at Eskilstuna in 2007 . . . a favourite memory.'**
>
> **Kylie Adams**

I had been to Poland several times but had surprisingly only joined Leigh at Leszno once by the time he was granted his Jubilee meeting in 2005. We have great memories from Leigh's years racing there and he's met a lot of good people in a place which has become his third home. His Jubilee brought home what an effect he has had on speedway in Poland; the Leszno fans regard him as God. I remember sitting in the grandstand at the first Grand Prix in Leszno in 2008 which Leigh won. I had forgotten Declyn's ear defenders and he was agitated not only by the noise, but also by the over-enthusiastic Polish fans. When the Polish riders came round on parade the crowd went wild, which made Declyn stress even more. But to his amazement the crowd went just as wild, if not wilder, chanting 'Leigh, Leigh, Leigh Ad-ams' when Leigh paraded. Suddenly he realised their enthusiasm for his dad was just as strong and he had an immediate change in attitude!

It was emotional watching Leigh race in his last ever GP at Bydgoszcz, and I'm sure we will all eventually miss being part of the GP. There is no doubt that unless you're finishing on the rostrum at every round, there's not huge financial gain except for the sponsorship you pick up along the way. But you don't do it for that reason, when it's a World Championship you just put everything into it. We also got an awful lot out of it, and have many great memories to take away with us. But I believe Leigh has chosen the right time to move on.

There are times when some people may think Leigh is unsociable or rude, but I think it's simply his desire for his own personal space, something everyone is entitled to. To be honest Leigh is not a very sociable person unless he knows you really well. But there are occasions when the pressure of everyone wanting some involvement in his life is overwhelming and he's got to take a step back. You can give some people an inch but they take a mile, so he knows it's important to be aware and stay in control. For instance, Leigh admits to me that two days at a time in Poland is enough for him as it can be a very demanding place in terms of fans, sponsors and press. He occasionally gets fed up with signing autographs and doing public appearances whichever country he's in, but I remind him that his fans adore him and he's making their day! There are only a certain number of people in this world who have generated such interest in themselves and deep down I'm sure he's proud to be one of them. I know I am.

Kylie with Declyn and Casey at Eskilstuna, Sweden, in 2007 after Leigh had won the Swedish Grand Prix. (www.mike-patrick.com)

8

The Best Laid
Plans

L eigh Adams swore. In fact, he was so frustrated by the state of the
Brokstedt track in Germany that when the world's press arrived in his
pit to get his reaction to Australia's performance in the 1994 World
Team Cup Final, the normally amiable Adams' response was unprintable. It
was his team-mate Craig Boyce who eventually put a sentence together that
described their annoyance with the slick nature of the surface – although
once the journalists removed the profanities there wasn't much left to print
except, 'Pathetic, concrete, the M1, disgusting, a waste of tyres, the worst
surface I've ever ridden on.'

This meeting, where the Australians only just missed out on a bronze
medal when Boyce lost a run-off to Denmark's Tommy Knudsen, brought
an end to what was, ultimately, a disappointing international campaign for
Adams. It wouldn't be the last time that Leigh would be disappointed with
a track surface and as he continued along his career he, along with many
other world stars, would continually be dissatisfied and frustrated by the
policy of producing slick surfaces.

'When you get a really slick track it's hard to get hooked-up to go fast, I
like to chase the dirt,' he says. 'With a grippy track you can be off the money
a little bit with your set-up, but with natural ability you can ride and be fast.
I tend to like a little bit more grip. I've never had so many slick tracks as there
are in the Grands Prix – compared to your normal league matches, they're
extremely slick, which is probably why I struggled, especially in 2009 . . . they
were terrible. They were either slick or wet. When we've had a grippy track
or a well-prepared track like at Peterborough for the World Cup qualifier the
racing is better, and everybody said what a fantastic meeting it was. So it is
frustrating and it does piss me off a little bit. At the end of the day you can't
let that affect you, you just got to get on with it and go racing.

'Bradford was a perfect track for me, and Leszno; they had a little bit of
banking where you can use it to work your magic and pass people. I found

Bradford so good for that, and you could use the banking to your advantage and sweep off the corner and pass. If it's a big, flat, slick one, it's so hard to get things working. And then it comes down to getting your bike set-up. That's where I might have been a bit lazy early on in my career because I relied on my natural ability to win races. Swindon's nice – 2009 was very good, lots of overtaking. You could come off the inside, run in and turn back and get a run on people. The last few years it got to the stage where you were running the fence, you'd get on the dirt line, come into the corner and skim the fence.'

Disappointment in the world team meeting in Brokstedt was followed by problems with transportation. Jason Crump was a non-riding reserve for Australia and his van had broken down.

'It was a JT Commericals' transit and we had Owen Brothers because Randy was with me. So there was a bit of rivalry there because JT and Randy were friends and used to go to the auctions together. He was a bit of a mechanic, had a rough idea, and he had a look under the bonnet and it was something to do with the fuel pump, so it wasn't something that was going to be fixed overnight. We were driving back straight after the meeting to England.

'So Streetie, Broady, Randy and Tim (Osmond) mocked up a tow hitch. There were some big bits of pipe that divided the pit lane off from where you'd come in and out, so we pinched a bit of that and cut out some u-shackles and hitched Jason's van behind mine. On a tow rope you've got to be on the brakes and be alert, at least this way you're actually pulling the van and they're getting dragged along. So we towed him all the way back from Brokstedt, Germany, to England.

'It was really early in the morning and we were near Brussels and Randy was driving my van and Streetie was at the wheel of Jason's. Randy is a pretty wild driver at the best of times. We were coming off a slip road onto the motorway, and Randy was going way too fast. I was thinking, oh no, we're both going to get tipped over here! Somehow, Streetie managed to steer it around. When we pulled up Streetie goes, "Bloody hell Rand, bit fast there!"'

While travelling around Europe can grind you down as the year wears on, there is also fun on the road. Sometimes this is generated by boredom, such as a food fight along the motorway at 4 in the morning! At other times, as Tim Osmond recalls, it was just pure devilment.

'We were on our way to Vetlanda and we stopped at the services to get some fuel. Crumpie and Boycie were there with their vans, and I think it was Rune Holta that was following. They were talking among themselves and they said, "Are we going to do a runner, or what?" And they said, "Yep, we'll do a runner." I didn't realise what they were talking about, but "a runner" meant that they were going to run the queue at the border crossing in Poland.

'So we pulled out of the queue and took off down the side road. All these people were throwing fists at us and banging on the van. Suddenly this truck pulled out and stopped us. We hollered out that we had to catch a ferry or something, then he backed in and followed us. We got through, but someone stopped Rune Holta and cut his tyres! That was exciting for a while – I thought the Pole cats were going to get us.'

By now Leigh had carved himself a reputation as the consummate professional, and when he won the Australian Championship for the third successive season, there was every indication that he would continue his climb up the international ladder.

History may well record Leigh Adams for being the ultimate professional, but he will also be remembered for his smooth-as-silk style. He's not a spectacular hanging-off-the-bike type of racer like Simon Stead, but a more compact and controlled rider in the mould of his hero Hans Nielsen. He's at one with the bike, has superb throttle control – better than some World Champions – is skilful, and his height and weight are ideal. A classic style, he can seemingly put the machine where it should go at will. The Australian has attracted some nicknames for this approach to his racing such as 'the Sultan of Slide' and 'The Armchair Thriller' – interestingly, Australia's first double World Champion Jack Young was also famed for his 'armchair' style of racing.

John Adams recalls, 'There is a really good photo of him and Phil Crump that's on the wall at the Mildura Motorcycle Club, they're side-by-side and have similar styles. They're low and someone reckoned that they both fell off afterwards, but I don't think so. Leigh's always had that smooth style and is really skilful.'

1994 was going to be the last year of the old World Final because the FIM had announced that the Grand Prix would be introduced the following year. Therefore, making the final was the main target for Leigh to make sure of his place in the GP series, and to build on his World Final debut from the previous season. However, when he resumed the World Championship trail at King's Lynn as the defending Commonwealth Champion, he had his first indication that his fate could have been in the lap of the gods as he arrived at the tapes for his fourth race. Already lined up with his rivals, he looked down at his machine, and to his horror the fork leg had come loose! He admitted that it was a bit scary to roar off the start line knowing that a vital part of his machine wasn't secured together, but he managed to get second and seal his place in the next round – he finished fourth overall.

The picture that hangs on the wall at the Mildura Motorcycle Club: Phil Crump and Leigh Adams get down to it. (Mildura Motorcycle Club)

Such happenings are rare indeed for the meticulous Australian and Randy Owen would certainly have been shocked by this incident, especially with the contrasting experiences he had with Leigh and his other sponsored rider, Paul Fry.

'You couldn't fault Paul Fry's effort on the track, but his preparation left a lot to be desired. When I helped him in the pits one night I was forever tightening things up and putting things back on that had fallen off. I always had spanners in my hand.

'It was totally different when I helped Leigh, though,' he smiles. 'I was there with my spanners at the ready when he came in and there was nothing to do. He was sat there looking at me with my spanners as I went round the bike, checking the seat was secure and things like that, wondering what I was doing. There was nothing to do! Leigh is so professional that he doesn't break down very often and it was the total opposite to Fryer.'

Some riders are more mechanically minded than others. There are plenty who have gone on to become engine tuners when they retire. Some tinker and fiddle around with their set-ups, while others are quite happy to sit back and just ride the bike.

'I'm in the middle,' Adams assesses. 'I've never been a rider that does his own tuning. I think I've got a really good feel for the bike, what's fast and what's not, and what it should be doing. I never got involved with the tuning. I know guys who did their engines from top to bottom, but that has swings and roundabouts. I didn't get screwed up, I trusted the tuners I had, I'd just get on and ride them and say, "Don't like this, or I like that." But I have also seen the other side when the riders do the tuning themselves, and nine times out of ten they'd screw themselves up because they knew too much about it. They get a quick engine and pull it apart to try and find out why it went so quick.

'Guys like Tomasz Gollob, he's got twenty engines and he knows so much that he actually confuses himself sometimes. Even now, in the back of his van, he's got six engines, and that's not including the three he's got in his bikes. He is dropping engines in and out of his bikes non-stop, but I think if he actually got back to thinking about riding bikes, which he does pretty well, he may have been World Champion.

'Speedway is a mental game. So they'll try a certain camshaft, have a good meeting and think that was the be-all and end-all, and off they'd go. But they do a full circle and come back to where they started. I know enough; like that compression ratio was good with that cam, and so on. Maybe I should have got more involved, I don't know. At the start of the year you get a new engine, you run through a few things, try and get it right to make sure it feels good.'

At this time Leigh didn't have a full-time mechanic and was hoping that his Aussie spanner-man Tim Osmond would come over to help him out. Rod Colquhoun had been wielding the spanners when he wasn't racing himself, and despite a busy build-up to his next World Championship round he qualified comfortably. When he was drawn at Bradford (one of his favourite tracks) for the semi-final, everything was going according to plan. Fortunes in speedway can change in a split second: and it only took a few seconds to throw Adams' 1994 ambitious plans into disarray.

'I was riding at Ipswich in a four-team tournament for Arena when I crashed. It was my fault,' Leigh says honestly. 'It was really grippy, and I crashed with Dave Mullet who was riding for Reading. I came up the inside to pass him, but I picked up a bit of grip, hit him, and we both went straight through the fence. Typical of Ipswich, I landed on the stock car track with bits of wood and fence going everywhere – there was no air fence back then. I was pretty lucky because I ended up right out on the stock car track and it could have been a lot worse. But I broke my middle finger.'

The accident came just over two weeks away from the World Championship semi-final at Bradford. Still, in true speedway rider fashion, Adams was determined to ride in the meeting – after all, others had kept their dreams alive by racing with worse injuries than a broken finger. He rode four practice laps the Friday before the meeting at Arena and, as a result of those laps, he knew that he faced an uphill struggle.

'Ivan Henry was very good then, he took me to the physio, Brian Simpson, non-stop, trying to get it fixed. In fact, Simpson actually came to the Bradford meeting and pumped a heap of needles into my fingers just to kill the pain. Just through the vibration coming from the bike, the pain was unbelievable. I had my grip done old style, all rubber bands, just to stop the vibration, but it was awful.'

To make matters worse, his machine spluttered to a halt in his first race when his ignition failed after he dropped the clutch. He added just a further two points to his name, and with the qualification impossible and the pain not easing, he withdrew from his final outing.

'I just couldn't hold on and I really struggled,' he remembers. 'That was awful because I had a pretty good season that year through the qualifiers and Bradford was one of my favourite tracks. To go there with an injury is pretty hard, but I loved Bradford, had some great meetings there, so to bomb out of that was terrible. I knew the Grand Prix was in the following year so that put me out for the next year. But that's the ups and downs of speedway – these things happen. I did my best to get my finger fixed, but it just didn't work. If it happened now, it would probably be different because your pain threshold is better as you go along and you learn to get by. I've ridden with an injured shoulder which was pretty painful so I guess you're stronger mentally.'

However, at the time of the Bradford meeting Leigh was sitting in second place in Britain's Division One averages, and there would be many riders who would gladly swap their campaign for the one that Adams had endured, but for the Aussie, who had set his standards very high, that one major disappointment blighted his year.

Missing out on the World Final was very disappointing. This meant that one of the most promising young riders in the world, and one that was making genuine strides on the world's stage, would be missing from the first ever Grand Prix series in 1995. Still, as the FIM had failed to deliver the year before, there were many sceptics who wondered if they would succeed this time.

Nonetheless, Australia had stolen a march on the world's governing body by arranging a thirteen-round, International Masters Series in Australia during their 94/95 season. Not only had they dwarfed the FIM's paltry six-round series, they had also secured the appearance of new World Champion Tony Rickardsson, the previous year's title holder Sam Ermolenko, and the World Longtrack Champion, Simon Wigg. The series attracted a lot of media attention because of its strong line-up.

Leigh returned to Australia knowing that he couldn't be World Champion in 1995, but would have to spend the European season trying to qualify for the competition in 1996. A new era was under way, and instead of being at the centre of the action, he would be sitting on the sidelines.

The Masters Tour

The Australian International Masters Series was the brainchild of David Tapp. Although the Aussies were an emerging force in world speedway, the sport Down Under wasn't really going anywhere. A Test series against the old enemy England had proven to be popular with enthusiastic crowds, but the entertainment on the track didn't always live up to its top billing. Moreover, the Aussie promoters were disappointed with the make-up of the English Lions team who were missing their star names like Gary Havelock, Kelvin Tatum and Chris Louis.

Speedway was changing, and Australia needed something fresh to attract attention and to make the most of this exciting new generation of Australian racers who were enjoying a lot of success overseas. Tapp had already shown that he had the media connections when his company, Speed Machine, had put together a thirty-minute speedway TV show that was broadcast on Channel 9 just before the cricket. Such valuable exposure gave the sport in Australia a boost.

But when Tapp first announced the series in 1994, there were many who didn't believe such an ambitious undertaking would happen. In fact, petty jealousies did make life difficult for him and some false reporting cost the series a $12,000 sponsorship. However, not only did it come to the tapes during the 94/95 season, but it went on to be staged for a further six seasons. It was often referred to as a 'tour' because the series raced exclusively in Oz during a six to eight-week period from January through into February and, just like a music tour, the series had its own truck and bus that transported the bikes, riders, mechanics, wives and girlfriends. They all stayed in the same hotels and they all queued for the same washing machines.

'After the meetings you can imagine all the gear was sweaty and what have you, and everybody would be lining up for the washing machine. Meanwhile, the truck would go off with all the bikes to the next venue,' Leigh remembers.

Although it sounds great to have your bikes transported for you there were drawbacks to this. Your bikes wouldn't be the only thing going in the truck because other equipment accompanied your racing steeds, in particular the tyres, as Adams discovered.

'The first year I went separately, I did my own thing and drove. The next year, from the Perth leg, I got the truck to take my bikes to Perth while I flew there. The truck carried that many tyres the bikes ended up knackered at the end of the series, not because of the racing, because of just being loaded into the truck. Everybody had tyre marks on their machines; you never took a white bike to Australia because it just got hammered.

'It was a great atmosphere though because everyone socialised off the track, but when it came to the racing it was really good and competitive. That's what made it; it was like one big family doing this big circus. That's what made it so special and we'd all be in the same hotels.'

It was a bit like a travelling band, and there are thousands of stories from the riders who took part. 1996 World Champion Billy Hamill rode in the 1999/2000 series and he said that it was the closest he had ever been to being on the road with a rock band. And there was certainly some fun to be had, although it was a big eye-opener for some of the visitors. Jacob Olsen raced in the first one and when they got to Mildura he decided to sample the delights of water-skiing on the Murray River. He soon regretted it! He crashed on the water, injured his back and had to go and see a chiropractor to get it right.

'It wasn't so much the water skiing, we've got these inflatables that we tow behind the boat and we used to make them crash out of those pretty hard,' Leigh says. 'That's the thing about Mildura, our pride and joy is our river. It was tradition, Phil used to do it when all his friends and rivals came over, and I still do it now whenever anybody comes. A few cold beers in the boat and off you go – it's good fun.'

New experiences weren't just confined to the foreigners either. Mischievously Kylie was set-up for a travelling experience of her own, as Leigh explains.

'I can remember the first year we drove over to Perth and Kylie came with us. Randy joined us in Perth. Kylie had never driven across the Nullabor Plain before and we're talking 3,000 kilometres (1,864 miles), so it's about a thirty-hour drive. She hadn't done it and Randy hadn't done it either, so he would join us for the trip back and we thought it would be a good experience. Basically, you come down a big hill and then off you go – you just drive, it's 100 kilometres (62 miles) of dead straight road, no corners at all. Obviously we didn't tell her any of that and we said, "You can drive here, Kylie." After a little while she said, "This is very straight," and we just sat there laughing.'

The parallels between the International Speedway Masters Series (ISMS) and the Grand Prix were not lost on either Tapp or the on-lookers. Stealing a march on the FIM wasn't difficult with the way they fudged many issues with regard to speedway, but the series also showed the way forward.

'He pretty much did it exactly the way it should be done,' Leigh praises. 'I don't know whether the Grands Prix followed suit directly, but when we went to Olympic Park, Melbourne, we built a track. A few years later the GPs were building temporary tracks. We didn't think about it at the time, but here we were and you just got on with it – but it was a crap track!'

Tapp's showmanship and professionalism also extended to press day. 'Press day was always a big thing and we were all randomly selected to do them, depending on the rider, the Aussie guy might do his local one and a few others while the foreign riders would share it around,' Adams explains. 'The first couple of years were big deals. You had to turn up and it was stated in your contract that you had to wear your team shirt, or the one they supplied, mechanics had to wear co-ordinated shirts, be clean shaven and no earrings. You'd do interviews, do a couple of wheelies, a few starts and nine times out of ten it was in 40°C heat.

'I remember doing press day in Townsville and it was hot and humid – the humidity is a killer, it slaughters you and saps your energy. It was the luck of the draw if you got drawn on that one, while your mates were sitting by the swimming pool at the hotel.'

The first staging of the thirteen-round series was anything but a red letter period for the Australian riders as they failed to win a round. Leigh's best performance was third in Mildura. However, fresh from his World title success, Tony Rickardsson was the overall winner finishing three points ahead of Simon Wigg, with Sam Ermolenko third.

'Tony was always competitive,' says Leigh. 'That first year when he won the series, he got to the end of it and he didn't really have a mechanic, so he was doing most of it himself. We laughed at him because all he did when he was at the Langdon's was put a helmet cover over his clutch mechanism and wash his bike rather than take it apart – that was it. And then he went out and smoked everybody!

'Olli Tyrvainen linked up with Tony during that series and they used to knock around together and have a good time. Olli went to work for him in the end, they were "the dangerous brothers". When it came to the racing, Tony was always serious. You could have a good laugh with him, but he knew when to turn the switch on. As soon as he pulled on his leathers that was it – he was all business. Afterwards, even in the changing rooms, he would sit back, relax, and have a beer like the rest of us.'

Leigh finished sixth and recalled that the Aussies were caught out by equipment. Laydown engines were becoming the engine to have, especially on the big tracks. Tony Rickardsson had won the World Championship riding one and Simon Wigg and Sam Ermolenko both had them. Although they were not widespread, the Aussies were at a disadvantage.

'It was a piss take for all the foreigners to come over and smoke us. So we had to go back to the drawing board and bring better equipment. The first year the Aussies were nowhere and we had to smarten up our act and the next year we got things together.'

Tony Rickardsson wins again in Australia; this time he's flanked by Aussies Jason Lyons (left) and Leigh. (Adams Family Archive)

The following year it was a different story. Even though British Speedway had banned the laydown engine, they were becoming the norm and were commonplace in the new Grand Prix competition.

Leigh Adams had secured backing for the new series from Series 500 Car Care Products, and after Boyce's high-profile flooring of Poland's Tomasz Gollob, it was announced that he would join Adams in a 'Series 500 Super team'. Subsequently, both riders were much better prepared for the 95/96 competition, especially Boyce.

'Ivan Ballantine of Series 500 Car Care Products came in and he sponsored us. He was a clever guy with the way he went about his deals, he put us on incentives, never really forked out a big lump sum – it was always per round and things like that and that was always a good incentive. As it turned out he became a family friend and came to our wedding, he was a multi-millionaire and was just one of the boys who enjoyed his speedway.'

Before all that could happen, Leigh had a very important date to fulfil on 30 November 1996, when he was tying the knot with Kylie.

'One of the best days of my life,' Leigh smiles. 'Andrew, my brother, was my best man and Kylie had her sister, Sharolyn, as her first bridesmaid. It was a cool day. We had an outdoor wedding at a winery called Wingara Winery and they had a big lake that they used for their irrigation – it was beautiful, a really nice spot. There were loads of friends there and sponsors. We didn't have too much time for a honeymoon, but we went to a place called Daydream Island in Queensland.

'She comes from a strict family, a good work ethic and she's always put a lot into the relationship and my racing. Even now they say, "Oh what do you do for a job?" and I think she feels like hitting them sometimes because they think that she is living the life of a speedway rider's wife – and it's not like that at all. She sorts the logistics, flights, running everything, looking after two kids, running the house, and she's like a single mum sometimes. She puts in a lot of work. I think she has the hardest job, but she's pretty cool and it's been good.'

If anything, the second year of the Masters was even better than the first. All the main players from 94/95 were back, including the defending champion, Rickardsson. Craig Boyce became the first Australian to win the competition, with Sam Ermolenko second and Rickardsson third. On the back of a dramatic year in the Grand Prix, Boyce was on top of his equipment this time.

'He went out and got (Klaus) Lausch engines, carburettors and everything and he just blew us away. He made us look stupid, he was awesome that year,' says Leigh.

Leigh wasn't able to improve on his sixth place from the previous season, but he was involved in one of those classic races, the kind that sticks in your memory. It was the Grand Final at the Exhibition Ground (the 'Ekka') in Brisbane, held over five laps and a three-rider duel lasted the whole race, and with it being staged on a D-shaped track, it had the added element of breathtaking spectacle.

'It was Sam Ermolenko, Tony Rickardsson and myself; it was good, full-on, five laps, swapping and changing. Sam was running wide, Tony was on the inside, and I was poking my nose in. Tony won it, I was second and Sam was third. It's good to be in a race like that, it feels pretty cool afterwards – I like it. It's even better when you win. If you have a really good race, it just flows. If you pass somebody, set up a good move, it's cool, but this was five laps, full-on and really serious. It's getting harder to do now, because everything is so fast, so to have a really good, close race for four laps is really difficult, mainly because the bikes are so quick.'

David Tapp was more than just the promoter of the series – he orchestrated the whole thing from signing up the riders, getting the venues, doing the introductions and even personally provided the commentary and interviews for the TV and videos. Luckily, he was a natural showman and his media skills ensured that the competition reached the parts that other speedway meetings didn't.

However, it was while he was introducing the riders that his combination of showmanship and his skill with words, gave Leigh Adams a nickname that stuck.

'His forte was on the microphone. Back then we used to have a one-lap dash, and he was trying to bring things in line with sprint cars because they always did a dash. The presentation used to be a long, drawn-out process and Tappy used to have nicknames for everybody. I was "The Book" because I had a perfect style and never got out of control. Todd (Wiltshire) was "The Freak" because he came back after being split in half and was stitched together.

'He used to dramatise it all like, "This guy had fifty broken bones in his body and look at him, he's back!" All that sort of stuff. He had nicknames for everybody and we used to laugh on parade, "Tony Kasper, fifty-nine-times Czech Champion", how can you get fifty-nine-times Czech Champion? We used to take the piss out of Tony over that. So yes that's how "The Book" started and it has stuck ever since with magazine articles and things like that.'

The schedule remained at thirteen rounds and continued at ten or eleven rounds until its final staging in 2000/01 when it was reduced to a mini-series of three rounds. Even by today's standards, thirteen, eleven, or ten rounds, within a short space of time, across a country that's listed as the sixth largest

Australian International Masters Series boss David Tapp interviews Leigh.
(James Baker)

in the world, could be exhausting and hard work for the riders and their machines.

'I can't believe the amount of travelling we did, and it didn't get any easier,' Leigh reflects. 'We went to some weird and wonderful places. Mount Gambier was a sprint car track, and it was a big, banked thing. The track wasn't that big, but it was renowned for sprint cars. I wasn't due to do press day, but the vibes from the riders who did said that it was rough and horrible. Honestly it was one of the best tracks that I've ever raced on – it was awesome. The guy who prepared it was a sprint car driver and he sort of knew what we wanted. It was like Bradford, really banked on both corners and the straights. The only problem was the start/finish line on gate four, because it was so banked you'd actually slide down towards the inside a little bit, which was a bit difficult. Everyone was blown away by it – it just proved that we could go on a sprint car track and do it. This guy smoothed it all out, and put this sand on top, like granite sand, and he top-dressed it and that was our racing surface – really good. We've been back a couple of times since and it's been the same.

'The problem with racing speedway on sprint car tracks is the weather. If it was really hot, the clay would get hard and bake under the sun, and it'd go like a blue groove. If it turned wet, there was just no chance. One time at Parramatta it rained and the meeting was called off. We could hardly get out of the pits in the van, the wheels were just spinning and everyone was getting bogged down. When you walked, you'd grow taller from the clay building up on your shoes.

'I'm quite proud that I got to ride at the Sydney Showground and the "Ekka" at Brisbane, because the kids now are never going to ride on those tracks. They were famous, and Wayville and Claremont to a certain extent. You don't think about it at the time because you're chasing prizes, but you sit back and think how famous the Sydney Showground is with all the greats, Mauger, Olsen, and all the Test matches. I rode there once, when Dave Lander had put together a Test match against England. In fact, that was the last ever Australia v England Test match at the Showground on New Year's Day, 1994, which we won. I was on a maximum, but I missed the start in my last race and clipped Steve Schofield's back wheel and crashed. I can remember when I was young, Phil Crump was always shooting off to ride at the Sydney Showground or the "Ekka". And then you're racing there yourself. As I said, you don't think about it at the time, but now you think, how cool is that? It's such a famous venue. Sydney and Brisbane were very narrow and really big, fast things, but not totally away from conventional speedway. I used to like it; I had some great meetings at the "Ekka".

'We did one in Canberra, what a disaster! It had really old facilities and I think Tappy just wanted it because it's our capital city, he must have been feeling patriotic or something, but it didn't work at all, it was terrible.'

Once again, off the track there was plenty of fun and mischief to be had, and one incident when they arrived in Mildura sticks in Leigh's memory. The Swede Peter Karlsson took part in the series and he had ace engine tuner, Carl Blomfeldt with him. Hailing from Canada, he may have been a bit of magician with engines, but he certainly couldn't be described as the most athletic of people. Nonetheless, hanging out with enterprising young Aussie blokes meant that he wasn't left out of the fun, no matter how crazy it got.

'We got him to ride a bike down a hill!' Leigh laughs. 'It's a massive big hill near Mildura and it comes down to a flat green and then to a bit of a drop into the river. The people that own the property, their kids have got a pushbike and they race it down the hill and jump into the river. We were all messing about doing that and it was actually Jason Crump who said, "Come on Carl, it's your turn."

'Carl was sitting back with his Diet Coke, and he said, "Man, I wouldn't do that, you'd have to give me two hundred bucks to do that." Just to get out of the chair was an effort for him. Well, Jason being Jason, got $10 off of everybody that were there and sure enough we got $200 in the kitty. So off he went, up this hill, and it was the funniest thing I've ever seen.

'If you can imagine Carl, on a rickety old pushbike, coming flat-out down the hill – let's just say he didn't look like a natural. Well, everybody was jumping and kind of going in wheels first. Not Carl; he just went down the hill, jumped, and went in head first! He didn't lift it when he jumped, he just rode it and as he jumped, the front tipped over and back of the bike kicked him like a mule!'

David Tapp always presented himself and the series very professionally. Therefore, he expected the riders to display the same level of professionalism. He was quite aware of some of the wild times the riders were having away from the track, but as long as it didn't interfere with the series, or sour its reputation, he turned a blind eye.

Steve Johnston isn't what you'd call a quiet person. He likes to enjoy his racing and a party. As a result of this competition, despite their quite different personalities, Leigh and Johnno became very good friends – occasionally, when he's not riding, Johnno will mechanic for Leigh.

When Johnno joined the series he provided a lot of humour during the long-hauls across the country. Sometimes, though, he went a bit too far. For example, the riders' wives and girlfriends that were holed up on the bus with their partners were not too impressed by his flatulence, and even less so when he was being creative with a cigarette lighter!

Famously, Steve missed a press and practice day because he was in court for doing a streak during a football match! Tapp saw an opportunity to capitalise on the publicity generated by Johnston's streak.

'We wanted him to do a lap nude,' recalls Leigh. 'Before each series Tappy would get us all together and lay down the law and run through the rules. Johnno was there and we were congratulating him on this streak. The press had picked up the fact that he couldn't do press day because he was in court. So we were thinking of things he could do and he said, "Look, I can do anything, as long as these guys subsidise me when I'm in jail making number plates." That's what they do in jail, and that was typical Johnno, quite witty. But he never did, he was quite well behaved.'

However, Johnno got tired of travelling on the bus. So Leigh suggested that they form a team together because Steve is another one of those riders who could achieve a lot more if he was a bit more professional.

'He said that he couldn't do all the travelling in the bus and it just wore him down. We were pretty lucky because I had my own van, we could wash the bikes when we wanted, and we had our own transportation to go and get food when we wanted. You can imagine in the bus you've got to wait for everyone to arrive, and everyone to wake up in the morning before you start travelling and the days were long. We had the flexibility to travel through the night when it was cooler, and we had a base, or knew people on the way to stay with.

'So we came up with a team thing. We had the same suits, same bikes and got a sponsor together. I still had Series 500 sponsoring me and Johnno had Biketrader, and Tucker Time came in and gave us a fuel card. I took him around with me, we had a trailer behind the van and we ran under the same tent. During the first part of the trip we got him going pretty good. We had him on light beer and he was pretty well behaved, but then his results were just terrible and he wasn't winning anything. Then he went back on heavy beer and his results started to pick up!

'Then we went to Perth, and if we had a day on a Sunday when we didn't have to fly back, he'd put a party on at his house – this happened a couple of times. It was a barbecue and everybody turned up. But Johnno's mates were pretty wild and they had a helmet set up with a funnel and a big hose running down, and they'd pour beer in and you had to drink it. Everybody had to have a go, including myself, Randy Owen was there, the girls were excluded, but all the guys had to have a go at this.

'As the day went on, Johnno kept using it and his mates were tipping all sorts into it, and he just kept drinking and drinking. By the end of the day he was wasted. I think he tried to get Rune Holta to have another go, so he grabbed him, but he'd already done it and he didn't want to do it again. Johnno wrestled him and it ended up in a big fight.

'Tappy was disgusted and he was going to kick Johnno off the series, and I had to put out a few fires. He was fine then. I think I may have wrecked him by trying to keep him on the straight and narrow, and it built up and built up, so when he got with his mates he just exploded. It wasn't in his make up to be all professional, he couldn't do it. It was good for me, and I had a great trip, a great laugh and there was never a dull moment even though the travelling was long. But if you went anywhere with Johnno, nine times out of ten it ended up in a fight. He didn't mind a scrap, although he's calmed down a lot now.'

> **'If you went anywhere with Johnno, nine times out of ten it ended up in a fight.'**

However, during the 96/97 series, Leigh Adams brought the consistency that he showed around the world Down Under. He enjoyed a tight battle with Craig Boyce and the heat was turned up on their rivalry during the Grand Final in Townsville when Boyce crashed while chasing the Mildura rider. Despite his vociferous protestations, Craig was excluded and Adams took his third series victory. The championship remained tight and came down to the final race of the final round on the spectacular track in Brisbane.

Boyce had first choice of gate positions and, even though most of the previous races had been won from the outside gate, he chose the inside. Leigh was amazed by his decision, but took full advantage and chose the favoured outside. If Adams defeated Boyce he was the winner; but for Boyce to retain the title he had to finish first or second, and defeat Adams.

The monthly magazine, *5-One*, carried a big feature on the series in its May 1997 edition and Tony Jackson wrote of the final, 'The first attempt to run the final was stopped due to an unsatisfactory start, although it looked perfectly okay to me. Maybe it was just to increase the tension a further notch. As they exited turn two it was Boyce who led, but not for long as Adams flew round the outside as they went down the back straight. Boyce had no answer and by the second lap was visibly slowing, dropping back before pulling up with a blown engine, the title belonged to a jubilant Adams.'

Jackson's comment that the first attempt to stage the race was stopped to possibly 'increase the tension' could have been more than just an astute observation on his part, because Tapp wasn't opposed to bending the rules in order to improve the show.

'There was a bit of that with Tappy and he could have done. He was a showman and he wanted to put a show on, which he did,' agrees Adams. 'The referees were so inconsistent when we raced in other meetings in Australia. One of Tappy's stipulations was, where possible, we had one referee do the whole thing, Gavin Wilson. He was fair but he also wanted to put on a show. He didn't break the rules, but if the two minutes was on and it went to two minutes, ten seconds, he'd let it go.'

The following year Leigh retained the title and by now the Australian riders had turned their fortunes around from the early years with the top six places all filled by the home riders. Although there was a lot of fun, the racing was always serious stuff. Leigh was looking good to win it for a third time, although by now Jason Crump was up there with his fellow Victorian racer as one of the world's leading riders and was eager to win the Masters. It was proving to be very competitive, but Leigh's series came to a painful end at Warnambool.

'I was leading the final when I broke a primary chain. It was a massive track and there were six riders in a race. I had a pretty good race going on with Crumpie, but it broke on the back straight and I just cringed. I thought, oh here we go. Everybody got by me except Rune Holta, he hit me just on my arm and I got a big tank-slapper and just buried myself into the track – it was a clay track and rock hard. I went straight down, got flipped over the high side, landed on my head and compressed my back. I was just in pain. I was sparko'd, knocked out, and was just talking shit. I kept asking Kylie about ten times, "How's Dec?" And she said, "He's fine." And then I'd ask again, and she said, "Yeah, still fine!" I went to hospital, but they released me and I rode the next day.'

By the time that the 1999/2000 series kicked off, demands on the top riders in Europe had grown considerably – especially if you were a Grand Prix rider. In addition to the World Championship, the riders were racing in three leagues, the British, Polish and Swedish, on a weekly basis. Therefore, the days of attracting the likes of Tony Rickardsson were fading away because they wanted to spend their winters recuperating.

Nonetheless, Adams began the championship determined to win his third title. He won the first three rounds in Brisbane, Lismore and Gosford – he was flying. Unfortunately, success can be a catalyst for jealousy and his dominant performances fuelled rumours that he was using oversized engines.

'There used to be a couple that went round with the truck, Pat and Bob Levy – he was a good sidecar rider. They did every round. He drove the truck and they were known as the mum and dad of the kids because they looked after everybody. We'd done a few rounds and there were all these rumours floating around, it didn't come to me, it went through my sponsor, Dave Parker of Fraser's Imports, and he owned the bikes. He heard from Bob and Pat that they were accusing me of using big engines because I kept winning everything. When you're going good everyone points a finger at you, there's no competition so you're going too good.'

Leigh's long-time mechanic, Tim Osmond, got to hear the whispers from the referee, Gavin Wilson.

'It all started earlier at Mount Gambier, there were a few people saying that we had a big engine, titanium con-rods and all this sort of thing. The referee got me on the side at Claremont, he said, "There's a bit of drama happening, there's a few people complaining about Leigh's engine." John Titman's lad, Kevin, was looking after Ronnie Correy at that time, and he said that we had a titanium con-rod made by a bloke in Adelaide, which we did have, but that was for a long track engine which didn't run under speedway rules at the time. That blew up and bent the rod anyway. He said that the rod was in it and all that sort of thing.'

However, it really reached a peak when Leigh won another final, and Tim was surprised to hear Pat Levy's comments.

'She said to me in Adelaide, "Leigh winning all the time is spoiling the series" – I didn't take much notice of it. She was on the infield at Bunbury when Leigh won the final and she said, "Oh illegal engines, it's spoiling the series," and jumped up and down about it. Put on a hell of an act. Kylie had a bit of a go at her the following morning she said, "Leigh wants to win; where are all the other boys at the moment, Pat? In bed after their night at the pub. Do you know where Leigh is?" "No," she said. And Kylie retorted, 'Gone out for a jog'".

Leigh Adams remembers, 'I had a big set-to with them and approached them saying, "Look, I am not a cheat, blah, blah, blah," and we had an argument. It wasn't just them; it was the vibes going around. They were the ones who let it slip out of their mouths even though it was other people spreading it around, and when they came out and accused me – that pissed me off!

'The next meeting we flew to Kalgoorlie and, unluckily, I didn't make the final, I ran sixth or something. Since then, I've heard it mentioned that once it was rumoured that I was using big engines, I happened to have a bad meeting. It was a shame, it would have been nice to have gone out there and won the meeting, but I didn't.

'It pissed me off because I have never cheated in my life,' Leigh says. 'They had never been there and done it and realised what it takes to get to that point, to start winning and have a successful run. You can do that to anybody, you could probably have done it to Tony Rickardsson when he was dominant, and Emil Sayfutdinov had it because he was on a bit of a roll. That's pretty disheartening when people come out and accuse you of that. We're not that stupid, we put in a lot of work to get to where we are. I told them too. It caused a few rucks and Tappy was always apologetic and trying to tame everything.

'At Bunbury all the bikes were going back to Adelaide so we had a bit of time. So to prove my point, I stripped my engine there and then after the meeting, and they were all apologetic, they didn't want me to do it, but I was so pissed off with them. I said, "Look I am going to strip it," and they said, "No, no you don't have to do that."

'We nipped it in the bud and did it there and then in front of everyone,' Tim adds. 'We had to clear his name. He's got a good name and has never done anything wrong. Sam Ermolenko and Steve Langdon did the measuring. They took a fuel sample, measured it, whipped the cylinder off, checked the valves, confirmed it had a Jawa con-rod and it was all legal.'

Although it was an unpleasant experience, and upsetting for everyone connected with Leigh, he didn't dwell on it.

'I'm the type of guy that gets over it the next day, and gets on with things. I just forget about it,' he says.

Happily, he won the overall competition which proved to be the last one of any length. Just for good measure, he also won the series' swansong the following season, a three-round mini-series that included American World Champions, Billy Hamill and Greg Hancock.

At its height, the International Speedway Masters Series put speedway racing back on the map in Australia. The riders who raced in it all have fond memories of their time on tour in the Masters. But it would be very difficult to attract the same sort of field for a similar competition now.

'It came on in leaps and bounds,' says Leigh of the tour's impact on speedway in his home country. 'Speak to any Grand Prix rider and they will say that they couldn't do the Tapp series now. Physically, you've got to shut down and finish; you couldn't even think about doing an eleven- or thirteen-round series. You're struggling to do a two- or three-round series after a year in Europe. That was the closest we ever got to holding a so-called World Championship on our home turf. You couldn't do it now, but it was good fun – I loved it.'

10

New Challenges

With shields and batons, the riot police menacingly moved into the Bydgoszcz crowd and brought some order to the disgruntled Polish fans who were angry that the referee had excluded Tomasz Gollob for the cause of the stoppage. Leigh Adams sat in his pit waiting for his first ride in heat 12 of the 1995 World Team Cup Final against the unbeaten Danes. It would prove to be his only outing as they trailed the Danish duo, Hans Nielsen and Tommy Knudsen, who emphatically stormed to glory on a difficult surface to win another world crown.

Crowd trouble was nothing new in Poland; the supporters were passionate, vociferous and loyal. Leigh had experienced it before and soon learned to focus on the business of racing.

'You always get it in Poland,' he says. 'We have local derbies and it's so irate, it's crazy. If you go to Zielona Gora the fans there are over the top, but that's their passion, that's the way they are. Gorzow is the same. I remember riding up to the start line at Zielona Gora and the crowd are right on the fence, and you can see them. I remember someone in the crowd tossed a rock at me and it hit the side of my helmet! The way they think is totally different to Sweden or England, but that's the way it is. They've got their supporters club, their hooligans and stuff like that, which is the same sort of thing as football.'

Earlier that year, Leigh had signed to ride for Vetlanda in the Swedish Elite League. Despite the fact that the league had opened its doors to foreign riders in 1989, this was the first time that he sampled life in the top Swedish League.

'There weren't as many foreign riders as there are now. Vetlanda contacted me and we did a deal and I remember driving over with Randy and Kylie and we dropped the bikes off. We turned up at this little town, a great speedway venue, and it was a good club. My bikes in Sweden were dealt with by a guy from the club who used to take them to a motorbike shop and clean them.

'Sweden is more a club-orientated set-up. It has a family atmosphere that involves the club and the crowd, and they're not so vocal. Fantastic tracks, always good, always prepared well and it didn't matter about the weather conditions because they had it sorted. They were on the button. Vetlanda was a stepping stone before I went to Kumla for a couple of years and then off to Avesta.

'But Sweden was quite steady and drawn back from everything. The most exciting thing they did was drink coffee! Serious! That's all they did. The kids used to drive up and down, pull up, go in, have a coffee and then do more driving up and down the street.'

As we've read from Kylie, her husband has developed a taste for coffee and, as a result of many years racing in Sweden, that nation has encouraged his infatuation with the beverage.

'It's really strong coffee and I got the taste for it. I'm always up early and go straight to the airport and check in. Then I go to Starbucks, which is my little treat – I love them! I don't like the Red Bulls, I just sip away at my coffee during the meeting. I definitely drink too much – I am an addict,' he laughs.

The Swedish League had been growing steadily, and it was just bubbling but not quite ready to bring to the boil just yet. That would come later from the heat generated by Tony Rickardsson's domination and Leigh would find himself at the centre of it. However, as the 1995 season commenced, he was still smarting from the World Championship elimination that he had experienced the year before. His priority was to get his dream back on track by qualifying for the Grand Prix in 1996. He safely negotiated the Overseas Final – losing a run-off for the title to the fast-emerging Ryan Sullivan – and then headed to Elgane, Norway, for the Inter-continental Final. Leigh said that the venue felt like going to the ends of the earth, but he booked his place in the all-important Grand Prix Challenge meeting by winning a run-off for third. He actually clipped the fence just before he set-up the move that would take him past Brian Andersen.

However, he faced a dilemma over engines. The Grand Prix Challenge would feature the bottom eight riders from the GP series, and the majority of the GP field were using laydown engines. These engines were banned in British Speedway and only the top six (plus two reserves) would qualify for the following year's World Championship.

He'd used upright engines at Elgane that were tuned by Carl Blomfeldt. But even in that round there were riders who were coming out with laydowns. It wasn't just a case of riding a laydown engine, the characteristics were different and you couldn't afford to be thinking about the engine and how to ride it with a World Championship place at stake. Although he had been testing laydowns with Blomfeldt, he decided to call Otto Weiss and a hush-hush testing session was set-up for him before the Challenge meeting in Italy.

'I realised that I had to go laydown because everyone was so much faster. I had been trying the laydowns abroad, but I didn't feel that they were quite right. We couldn't run those types of engines in England, so I called Otto, flew to Munich, and I did some testing at Landshut. We got all the carburation sorted and I felt pretty confident, so I rented one from him.'

Nothing could be left to chance; it was vital that every detail was attended to because he felt his whole career hinged on this one meeting. Although he had his upright machine as well, which he said also felt good in practice, he rode the laydown from Weiss and won the meeting. He was only beaten by fellow Otto man Marvyn Cox, who finished second.

'Cocker was on Otto's stuff for years and years, and I didn't want to leave anything to chance after the disappointment the previous year. I made good starts, and the bike was so strong early on. To win that meeting was a great relief because I had focussed on that all year, and those Challenges were tough meetings.'

Less than a week later he was at his old stomping ground Swindon for the revamped Premier League Riders' Championship. The British League had combined both leagues to create a twenty-one-team competition. Adams would represent Arena-Essex at Blunsdon in a mammoth twenty-six-heat tournament that included a winner-takes-all Grand Final.

Along with fellow Aussie Jason Crump, he led the qualifiers with 11 points. From his last programmed ride to the Grand Final, he had to wait six races and during that time he may have been caught out by changing track conditions. He finished a disappointing last behind the winner Gary Havelock, Billy Hamill and Crump.

> **'I dominated that meeting, but totally screwed it up.'**

'I dominated that meeting, but totally screwed it up. I had first choice of gates and I chose gate three and blew it,' he laughs. 'I had won from that gate in a previous race, but the meeting dragged on and it was the slickest of the whole lot by then. Havvy came up to me, laughing, and goes, "Man I can't believe you took gate three." It was rider error.'

However, he soon discovered that there would be no room for rider error in the Grand Prix series. He made his debut in front of 26,000 fans in Wroclaw, Poland, and in those days the format was the traditional twenty-heat, sixteen-rider formula, followed by four finals where the big points would be scored. To explain, the top four scorers would compete in the A-final to decide the rostrum places, the next four the B-final and so forth.

A seized engine in his final outing meant that he would contest the D-final, dubbed the 'desperate final' by some. His debut ended painfully after a clash with fellow countryman, Crump.

'It was the first corner, I was running round the outside and he came up the inside. It was a normal Wroclaw incident really, the corners are so wide and then they funnel into nothing. I was on the fence, but he came across the inside to stop me and it stopped us both dead. I was sent flying and landed straight onto my collar bone. As soon as I got up I knew it was broken and that was it. Welcome to the Grand Prix! I ended up going out pretty quickly.'

In those days the bottom two scorers would drop to reserve for the next round and the two reserves would step up into the meeting. It was a disappointing start to his Grand Prix career and, if he was fit, he'd go to the next round in Italy as a non-riding reserve.

'I remember travelling back to England from Wroclaw, pretty uncomfortable with a broken collar bone. In that time between the two GPs, my mechanic, Chris Penny, said that he was going back to New Zealand with his girlfriend. So there I was: no mechanic, broken collar bone and reserve for the next Grand Prix. I was sitting there wondering what I was going to do. I was in the shit, big time.

'We all went to the Wheatsheaf pub in Stratton, everybody used to go down there. I had my arm in a sling, but was still planning to go to Italy. I was talking to Terry Broadbank, who used to mechanic for Tony Olsson for many years, and he said, "I heard that you're struggling for mechanics." "Yeah, Chris has just left me," and he said, "I'll help you, I'll come out with you to Italy for the Grand Prix." I said, "Yeah, that'll be cool." In the end, because I was only reserve, I got hold of Norrie (Allan) and he agreed to take a bike out for me. I had one bike, flew out with Broady and struggled around in practice, and then just sat it out and watched. That was the beginning of Broady as part of my support team and he hasn't missed a Grand Prix since. Obviously I've had a lot full-time mechanics, but he's been to every GP.'

It was while he was in Italy that he was party to the solid block tyre controversy that threatened the future of the series. The FIM wanted to introduce a tyre without slits in the tread, but the riders maintained that they were dangerous. As a compromise, it was agreed that they didn't have to use them in the series, but must test them during practice.

'We tried them there, but because they were solids, as soon as you hit a wet track or something, they'd just spin up, the bike would want to turn around because it had no grip trying to hold it. You can imagine with slits in the old tyres, you had edges helping you, because the knob on the tyre would squash into the track and grip the surface. I can remember Hans Nielsen did a lap and pulled onto the centre green because he wasn't happy with them.

'The Grand Prix Riders' Association was big then, and Steve Brandon was the secretary and he had his battles and his fires to put out with the solid block', recalls Leigh. 'It was bubbling all year; we didn't have to run them in the Grand Prix, but in other FIM meetings they had to ride them. Next year they were out – finished. Ole Olsen was the one pushing it and Hans was opposing it – the old rivalry. I think Ole thought it would slow the sport down and every year they were bringing something in to slow it down. When the laydowns came in they tried to bring in fuel injection because that would have been the simple way to work on a laydown. I think Sam Ermolenko brought one out and then they banned it. Silencers were always an issue. It's only been the last six or seven years when things have been settled, it's been run pretty smooth until the silencer change for 2010.'

Few riders were using upright engines now, and Adams had also switched to the laydown and he confesses that it took a while to get them dialled in.

'It was very difficult, I'll admit that. It wasn't only the transition of the bike, not so much the riding style, I still think that was the same, but you had a lot more revs and a lot more entrance speed into the corners. But now it's so quick and bang, you've got to make your move. A guy might come into the corner and lift, and within a split second you've got to turn back and go underneath him. So, yes, things have changed, and laydowns brought that in.

'The transition was really tough for me. I was GM, which most people were. When they went laydown, for some reason the GMs struggled to get going. I think the biggest thing was that they converted upright engines to laydown and they just didn't work. Carburetion was the biggest issue; but the Jawas hit the button straight away and they obviously developed it through Klaus Lausch. The long and grass track racing had gone laydown the year before, so Jawa were a step ahead. Also, frames were an issue; and we were all trying to develop what Jawa already had, so it took a year or more to get on the pace. I had to try and get them handling right, and get the carburetion right on the laydown.

'I can remember in Sweden being one of the last ones still riding the uprights. I can remember riding against Mark (Loram) and Chris (Louis) and they all had laydowns. But we were still running uprights in England. To be honest, it wasn't until I went Jawa in 1998 with the laydowns that I got going. I think that was the same for a lot of the guys. Tony Rickardsson was on the Jawas and was a factory rider, but the engines blew up a lot. I can remember him telling me that he blew fifteen engines that year he won the World Final.

'I still believe the uprights were always more vulnerable to flip, hit a rut and the front wheel came up a lot quicker. I've watched Ivan Mauger and Barry Briggs on DVD and the style then was off the throttle, lean it over, pick the bike up, grab the throttle and go. Not so much in Bruce Penhall's era, that was more understeer, everything was just beautiful. Now it's just attack, full-on, flat-out and chase the dirt. It's all about keeping your momentum. If you go to pass someone and you don't pass them cleanly, it can ruin your race – you can lose five metres and that's it.'

'If you go to pass someone and you don't pass them cleanly, it can ruin your race.'

Leigh changed tracks in England in 1996 – not clubs, tracks – to the revamped London Stadium at Waterden Road, which used to be the home of Hackney until they closed at the end of 1990. The stadium was refurbished and held the previous year's British Grand Prix. As the sport in the nation's capital hadn't been represented since Wimbledon closed down in the middle of 1991, the Arena promotion decided to move the Hammers team to the new venue and call themselves the London Lions. Unfortunately, it just didn't work out and they only stayed there for one season.

'Previously I only rode there in '89, and I remember it was a tough track. It was banked and you'd get right up on the fence and run around the outside. Andy Galvin was there and he would stick you through the fence as quick as look at you. I struggled a couple of times when I went there with Poole, mainly because guys like Galvin and Steve Schofield were so dominant. But London didn't work, it was tough. The whole set-up went there, what a disaster! It wasn't good for racing, the track was too narrow, square and horrible.'

That wasn't the only move either. In Poland he signed for Unia Leszno and began a relationship with the club that seems likely to last until the end of his career. In fact he's been there so long that the club officials forget that he's Australian and regard him as one of their own. Irek Igielski is the Managing Director of the Leszno Speedway club and he regards Leigh Adams as a hero.

'He should have a statue in the main square because he's one of the greatest speedway riders to have ridden for Leszno,' he praises. 'I have wondered a few times how it is that he looks so smooth, and so easy on the bike, especially when you look at some of the Polish riders. The bike is driving the rider, and the rider is following the bike, but not Leigh. It is such a pleasure to watch him race.'

Nonetheless, when Leigh finished second in the B-final of the Swedish Grand Prix and was averaging close to 10 points a meeting for London, combined with the fact that the British round was due to be staged at his home track, many people believed that the stars had aligned just right for him to take his first GP win. Sadly, it wasn't to be; it was a nightmare.

During practice, he was forced to take avoiding action when Peter Karlsson went down. He dislocated his shoulder in the accident. If that wasn't bad enough, the following morning he awoke to find that it had frozen and he couldn't lift his arm higher than shoulder height. However, strapped up, he was determined to ride but he missed every start and finished in a lowly fourteenth. The Grand Prix Challenge was beckoning, and to make matters worse his Australian rival, Jason Crump, won his first GP.

A victory in the D-final of the last Grand Prix couldn't prevent Adams from travelling to Prague for the Challenge. Once again it was destined to be a tough meeting because only the top four would book their places in the 1997 GP. Furthermore, to add to the difficulty, all the competitors would be using the much-hated solid block tyre.

'I remember Tommy Knudsen crashed in his first ride, splattered himself on the pit bend, and there was a huge uproar afterwards – "Get these tyres off, call it off and so on . . ." I was positive that would be the last straw when Tommy went down.'

Despite the protests and another crash that ruled out Russian Rinat Mardanshin, the meeting went ahead still using the solid blocks. After running a third in his first race, Leigh found himself topping the score chart with Simon Wigg and facing the popular Englishman in a run-off to win the meeting.

'Wiggy came up to me, because he was in Czecho and was a works Jawa rider, and asked me, "Can you help us out?" It was quite big for him to win it. I didn't care, I was just happy to be in the Grand Prix for the next year, so I let him win. It didn't mean anything, it would have been nice, but it didn't bother me, I just wanted to qualify – it's survival.'

And survival it was. Leigh said that he struggled in the GP for a lot of years and he earned himself an unwanted name tag of being a 'Challenge Specialist' – along with Britain's Andy Smith.

The American duo of Billy Hamill and Greg Hancock had broken new ground by forming a Grand Prix team with Exide as their main sponsor in 1996. With Hamill winning the world title and Hancock third, it was very successful.

Through his company, Owen Bros Commercials, Randy Owen also sponsored Mark Loram, who was also in the GP series. Therefore it was decided to follow Exide's example and Adams and Loram teamed up for 1997 to form Team Owen Bros Racing.

'Randy had been helping me every year and been to every Grand Prix,' Leigh says. 'We saw what Hamill and Hancock had done with Team Exide and it looked so good. It was Randy who wanted to do it really. We'd been friends for a few years. He started helping Mark the year before, and I guess he liked a British racer.'

Owen remembered it as being a memorable time for him, and he liked having two riders in the series. The whole thing was colour-coordinated in red and white, the vans, suits, mechanics, but it was Leigh who went to all the trouble of making sure it looked professional.

'Mark was pretty casual about it, he didn't seem to care what colours we raced in,' Adams reveals. 'We came up with what we came up with, which was a blend of my colours and his. It had to be red, I was red and he was red and white. I had to organise all the covers, the mechanics' clothing, sponsorship, and Randy did a couple of vans the same and it was cool – really good. But if you speak to Greg or Billy, as you know, speedway is not really a team sport. For some reason it just doesn't work. Speedway is an individual sport, it really is. Yes you're racing for a team in the leagues, but it's still an individual sport, you still go out, do your own thing and win your own races for yourself even though you try to help your team-mates.

'Randy was happy, it looked good and it looked professional. There was no benefit racing-wise, Mark did his thing and I did mine. We did it for Randy, he wanted it. I put all the work in to make it all work, and Mark reaped the benefits. There was no more money involved or anything like that.'

'It was good to be able to say to my customers that I had two riders racing in my company colours in the GPs,' Randy says. 'Leigh was professional, while Mark is more easy-going. But Norrie Allan was working with Mark and there was a bit of friction there from before. Unfortunately, Norrie was a bit of a wind-up artist and that did spoil it a bit.'

In 1997, Adams' GP performances found him still battling in the C and D-finals and once again he had to negotiate the cut and thrust of the Challenge meeting – this time in Wiener Neustadt, Austria. He finished third, which would have given him first reserve for the first round, but the FIM changed the format during the close season for 1998 and also increased the number of competitors from sixteen to twenty-four.

The new system was a ruthless knockout formula, which meant that if you finished third or fourth twice in a row, your evening was over. Although popular with supporters and the TV because it encouraged riders to take risks, it wasn't so pleasing for the competitors – especially for smooth racers like Adams and the reigning World Champion, Greg Hancock. Hancock in particular made no secret of the fact that he didn't like the system.

'The knockout was cruel but kind,' Leigh reflects. 'If you got onto a bit of a run, you had gate one. And I can remember Tony Rickardsson had gate one in every race, he kept winning, so it was gate one, gate one. It was a bit of lottery because of the way the gate draws were. If the outside sucked and gate one was dominant – that was it. I can remember Billy (Marcin Mroz, mechanic), was helping Smudger (Andy Smith) then, and he used to drop out pretty quick. Billy was packed up, in his normal clothes talking to me during the meeting. I think I had a few meetings where I transferred through quite well, but I still didn't make a final.'

He may not have made a final but he was mixing it. He had a run-in with Billy Hamill at Linkoping, Sweden, which left him nursing an injured hand. At the time he said that he was 'screwed' by the American and questioned the tactics that some riders were employing.

'Billy was always a very hard rider, not dirty, but hard – he wouldn't stuff you,' Leigh considers. 'I had my hassles with him but nothing serious. We all know a hard first corner, and we all know when someone is just going to ride someone into the fence. A rider knows how far you can push a guy until he can't turn, bails out and hits the fence. Just blatantly sticking you in the fence – that sucks doesn't it? Give me room to race is my motto, that's the respect I would want if I was on the outside and I always do that for anybody else. And maybe I've been too kind in the past and that has been my downfall, but I always respected that.

'Grand Prix riders will take it to the limit, definitely, but in general they're pretty good now. Eleven Grands Prix is a hard old battle; it's not only hard mentally but hard on the body. It's hard going through all those meetings, but to finish first, first you've got to finish – you've got to be there to score the points.

'We all gotta live and we all gotta ride another day. There's not that many dickheads around nowadays because we're doing too many meetings. Look at Lukas Dryml, he's a fine example. He came into the Grand Prix and was prepared to stick people in, but he had a couple of crashes and is gone – never to be seen again. You can't do it. The word gets around if anybody is being dirty and you have too many meetings nowadays and you'll always get caught out.'

However, there were other factors coming into play that affected the international rider. Riding in three leagues, a Grand Prix and other international meetings were taking their toll on all top-line racers, not just Leigh Adams. He remembered the 'mad month of May', which was particularly hectic because the Swedish League began that month and the World Championship series usually commenced then too. Possibly it was the intensity of the schedule which meant that his average for Swindon slipped below 9 points for the first time since 1991.

Speedway Star's editor, Richard Clark, sampled the 'mad month of May' for himself in 2007. He spent a long weekend with the Leigh Adams team, taking in the Swedish Grand Prix at Eskilstuna along the way. The early starts certainly got to the pen-pusher who, in a revealing article, described Leigh's necessary wake-up calls as a 'menace' – it appears that the journalist was more comfortable witnessing the last rays of a setting sun than the first streaks of light that accompany an approaching day.

However, not only did he document the racing and the characters he encountered along the way, but also the unexpected travelling mishaps, courtesy of the airlines, that are part and parcel of an international rider's working week. Clark found it exhausting, and although he believed that they led a remarkable life, he concluded that he was 'looking forward to a busy day in the office.'

Happily, that busy schedule hasn't prevented Leigh from being present during the birth of his two children, Declyn and Casey.

'I don't know how, but I managed to fit it around my racing somehow,' he grins. 'When Declyn was born we had some friends staying with us, Steve and Jo Carter, Steve was a mechanic for me. They had come over for a barbecue and were expecting a child of their own. I had just returned from a racing trip and was having a beer with Steve, just cruising along, when the baby started to come and Kylie was having contractions. I just kept having a beer, just made sure she was alright and carried on having a drink with my mate! All of a sudden Jo came out, she was all concerned and she said, "This is it." I was like, "Whoa!" you're kind of prepared for it, but you're not when the time comes, so it takes you by surprise a little bit. So off we went to the hospital and it was all straightforward, to me anyway, probably not for Kylie! But at 4 o'clock the next day Declyn was born.

'Casey was a bit different because she was always very small and they were always concerned about her. Kylie had to go to the hospital regularly to make sure everything was okay. Casey actually came three weeks early. I was meant to ride in the Elite League Riders' Championship in Poole, but Kylie's waters had broken. I flew in from Sweden and went straight to the hospital. In the end we didn't have her until Thursday. I didn't faint or anything at either of them, it was cool.'

Leigh was back at Swindon in 1997 and felt relieved to not have to negotiate London's congested road system on a weekly basis. Personally, he had another consistent season for the Robins, but the team was mediocre in the new Elite League. The following year it was a case of déjà vu as Swindon ran their home meetings on a Thursday with predictable crowd levels. But it was that or no speedway at all. This was also the season when team suits were introduced – for some strange reason green was added to the colour scheme – but they were worn over their existing leathers or Kevlar suits, not like today.

'The clubs had spent a lot of money on these race suits and Simon Wigg pioneered the whole thing,' Adams points out. 'Television was probably what Wiggy was looking at and I can see what he was trying to do, but they didn't last long. We found that because it was tight, it used to pull on your arms, and you'd get arm pump. We had to cut and alter them, and some guys chopped them off and just had tops – it turned into a shambles. I had my normal leathers on underneath, so it used to bind up on your arms.

'I can remember we did a couple of months with them and then we had a crisis meeting about them and Wiggy got stressed out. It was really bad because he had sourced all these companies to design and make them, and he'd put a lot of work into it. The concept was perfect but, unfortunately, it just went the wrong way. Had he gone about it with Kevlar suits, it would have been perfect. Two years later we got team suits again, this time in full Kevlar.'

> **'Television was probably what Wiggy was looking at and I can see what he was trying to do, but they didn't last long.'**

In 1998, Leigh switched from GM engines to Jawa, now called JRM – Jawa Racing Machines. Even though the American duo of Hamill and Hancock had won the World Championship on GM engines, it was still felt that Jawa held the edge over the Italian-made GM when it came to the laydown engines.

'I went back to Australia, and did a deal with a good friend of mine, Dave Parker, of Fraser's Imports. He was the importer at that time. Jawa was pretty dominant then with Tony and Hans Nielsen. Dave Parker helped me get a sponsorship in Europe as a factory rider. They were the engine back then. I was a factory rider which was pretty good.'

In other forms of motorcycle racing, being a factory-supported rider can be a big advantage. Many racers spend their whole careers trying to secure a plum ride with a leading factory team like Honda or Ducati. However, having factory backing in speedway doesn't carry the same sort of rewards, as Leigh explains. 'You've got your contract from Jawa and it's something like five bikes that they give you. Under the contract if you become World Champion your bikes are free. If you didn't, it was scaled-down a percentage that you'd pay for your bikes. It was always a good deal, but you had to go to Czecho to pick them up, bring them back, strip them down, start again, tune them up, and all that sort of stuff.'

Although Adams finished the 1998 Grand Prix series by winning the Consolation Final in the last round in Poland, once again he had to travel to the Challenge meeting to make sure of his place for the next year.

It was little easier with eight riders qualifying, but there was very little room for mistakes because they used the knockout format. However, on the big, wide open spaces of Pardubice, Czech Republic, Adams made no errors and won every race on his way to victory. Afterwards he praised engine-tuner Peter Johns for his blinding speed, and his dream of being World Champion was still alive.

'Those meetings were horrendous, one little slip-up and that was it. It was just a mental thing back then. I could run my Grands Prix and not make a final, but when I stepped back into a Challenge I could beat all those guys.'

There was little doubt that Adams had the talent and the ability to race at the very highest level, but he had yet to transfer his outstanding consistency from his league racing to the world's stage. In 1999, though, that would begin to change, and he wouldn't ride in another Grand Prix Challenge again.

11

The Turning Point

Belle Vue Aces' boss John Perrin was furious with Leigh Adams and blasted, 'I don't need people like him. I had an agreement with Adams and it was concrete, the whole deal was done. He should stay on the sidelines as far as I'm concerned.'

Perrin, who could be a volatile person at the best of times, was convinced that he had reached a settlement with Adams to ride for Belle Vue in 1999. The Australian admits that the Aces' promoter was right to publicly criticise him.

'He had a right to blast me because, verbally, we had a deal over the phone. We thrashed out a contract and I said, "Yeah, no worries, that sounds good." We were going to link up and sign the contracts. But then, out of the blue, Tony Rickardsson got involved at King's Lynn, and the promoters were Brian Griffin and Mike Western. It happened so quickly, they set up a deal and that was it. I weighed it up: going to Belle Vue was probably my worst track in the world and King's Lynn was my favourite track – so that was it, there was no extra money or anything like that. I didn't sign or shake hands, but he got on his high horse and slagged me off.

'At the end of the day I was looking after Leigh Adams. I knew I could score points for King's Lynn and to be involved with Tony helped me so much – that was my first year with him. He was getting some success back then and was World Champion, with Carl Blomfeldt, there was too many pluses there to give it away. Every time I went to Belle Vue John would slag me off. I don't regret any minute of it because it was the right decision.'

When you look back at Leigh's career, unlike some of his rivals, he's had an uninterrupted presence in British speedway. It says a lot about the instability of the sport in the UK that, more often than not, he's had to move clubs due to circumstances beyond his control. Owing to falling crowds and the high costs of holding Elite racing, Swindon eventually applied to join the more economically viable Premier League. That meant they couldn't accommodate Adams; and at one stage it really did look as though he would miss the 1999 British season. In fact, it wasn't until late April that he agreed a contract to ride for King's Lynn.

'It was a three-hour drive from my base near Swindon, cross-country all the way, not a motorway in sight, but that didn't bother me at all,' Leigh smiles. 'I had a great time and it was a fantastic home track. I had two really good years there. They had started off pretty bad, dropped Tomas Topinka and brought me in, and then got on to a bit of a roll.'

His impact was immediate; he scored a paid maximum on his debut against Eastbourne and Lynn's co-promoter Brian Griffin later said that his arrival turned the whole situation around. 'In terms of professionalism, Leigh's exemplary. What astonished me were the benefits he gained from being with Tony and being at King's Lynn. In heats 13 and 15 you need a powerful spearhead, as the expression goes in those two you throw a couple of grenades in. We never lost a home match when Leigh arrived.'

The Adams/Rickardsson spearhead was one of the strongest in the league – four years later they would team up again at Poole to devastating effect.

'He had his big motor home and I had my little one, and we'd camp out and have a few beers.'

However, Leigh would eventually ride with the Swede at the Masarna club until Tony's retirement. His professionalism and dedication was legendary and, understandably, this rubbed off on Adams.

'We were doing the GPs together, he had his big motor home and I had my little one, and we'd camp out and have a few beers. This was where the friendship started. Tony was the hardest man to beat and a rock-solid rider, he'd race you hard, but he wouldn't stick you into the boards.'

Rickardsson used a sports psychologist to help him focus and hone his skills. Having witnessed at close quarters how professional and talented the Australian was, he was also baffled as to why he couldn't bring that form into the GPs.

'I was just sitting on a plane with him, and he said, "Go and see somebody." And it wasn't until then that I thought about doing that. It's like releasing all the stuff that's been built up inside, you release it and you get a fresh start. You get all your demons out and you've got a fresh field and off you go.'

Leigh being Leigh, it wasn't something that he did straight away. He had to think about it first. Kylie did some research on the subject and he went to see a hypnotherapist, although how much benefit he got from it is open to question.

Sky Sports began broadcasting live Elite League matches in 1999. King's Lynn was one of the earliest teams to be featured, but travel disruptions put Leigh and Tony's participation in doubt.

'We were in Sweden on the Tuesday,' Leigh recalls, 'but when we got to Stockholm the first flight got cancelled, and the next one got delayed and we thought, what are we going to do? We were really struggling because we had to get the next flight into Stansted. But it wouldn't arrive in time for us to drive to the track.

'So, Brian Griffin, who was instrumental in everything, hired a helicopter for us. We flew into Stansted, went through passport control, and they chauffeured us through to the other side of the airport where Tony and I jumped into this helicopter. We landed in the stadium's car park out the back. After all that, we were actually early; it was just the driving time which meant that we wouldn't have got there on time.

'I don't know what it must have cost him. I remember it was important and Sky was just starting then and we landed in a helicopter, which I thought was pretty cool – that was Hollywood, an entrance in style.'

However, he certainly wasn't overshadowed by Rickardsson's presence. A friendship may have been formed, but he still wanted to be the number one at Saddlebow Road and beat him to the top spot. And he very nearly did by achieving his best average at that time of 10.67 – just 0.19 behind the Swede – and was regarded as a crowd favourite for the smooth way in which he would glide by his opponents.

Unfortunately, the side was a little too top-heavy to capture the league title and finished third. Disappointingly, there was no silverware to show for their efforts. Nonetheless, reluctantly, he did have a say in the destiny of the league title when he won the final heat against Poole that handed victory on the night to King's Lynn and the league title to Peterborough. Given his history with the Pirates, there were some who viewed the win as something more cynical, but the promotion had changed and there were no hard feelings on his part – it was just racing.

While he missed out on domestic honours, he didn't do so on the world's stage. Convincingly, Australia won the World Team Cup at Pardubice by defeating the hosts, the USA and England. Leigh led the score chart with 14 points and the team dedicated the triumph to their team manager Neil Street. Interestingly, although it was a four-team tournament that traditionally has one rider representing each team in a race, this time there were pairs.

On an individual note though, Leigh qualified for his first Grand Final in the Grand Prix series at the Swedish round at Linkoping, finishing fourth. Overall he finished seventh in the competition, which was his best thus far and, to his relief, he didn't have to race in the Grand Prix Challenge. But there was individual glory to saviour in the prestigious Czech Golden Helmet at Pardubice.

'I passed Tony on the third lap on the back straight,' Leigh says proudly. 'It was kind of the biggest thing that I won because in the GPs I hadn't won a final. Back then the Czech Golden Helmet was popular, everybody went to it. I can remember doing a press conference with Tony and he was pissed off! He was so professional that he actually said that if there was anybody that he was going to lose to, it was me. That was because we had become good friends and built this friendship. It was nice to beat him and I was a Jawa rider then so it was good to do it in front of the factory. And it was good for my confidence to beat Tony because he was the 1999 World Champion.

'It was six riders and six laps; and it's not a problem at all to have six riders because the track is so big – probably the only track in Europe where you can run six riders in a race comfortably. It's such a huge, fast track, and that was what I was used to in Australia, but it took me a while to get going on it. I had been there for world pairs and team cups, and I remember really struggling and having a hard time to ride the place because it was big, but it was still hard to turn. I had this theory that it was like a long track, I used to ride it like a long track, but it just didn't work. Then it clicked and I've got great memories of those meetings.'

Rickardsson's term at King's Lynn only lasted one season. He didn't even ride in the UK in 2000, but the Adams/Rickardsson pairing continued in Sweden where they raced for the Avesta club, Masarna.

'We set the standard, speedway became popular in Sweden and Tony helped a hell of a lot to bring speedway on in general,' Leigh believes. 'Avesta was huge because they had the local boy in Tony, and later Antonio Lindback came into the equation. It prospered big time. The whole town got behind the speedway and we used to get crowds of 3,500 every week, which was unheard of because in Sweden the crowds were around 1,500 per week at most tracks. That year we just set records at every place we went to.

'Tony set himself up with a full-time commercial press officer and he chased the press to start with. He got them involved, built himself up and built speedway up. It all came swinging back after he had success because all they wanted to do was chase him. He'd done all the hard work, but then, probably, it was too much for him – he was non-stop. We were always on the same flight and I remember driving the rent-a-car and he would be on the phone for an hour-and-a-half with the press. He must have been sick of it. But Swedish Speedway owes so much to Tony and as soon as he left, the minute he walked out, Avesta just went downhill from there.'

38. Australian title No. 6:
Leigh went through the
night unbeaten to claim
the 2001/02 championship
at Wayville Showground,
Adelaide. Six-rider races
were staged during this
meeting. Leigh is flanked by
a glum-looking runner-up
Jason Crump (left), third-
placed Ryan Sullivan
(right) and fourth-placed
Todd Wiltshire (far right).
(James Baker)

39. A Grand Prix winner
for the first time at
Gothenburg, 2002.
(www.mike-patrick.com)

40. 5–1! Just how the Poole fans remember them. Tony Rickardsson (left) and Leigh celebrate another success for the Pirates during the all-conquering year of 2003. (Alan Whale)

41. The champagne moment. Celebrating victory in the Swedish Grand Prix in Stockholm with Jason Crump (left) and Tony Rickardsson. (Adams Family Archive)

42. Leigh picks up the Czech Republic Golden Helmet Championship for the fourth time. (Jarek Pabijan)

43. (above, right) Team Leigh Adams Racing at the British Grand Prix, 2001, with, from left to right: Peter Johns (engine tuner), John 'Dude' McLachlan, Leigh and Terry Broadbank. (Adams Family Archive)

44. 'Cardiff was always one you went to win.' Returning to the pits after the riders' introductions at the Millennium Stadium with the vast and always noisy crowd in the background. (www.mike-patrick.com)

45. Ready for the off from left: Greg Hancock, Nicki Pedersen, Tony Rickardsson and Leigh at Stockholm. (Dave Fairbrother)

46. A close encounter with 1997 World Champion Greg Hancock. (www.mike-patrick.com)

47. A rare breakdown at Wroclaw in 2004.
(Dave Fairbrother)

48. 'Advance Australia Fair' – Leigh's always been
proud to represent his country on the world's stage.
(Dave Fairbrother)

49. In discussion with Randy Owen. (Adams Family Archive)

50. The big, red motor home. (Adams Family Archive)

51. Like father like son? Son Declyn gets an early taste of racing on board Dad's restored Honda MR50. (Adams Family Archive)

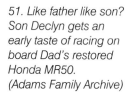

52. So close, yet so far: three years of successive fourth places in the Grand Prix was very frustrating. (www.mike-patrick.com)

53. Conference time in the pits as 'Billy' and 'Broady' listen to Leigh's instructions in the pursuit of more speed. (www.mike-patrick.com)

54. Focused, determined and in the zone, ready to chase the dream of becoming World Champion. (Dave Fairbrother)

55. Owen Bros: one of the longest sponsorships in the history of the sport. (Dave Fairbrother)

56. 'The Book', never out of control, the smooth style of a world-class rider. (Dave Fairbrother)

57. Pictured with Terry Russell at Cardiff. A chance remark from Leigh to Russell during his testimonial influenced Russell to take Swindon back into the Elite League. (www.mike-patrick.com)

58. *In action for Swindon on the inside of Poole's Bjarne Pedersen with Mads Korneliussen (blue) and Chris Holder bringing up the rear. (Les Aubrey)*

59. *Racing inside Nicki Pedersen. Leigh admits, 'I've got to take my hat off to him, he's become the complete rider.' (www.mike-patrick.com)*

60. The Men from Mildura in Grand Prix action: leading Jason Crump. (www.mike-patrick.com)

61. Leigh says, 'I've never asked my mechanics to do anything I wouldn't do.' Here he is lending a hand during a busy Grand Prix night with 'Billy'. (Dave Fairbrother)

62. *The whole team together after Leigh's brilliant 2007 Swedish Grand Prix victory at Eskilstuna. From left to right: Terry 'Broady' Broadbank, Marcin 'Billy' Mroz, Leigh, Richard Clark (Speedway Star editor), Tommy Cox and Mariusz 'Mario' Szmanda. (www.mike-patrick.com)*

63. *Leading Nicki Pedersen. (www.mike-patrick.com)*

64. The big-money final in the German Grand Prix at Gelsenkirchen. Leigh (No. 5) Jason Crump (1), Greg Hancock (2), and eventual winner Andreas Jonsson (4) exit the first bend. (www.mike-patrick.com)

65. Second in the world and the silver medal in 2007. (www.mike-patrick.com)

66. Receiving the bumps after clinching the Polish League Championship with Leszno in 2007. (Piotr Markowiak)

67. The triumphant Leszno team and the beaten finalists, Torun, pose for photographers after the 2007 Extra League play-off finals. (Piotr Markowiak)

68. *Nicki Pedersen goes down behind Leigh during the controversial heat 17 clash at Cardiff in 2008. (www.mike-patrick.com)*

69. *Anger, disbelief and shock were all on display for the world's TV cameras as Leigh argued his case over the telephone with referee Marek Wojaczek after his exclusion from the 2008 British Grand Prix. (www.mike-patrick.com)*

70. 'I don't race for records, but it was a nice one to have,' said Leigh after his record-breaking tenth Australian title. Over three rounds, he never lost a single race. Joining him on the podium are Chris Holder (left), Rory Schlein and Troy Batchelor. (Adams Family Archive)

71. The end of an era: Leigh was runner-up in his last ever Grand Prix at Bydgoszcz in 2009. (www.mike-patrick.com)

72. *Mother and father, Joan and John Adams. (Adams Family Archive)*

73. *The Adams family: Kylie and Leigh with their two children, Casey and Declyn. (Adams Family Archive)*

Meanwhile, in the British Elite League, King's Lynn had assembled what Leigh remembered as 'the Dream Team' – a mini Australia. Jason Crump, Craig Boyce and Shane Parker were brought in to join Adams and Travis McGowan who were retained from the previous year, while Tom Madsen and Steve Masters completed the side. Unfortunately, Mike Western departed the management team to be replaced by Nigel Wagstaff.

During their first eleven matches they only lost one meeting, to Coventry, and that set the tone for the rest of the season. The Knights remained in the hunt for the league title throughout 2000, but they came up short after they lost their showdown with eventual champions Eastbourne. Bringing in veteran American John Cook did help bring knockout cup success to Norfolk, but not the big one.

'Isn't it weird when you put a team together like that, and it just doesn't work out,' Leigh ponders. 'I've seen it so many times, like Belle Vue with Sam, Billy, etc., and it just didn't work. We should have smoked them all, but we didn't. Whether or not there are too many egos in there and they don't gel, I don't know. To win a league you need guys to come out of the unknown and increase their average by 2 points or more. If you look at this team, it just didn't happen. It came down to the last meeting at Eastbourne, which we needed to win, but we lost.'

It was a different story in Sweden though. Their league championship was already decided by a play-off system – that would be introduced to Britain in 2002 – and the Masarna side faced Rospiggarna in a ground-breaking final for the sport in Sweden. Both legs were held over consecutive nights, and Swedish Speedway hit unprecedented heights – the sport was booming. After Masarna won the first leg at Rospiggarna, 58–38, the Avesta town caught play-off fever and many stores closed for the afternoon or, at the very least, closed early so that they could support their club, Masarna. Consequently, the stadium was packed solid – the like of which had never been seen before in modern times.

'The attendance was over 12,000, which was unheard of back then for a league meeting,' Adams recalls. 'We set the bar that year for Swedish Speedway. We faced Rospiggarna, which was like our local derby – they were north of Stockholm and we were west. We just set records with 7,500 at their place and we won. We were such a dominant team that there was no way that we were going to lose. As well as Tony, we had Gary Havelock and Brian Andersen and we won the second leg, 51–45 and won the league.

'It was huge, to this day I have never seen anything like it,' he smiles. 'We had a street procession on the back of a fire truck and the whole town was out clapping us as we drove through – and this was 11 o'clock at night! They put up a big marquee for a party with a band. That was the start of big things in Sweden I think. Other clubs looked at that and thought, hang on, this is what we can achieve. The next year we finished second, but we ran strongly for a number of years.'

Although he qualified for his second final in Wroclaw, things were still tough for him in the Grands Prix. His disappointing performance in the final round at Bydgoszcz meant that he finished in sixth place overall. The fact that he finished top of the British Elite League Averages for the first time may have displayed his outstanding consistency, but this only highlighted the difficulty he was experiencing of transferring that devastating form to the top level.

Shortly before Christmas, the speedway public were stunned when Adams made a shock move to Oxford. After two impressive seasons at King's Lynn, it was reported that the Australian had become weary of travelling from his base in Wiltshire to Saddlebow Road, and a sponsor had also helped sway his decision. On the surface things were fine at Lynn and the Knights' supporters were sad to see him leave; the reality was quite different.

'I was owed quite a lot of money over the winter,' he discloses. 'To be fair, I did get it, but I had to wait six months or maybe more. It got very messy. I just kept contacting Nigel Wagstaff, threatening legal proceedings, take him to court, that sort of thing. We had it on a contract what the deal was. I kept quiet about it because I wanted what I was owed.'

Interestingly, in *Speedway Star*'s end of season review that came out approximately a month after Adams' transfer had been announced, Wagstaff gave a guarded clue as to what was going on behind the scenes when he said, '(He) puts his financial rewards in perspective with putting his neck on the line.'

'You always try and get more, every year!' Leigh declares. 'I always have a figure that I am after and work towards that figure. One was more money and another was to cut back on expenditure. I've always done my own deals. When you're young whatever the promoter throws at you, you tend to go, "Yeah that's good," because you just want to go racing. I knew the way to go about it and Norrie Allan guided me in that area. You get the gist of what other riders are on. If a rider came up and said "Oh I get this, and I get that" I'd take it with a pinch of salt because as long as I got my deal and get my money, I'm happy with that and that was what I was always after. I think it's worked out good for me over the years.

'If you speak to Terry Russell he will say that I have been pretty hard, but I've been fair and they've been fair with me. For the likes of Swindon, I've always put a lot into the club, perhaps too much, because I want success and as captain I'll push hard and push my team to be winners. That's what you want because if you're winning you get good crowds and stuff like that. I've always prided myself on that. When they've brought in pay cuts, that's a load of crap because you just get a sponsor to make up the deficit in some way. It still happens now in all sport. To be honest, I've always had good clubs, but I got screwed once in Lublin, they owed me money, and Waggy.'

Among his new team-mates was his friend Steve Johnston and rival Todd Wiltshire. Wiltshire had made a tentative comeback in 1997, but it didn't take long for the former world number three to get back into the groove. He raced in the 2000 Grand Prix series finishing eighth overall – that included a rostrum placing. Consequently, Leigh renewed his rivalry with the rider from New South Wales.

However, possibly enthused by his return to the world's stage, Wiltshire was eager to re-establish himself as the number one Australian in their National Championship; in fact, he was a little bit too keen to achieve that position at Murray Bridge.

Willing as ever to make a successful defence of the Australian title, Leigh smashed the track record by establishing a time of 59.81 seconds in his third race. Meanwhile, Wiltshire made his intentions pretty clear when he defeated Adams in heat 14 with one of his trademark lightning starts.

Both riders finished on 14 points and met again in the winner-takes-all final. By virtue of his win over Adams, Todd had first choice of gate positions and chose the inside, while Leigh took the outside. Mick Poole and Steve Johnston were the other finalists. Once again, Wiltshire stormed from the start and into the lead. But Leigh was not to be denied and constantly pressured him. Then, with half-a-lap remaining, he roared past his old rival on the inside and looked all set to take his sixth national crown.

'I was in front of him, and on the last corner I went a little bit wide, but I was still looking okay,' Leigh recalls. 'Then he came from nowhere, right from the kerb and chopped my nose off, and I was off the gas and went across the finish line in a bit of a mess. I was pissed off because I lost, and with the way in which he went about it.'

Peter White's report read, 'Wiltshire saw a glimmer of hope and went for an inside pass through the last corner. His front wheel lifted and into the straight he went, high towards the fence. With only 10–20 metres to go, Adams was forced to throttle off to avoid a collision and the title was Wiltshire's by a bike-length as the crowd stood as one to witness the most thrilling finish in the championship's history.'

As usual Tim Osmond was in Leigh's pit and he remembers, 'Todd got the jump on him at the start and Leigh was going round and round, reeling him in. Then I thought, he's gonna get him here, and he dived underneath, but then Todd just moved out and ran him out of room. He gave him no room at all. Leigh had to virtually shut down or crash into the fence – or crash into Todd, and then both of them would have ended up on the ground. Leigh got a bit cranky, and Todd said to me, "Have a word with Leigh, he's not real happy with me." I didn't say much, it was a bit of controversy but that sort of thing happens all the time.'

In full view of the public, a heated discussion between the two riders followed on the infield afterwards, and an angry and animated Adams was heard to say, 'I didn't think Todd was that kind of rider.'

'I just said, "If you're going to ride like that, be like that," or something like that. He didn't care, he had champagne in his eyes, and he just said, "I didn't mean to do it, that was the way it was, you gave me a bit of room and I took it." I was fuming, I was really pissed off. At the end of the day, I was annoyed because I had made a little bit of a mistake by leaving him a little bit of room, and was more pissed off with myself, so I took my anger out on him,' he laughs.

'I'd just signed for Oxford, but that didn't mean a thing really. That was the big thing when we went to press day, how is it going to be? I don't dwell on things like that; I just park it and get on with it. It was no big deal. We still talked and there was always a little bit of rivalry that went back to '89 when I first came over. But from a professional side, as a team-mate and all that, I didn't worry about it – I'd been there and done it.'

Speedway racing is competitive and intense. Therefore, in the heat of competition there are going to be clashes, differences of opinion and racing over the edge. Although Leigh admits that he's been over the edge himself, he's so skilful on a bike that he rarely has to step over the line to pull off a victory. But that frustrates some of his rivals and causes friction. One of whom was Scott Nicholls, who Leigh has had a few racing incidents with down the years.

'In '05, he stopped the bike completely in the middle of the corner at Coventry, I didn't get excluded but he did. He sort of ran across me, turned back, and I must have tapped his wheel and he went down. Another time he was in front of me, stopped the bike dead, and I ran over the top of him. I remember asking him, "Why did you do that?" At Ipswich in '09, I'd come off gate four and he was off three. It was towards the end of the year, so I don't know if he was frustrated with his year, but we got tangled up and crashed. We had another re-run and I had him covered, then the next minute he just rode straight into the side of me. There was no room, although he must have thought there was. There was a bit of a puddle on the track so I roosted him in the corner and he got all pissed off about that. To be fair, I've had a pretty

Gating alongside Scott Nicholls at Eastbourne. (Les Aubrey)

good run with most riders, it was only Scott that I had a few incidents with, but it's just racing . . . nothing too serious. He had a crap year in '09 so I guess it just built up.'

In 2000, Benfield Sports International (BSI), who had acquired the marketing rights to the Speedway Grand Prix, announced that the British Grand Prix was going to be held inside Cardiff's new Millennium Stadium. The announcement was both exciting and unbelievable. The stadium had been redeveloped a few years earlier and held the 1999 Rugby Union World Cup and it was the Mecca for Welsh Rugby. Therefore, for speedway racing to be staged inside this modern arena that had a roof was the equivalent of baseball being held at the Lords cricket ground.

'I didn't know much about it, all I heard was that it was all rugby there. I didn't realise that the stadium was so new,' Adams says.

Until the mid-1980s, the old one-off World Finals were staged before big audiences – in excess of 60,000 – at places like Wembley and Wembley was long-regarded as the home of the World Final. Since then, the sport's premier competition had lost its prestigious venues and was being held at traditional stadiums like Bradford, Coventry, Pocking and Vojens. Now, as the adverts said, big-time speedway was back.

Before that, though, the GP kicked off at Berlin's Friedrich Ludwig Stadium. It would be the series' first attempt at building a one-off or temporary track. Although affected by persistent rain, the first temporary track didn't auger well for the future. It was a messy, muddy affair on an already inconsistent and largely experimental surface, and it should have been called off.

'What a disaster, it was the most awful track you could think of,' Leigh candidly says. 'They had the track covered beforehand and they said, no big deal, but it was just drenched anyway. It rained throughout the meeting, the track rutted up and it was just a shambles. I can remember halfway through, we were all trying to get it cancelled, and I was going pretty good on points by then. If it had gone to countback I would have ended up second to Tony Rickardsson. I was pumped for it to be called off, but it wasn't, they ran the whole thing through and it was disgusting – horrible. I remember Tony wiping out Nicki Pedersen in the final. Then they had Cardiff straight after.'

Leigh arrived in Cardiff and was occupying seventh place with 12 points. Twelve months before the British GP was held at Coventry's Brandon Stadium and it was rumoured to be a sell-out. Like most of us, Adams wondered how BSI was going to bring the attendance up from 15,000. But he needn't have worried because the speedway fans responded in force with an official attendance given at 31,250. Being introduced to over 30,000 air-horn blowing, cheering and enthusiastic fans was a memorable experience.

'Cardiff was a bit rugged where they parked us up, I didn't realise it was called the Millennium because it was built for the millennium. It wasn't until we walked out on parade . . . it was massive, unbelievable, we were blown away. There is a great picture of us on the centre green and the whole lot of us were thinking, shit, what's going on here? Everybody used to talk about the Wembley days and how fantastic that was, and this was as good as it was going to get. I can remember being on parade and thinking, this is it, we've made it.'

12

Team Triumphs

'**T**he track was terrible; they had boards down and plastic on top of it. It was running down to the plastic and the plastic was coming up in the ruts of the track, it was really bad,' Adams recalls of the surface at the first Cardiff Grand Prix. 'I can remember standing there and watching Colin Meredith going out with a knife and chopping the plastic off, because it was exposed in a big hole on the first and second bend. I was thinking, Oh my God! Nobody worried about the track then, it was just the occasion.'

Getting the track surface inside the Millennium Stadium right has always been a problem. Despite all sorts of ideas and expertise employed to try to create a consistent surface, the track continues to break up, forming holes and ruts, which provides plenty of incidents for the spectators, but some very scary moments for the riders. During its first staging though, everyone was so overwhelmed by the spectacular setting and the occasion that the track's dangerous condition never came into the equation.

'It was all new, we were happy to be in this big stadium and just to go racing. No one worried about laying the track and having a good surface then. I didn't think it would stay as strong as it has. That is the showpiece of the Grand Prix now; it's pretty special and it was always a special weekend, it really was. For me, in the end, a couple of times, I drove home because the hotels were such a nightmare there. I'd come home after practice and then go back again because it was only an hour and fifteen from Swindon – it was virtually my home Grand Prix.'

Renzo Giannini was the president of the FIM Track Racing Commission and he was quoted as saying, 'Tonight was about history. The history of speedway has changed!' For Leigh Adams, his role in that landmark meeting was to finish with 8 points. A third in his first race meant that he faced an elimination heat in his second outing – third or worse meant an early departure. He won that race, but was then eliminated in his third outing.

'I think I was more excited about being there than trying to win the meeting – I was more worried about the occasion,' he confesses. 'I can remember Tony Rickardsson saying afterwards, "As soon as I walked into the place I thought, I gotta win here," and he won it.'

BSI also revamped the World Team Championship by making it a week-long World Cup tournament. Held at two venues in Poland – Gdansk and Wroclaw – Australia qualified straight through to the final by winning their round with the now established squad of Adams, Crump, Wiltshire, Craig Boyce, Ryan Sullivan and Jason Lyons, with Neil Street as team manager. They met the hosts Poland, Sweden, Denmark and the USA in the first World Cup Final. Inexplicably, the organisers decided that five teams should contest the final, with five riders in each race – one from each nation. On the Wroclaw circuit, which was renowned for being narrow into the corners, this was challenging to say the least.

'Five riders in a race was just stupid,' Leigh says. 'We had the qualifier and we went straight through to the final. So we went to watch the race-off on the Thursday and there were guys crashing like you wouldn't believe, and we thought, you've got to get rid of five riders in a race. We already had six riders with the pairs a few years before, and this was the same. It was chaos. Wroclaw is a narrow track, it funnels, so you've got this big massive corner and then all of a sudden it goes really narrow down the straights, even with four riders it's a bit much.

'Five riders in a race was just stupid.'

'That was like the family, we ran with that group of riders for years and years,' Adams says of the familiar Aussie team. 'They hated Crumpie at Wroclaw and threw bricks at his van! It didn't affect us; we always had a really good atmosphere in the team. If there were any vibes we'd just put it aside and get on with it. Crumpie could fight his own battles and I can remember one time he put his ass up to the crowd, like spank my ass, and the crowd were just flipping out!'

Courtesy of Crump, the Aussies took the lead in the opening race and never let go. He remained unbeaten and Leigh backed him up with a 16-point return. With solid and valuable contributions from the rest, Australia had won the first of the new World Cups and their second world team trophy in three years.

'It was a big achievement to beat the Poles on their home turf – a great win for us. Back then we did have a five-man team, but then we started to lose guys after the second win. We won in Pardubice under the old system. This was the Ove Fundin Trophy, the new era. Everyone rises to the occasion, even now, all the riders get involved. I had all my mates over from Aussie and we had a couple of motor homes and we all drove into Gdansk. It was a really good atmosphere. It's a shame that they don't do it like that now. Now we have one in Sweden, we fly into Sweden, go back to England, then over to Poland later in the week.'

Sweden finished third in that meeting with, predictably, Tony Rickardsson topping their score chart with 17. Rickardsson mania was showing no signs of abating because the Swedish Grand Prix, to be held inside the Olympic Stadium, Stockholm, was announced as a sell-out during the run-up to the Cardiff round.

There was every reason to think that speedway racing was about to experience a new upswing in popularity, especially if you were attending meetings at Leigh's club, Oxford, in 2001. Many times the author decided to wait in the car park after the match had been concluded to let the traffic go. As the year progressed, late comers would park anywhere blocking any chance of an early exit, and when it came to the business end of the season, the car park attendants shut the gates and directed traffic to an overflow at the back of the Rover factory.

Adams was once again piling up the points for the university city club, and he received solid backing from fellow GP riders Todd Wiltshire and Brian Andersen. As he indicated earlier, in order to have a championship-winning team, you needed someone to increase their average by a good margin to make the difference. Oxford had that person in the shape of Lukas Dryml – and to a lesser extent his brother Ales. Mid-term, Lukas sustained a knee injury, which meant that Oxford took their foot off the gas a little bit and enabled Poole, that were led by Rickardsson, to close the gap and apply pressure at the top of the table.

However, when the Cheetahs went to Wimborne Road and held the Pirates to a draw in mid-June, it proved that the side possessed the strength in depth to still be affective while covering for Dryml's absence.

'It was always a tough place to promote,' Adams says of Oxford. 'Vanessa and Steve Purchase threw everything at it. We had a fantastic team and it was a solid team. I remember when they were assembling it and I thought, wow, the Drymls were pretty young then, Brian Andersen, obviously he had his collar bone problems, and Johnno was captain, it was good, we enjoyed it. Vanessa was like our mum and she'd make us sandwiches, we had special towels, all the home team had purple towels, and she took them home and washed them.

'Colin Meredith was a good team manager, he was also doing the track and he was good. He was pretty much running the whole thing. Oxford was always a shit track and always difficult to prepare. I don't know why, just

Oxford – the 2001 Elite League Champions celebrate after clinching the title at Ipswich. Standing, left to right: Colin Meredith (team manager), Leigh, Ales Dryml, Steve Johnston, Richard Palmer. Kneeling, left to right: Andrew Appleton, Brian Andersen and Todd Wiltshire. (Adams Family Archive)

surface-wise, there was always trouble with the dogs and they couldn't get onto the track early enough. But, to be fair, Colin did extremely well and he'd been there, done it before and was pretty level-headed. It was a good year.'

Indeed it was. This was the last top flight league championship to be decided over a season-long league campaign, and not over a series of play-off matches. Nonetheless, Oxford needed at least a draw at Ipswich to clinch their first league title since 1990, and it was the Aussie duo of Leigh and Wiltshire who did the business in the final race by filling the minor places behind race-winner Scott Nicholls.

There was hardly much time to celebrate because it was a double-header fixture and Oxford then raced the Witches again in the knockout cup semi-final, losing by 2 points on the night, and the same margin on aggregate. But that didn't dampen the celebrations.

'When Todd and Leigh went out there and did what they had to do in the last race it was a special moment for us all,' said skipper Steve Johnston. He added, 'Leigh and Todd kept their cool throughout it all, but I must admit it was starting to get under my skin and we had to keep our cool.'

After failing to make the semis in Cardiff, Leigh began the Danish Grand Prix at Vojens in the preliminary heats. He safely made it through to the 'Sweet Sixteen' and then into the finals. Starting from gate two, with Rickardsson inside him, he didn't quite make the jump and the Swede roared to victory with Crumpie in second. Significantly, Adams grabbed his first Grand Prix podium by taking third. Although it wasn't the breakthrough that he wanted, it represented progress.

'It took that long to get to a final and then it just dragged on and on to win one,' he says. 'There was a lot of racing and it felt like it was never going to come. The press were on non-stop, "When are you going to win one? You're the best rider in England, the best rider around the world in the leagues, top of the averages, when are you going to win one?"'

The weekend of 8/9 September 2001, was another typical busy few days for Leigh Adams. He had practice for the Polish Grand Prix in Bydgoszcz on the Friday, followed by the meeting the next day in which he failed to make the semis. On Sunday he scored 17 points for Leszno but couldn't prevent them from losing to Pila. Happily he had a day off on Monday before contesting the second leg of the Swedish Elite League play-off semi-final for Masarna against Vastervik, scoring 9 points and securing their place in the final.

As he prepared for the Swedish fixture, the world held its breath as hijackers crashed two airliners into the Twin Towers of the World Trade Center in New York City. All on board were killed and thousands more lost their lives as the towers collapsed approximately two hours after the first plane had struck the North Tower. Leigh was due to fly to England the next day to race at Poole. However, the airports were in a state of panic and security was stepped up. Sport didn't seem that important as the western world was in total shock, and it even crossed his mind that the fixture could be called off. Meanwhile, Kylie waited anxiously for news that her husband was safe and sound; whether he was racing or not, she wanted him back on terra firma.

'I remember when it happened, we had just turned up for the meeting and then we had to fly back the next day,' Leigh recollects. 'We wondered what was going to happen, we thought it would be chaos. Tony happened to be with us and I was riding for Oxford. You know what, it was the easiest trip that I have ever had. There was no-one flying, no-one at the airport and it was like a ghost town. We were panicking at the time and worried, but it was so easy because there was no-one at the airports.'

Ever the professional, Adams raced at Poole and scored 11 points for the Cheetahs. Flying is a necessity in a speedway rider's line of work, especially one high up the international ladder like Leigh has been. Therefore, he's had his scary moments, but he remains philosophical about travelling thousands of feet above the ground.

'I've never been too bad like that, I've always thought you can drive a car and crash, you can have a crash anywhere and die. Flying has never been an issue to me; I've never really thought about it, it's just a means of transport.'

However, during his early days racing in Australia and travelling with Phil Crump, his youthful innocence made him oblivious to a potentially serious situation.

'Trevor Harding ran an indoor meeting over in Perth and we were flying out the next day. We took off and the plane wouldn't climb, we were just floating above the mountains and Crumpie said, "There's something not right here," and I'm just sitting back, wet behind the ears, thinking, we're up, no big deal, and then an announcement came on saying that we'd got to go back. So we turned round, went back over the ocean and we had to dump the fuel out. I remember looking out at this big outlet at the end of the wing, it opened up and spewed all this fuel out. We landed and there were fire trucks and all sorts waiting for us.

'Honestly, when we landed, I thought, no big deal,' he shrugs, 'but now if that happened I'd be looking out thinking, My God what's happening here? Then we had to wait for another plane, but it was no big rush then, whereas now I'm more wary.'

BSI continued to expand the series, and it was when Leigh arrived in Stockholm for the final Grand Prix that he got a clue as to what was on the cards.

'This was weird, I went to the motel to check in, looked across and there was Dave Lander and another guy sitting at the bar. I twigged then, straightaway. I knew Dave Lander because he had done a lot of meetings in Parramatta, he'd done sprint cars and I'd been invited to some of his meetings. So I got talking to him and said, "What's the go?" There had always been this whisper of an Aussie Grand Prix, but it wasn't until I saw them that they said, "Keep it quiet, but this is what our plan is."'

Tony had clinched his fourth world title. He's regarded as a dedicated, ultra-professional racer, but there is a side to his character that few outside the sport get to see. Leigh recalled an incident after practice that showed a side of Tony Rickardsson that the public at large were not aware of.

'Tony wasn't shy to have a drink, whack the music up and enjoy himself,' says Leigh. 'I really respected him for that; he was one of the boys. When we were in Stockholm for a Grand Prix, he had this little mini bike that he was riding around and it was done up in his colours. They got it out and rode it round the car park, his mechanics were riding it and I was sitting there watching this thinking, this is going to end up in a mess. Susi's (Tomasz Suskiewicz, mechanic) girlfriend then gets on it and I'm thinking, this is going to end in tears.

'The next thing Tony gets on and off he goes and disappears. He goes out onto the track and decides that he's going to do a lap of the track, this is on the Friday night, after practice but before the meeting. He told me he went down the straight, got a big tank-slapper and crashed this little supermoto bike. When he crashed, he looked up and there are these two guys hanging over the fence thinking, what's Tony Rickardssson doing?

'I can remember him pulling up by his motor home – he was scarred and he had mud all down his face, and Carl Blomfeldt was standing there just shaking his head. We knew it was going to happen and it turned out to be Tony. He enjoyed himself more than anybody, but most people only saw the serious side of him.'

It wasn't until the end of October that it was announced that there would be an Australian Grand Prix in 2002 at Stadium Australia, Sydney – the 80,000-seater arena that was built for the Olympics. At the time Adams described it as 'awesome', and it was a dream for the top Aussie stars, and along with Jason Crump he did some promotional work at the stadium. With his best finish of fifth place in the Grand Prix, a league title with Oxford and he had retained the Czech Golden Helmet for the third successive year, 2001 was quite a memorable year.

> '*I can remember him pulling up by his motor home – he was scarred and he had mud all down his face.*'

The days of just having six Grands Prix a year were at an end. Competing in the British, Polish and Swedish Leagues, ten Grands Prix, the World Cup plus assorted international and open meetings, Leigh Adams' calendar for

2002 was looking hectic. And, for the most part, this was how it would be from now on. At one time or another, Tony Rickardsson, Nicki Pedersen and Jason Crump have all dropped the British Elite League from their schedules in order to cut down on the travelling and to remain fresh for the GPs. Leigh, though, has always felt that he needed to race in England.

'Why I've always committed to England, and Kylie and I spoke about this too, I always felt that I raced at my best when I was busy. Deep down I knew I had to earn my living. It's then that you've got to equal it out. If you're crazy busy you need good people around you to organise stuff. May was always crazy, everything started and by the end of the month you knew that you had done twenty-five meetings or something. At my height I did 118 meetings a season and the most I did was 121.

'I looked at Tony, when he finished in England, he went downhill and then you look at Nicki, he blossomed, but did it catch up with him in 2009? I don't know. You look at Jason, he had a fantastic year in '09 but the other two, Hans Andersen and Scott Nicholls bombed out, they came back didn't they because they felt that it wasn't enough for them without racing in England. Personally, I've always felt that I needed England. So no, I stuck to my guns, and thought let's go with what we know and I think that was the right decision.'

Leigh qualified for another final in the GP series, this time in Cardiff, but finished fourth behind an in-form Ryan Sullivan, Todd Wiltshire and Mikael Karlsson (now Max). He was making steady but unspectacular progress. However, Australia retained the World Cup with 'the family' defeating Denmark, Sweden, Poland and the Czech Republic at Peterborough.

With an Australian Grand Prix on the horizon, plus the fact that he wasn't in the series just to make up the numbers, Leigh decided that Tony's advice to seek help from a sports psychologist seemed like a good idea. He made an appointment to see Graham Sterry.

The Scandinavian Grand Prix was to be held in Gothenburg's Ullevi Stadium. It had made a return to the World Championship stage after it was one of the venues that used to host the World Final. A 26,000 crowd saw Leigh Adams take just four rides to exorcise a long-standing demon – to win his first Grand Prix.

'Tony was off gate one and he lifted and went wide, and I turned back underneath him,' he says. 'It was a normal man-made track, a bit rutty, but Tony hit the rut, went wide and I just ran straight round the inside. That was really special and we had a big party that night. Randy and I did an all-nighter and I was celebrating Casey's birth as well – we needed to celebrate that. The engine I used was called Casey because we decided if we got a girl we'd call her Casey. There was an Aussie bar called the Dancing Dingo, and we'd been there the night before and they sold Aussie beer. Well, we cleaned them out! I can remember walking out of one of the discos with Randy, and it was daylight! We just went straight back to the motor home, picked up our bags and went to the airport.

'The big question, which everybody asked, "How come you haven't won a Grand Prix?" To finally win in Gothenburg was a monkey off my back; I got that out of the way and I could get on with my Grands Prix,' Leigh says. 'I think I definitely became a lot better rider after that. Mainly because, you sit back and think that it doesn't worry you that you haven't won a GP, but everyone is asking you non-stop, so it's got to play on your mind a little bit.

'You know what, I only phoned Sterry beforehand to arrange a time to go and see him. When I went to see him, I said, "Mate you're not going to believe this, I just won a GP." Then we did a session or two and he said the reason I had won was because I had taken the first step in changing things. But we didn't really gel. I think the real reason I won was because I wanted to prove Clarkie wrong after listening to the song he had written for me which was called, "You're Never Gonna Win One"!'

Two more rounds passed before the big one for the Aussies, the Australian Grand Prix. Needless to say there

'A monkey off my back'.
Celebrating his first Grand Prix
victory at Gothenburg.
(www.mike-patrick.com)

was a lot of hype surrounding the riders from the home nation, but it was an anti-climax for Adams and the championship – Rickardsson had already clinched a fifth world crown. Sadly, Leigh could only score 5 points on a difficult track, on which Greg Hancock won.

'It was a bit of an anti-climax really,' Leigh agrees. 'Everybody just thought, wow, the Aussie Grand Prix is coming, Stadium Australia, everybody had this figure of 50–60,000 people packing the stadium out, but it just didn't happen. Don't get me wrong, it was a great event and a great achievement. But in hindsight, we would have been better off going to a 15,000-seater stadium and selling that out and having a great atmosphere.

'The track was a nice surface, but it had just one line because there was no banking. In fact it had adverse camber, off camber, because of the dirt. I think they ran out of dirt so they just ran it down and put up the fence. I can remember watching Tony riding his balls off and he couldn't do anything, and I thought that was disappointing because under normal circumstances he would be on the gas. I was happy with fifth in the championship. I was starting to think that we were getting the Grands Prix on track and I was enjoying them a lot more after I had won my first GP.'

Behind the scenes there was some controversy. The meeting hadn't been a financial success and any thoughts of another GP the following year were quickly squashed.

'BSI milked Dave Lander a little bit and I can remember Ole Olsen and John Postlethwaite flying business class to check the stadium out. I mean, back in 2000 they had just run the Olympics, so the stadium was definitely up to scratch, so that was a load of crap!' Adams reveals. 'Then they flew out again to check what size the track was going to be and all this sort of thing.

'Lander's just a normal guy and he'd promoted sprint cars very successfully. To think that he was going to put together an 80,000-seater stadium, God knows what sort of figures he was working on to make that work. I think we got about 28,000 in there, and that was very good, but in a stadium like that it looked like nothing. It was a little bit of a dud, which was a shame because it was a great facility, the best you could come across, hotels, bars, everything within walking distance, a great complex. If it had been done right, on both parts, I feel we would have been there now.'

Oxford couldn't repeat their league title success of 2001 and Steve Purchase was looking to offload the Cheetahs. Any chance that Adams would remain with the club was put beyond the question when the new owner turned out to be Nigel Wagstaff.

'For Waggy to come and take it over, how weird is that? Once bitten twice shy, I didn't go back there did I? When he wanted me back at Oxford, I said no chance. He was pretty pissed off because he thought that he got me as part of the deal', Leigh remembers.

'I can honestly say, the phone call came late from Oxford and I didn't have much on at all. I knew Poole weren't really settled, but I didn't think I would be able to go there because Tony Rickardsson was there and he'd signed a contract. It was really weird how it came about because I texted Matt Ford and said, "Hey Matt, what's the go, I'm free now, I don't want to go to Oxford, what's the situation?" Matt came back and said, "Give me a couple of days and I'll have a look to see what I can do." He came back and said he could fit me in, what did I want? Within a week we had a deal and it was all done through text messages, I didn't even speak to him. It was the best move I ever made, it was fantastic.

'Oxford was good, but it was a tough track to go to and it was always bumpy. It was starting to get pretty awful in 2002 and then Waggy took it over and it was just a disaster. It was always a tough place to promote for some reason, it was competing against colleges and universities and that. And even in 2001 when we won the league, our crowds were all right but not what they should be considering we had been at the pointy end for the whole year.'

Return of the prodigal son? Some thought so. However, the track had been altered and would turn out to be more to his liking, plus a new promotional team of Matt Ford and Mike Golding had joined Pete Ansell with ex-rider Neil Middleditch (Middlo) as team manager.

'The track had changed a few years before and I used to struggle with it – it was a tough track to go to. It's a good, pacey little track, and you've got to keep your momentum up because it's so fast. Nine times out of ten it means riding the boards and getting right out on the fence and skimming it. I can remember press day and watching Tony go round there and thinking, this is the only way we're going to be able to get it done. It was a really good move for me. Matt and Middlo were fantastic, I just can't speak highly enough of them.

'Plain and simple, I didn't think I'd ever go back there. It was a little bit weird going back because they always booed me as a visiting rider, because they remembered what happened in '90 when I left. Every rider's parade: "Leigh Adams! Booooo!" It made me more determined, but those supporters

> **'Oxford was good, but it was a tough track to go to and it was always bumpy.'**

were cheering me from the start – the vibes were good and it was a good little team. I loved it, and my results were showing that as well. I was back with Tony again in heats 13 and 15, riding numbers one and five – we never changed all year, a great relationship.'

The Adams/Rickardsson spearhead harked back to the King's Lynn days and, if anything, was even more effective than they were in 1999. Furthermore, Lukas Dryml who, when fit, had proven to be a trump card for Oxford two years before, also joined the Pirates and developed into a third heat leader – his brother Ales joined at the tail end of the season. Swede David Ruud and Pole Krzysztof Kasprzak also weighed in with good support, while Ricky Ashworth and Davey Watt shared the reserve berth.

No doubt Adams was given cause for concern during their first league match against Coventry which they lost, 43–47, when Bjarne Pedersen scored just 3 points. It was also an early indication that it would be the Midlands club that Poole would ultimately do battle with for the league's top honours. However, as keen as ever to see his team enjoy success, Adams confided to Matt Ford that he wasn't sure about the indifferent start to the season that Bjarne Pedersen was experiencing.

'Bjarne started the season really slowly. He was notorious for taking his time to get going. And I remember talking to Matt and saying, "What are we going to do about Bjarne?" And he said, "Just stick with him." This was early in the year and sure enough he got going, and towards the end of the season we were really solid. What a team – it was fantastic. It brought me on as a rider too, to be riding with Tony. I think I finished top of Poole's averages that year – beating Tony.'

In 2003, Leigh was granted a well-deserved testimonial meeting that was held at Swindon. He was still a Robins rider, but because they operated in the 'lower' league, Adams was prevented from racing for them by the rule book. Since their switch in 1999, the Robins had enjoyed quite a bit of success, they almost won an elusive league title in 2000, but added Knockout Cup and Jack Young Shield trophies to their shelf.

Swindon had always prided themselves on being a top flight club, so when Leigh's meeting included many stars from the Elite League such as Jason Crump, Joe Screen, Sam Ermolenko and Steve Johnston, the supporters responded in big numbers.

'Pete Toogood was still in control at Swindon and we put a lot of work into that. I had it organised the year before when I was at Oxford and I was good friends with Pete. I just thought I would run it there, and Swindon was still my home. Plus I was trying to organise it during the winter and I wasn't sure where I was going to be. The weather was pretty shitty leading up to it, and I can remember going to the track the day before the meeting and, because it had rained, we pumped the water off the track from the first and second bend.

'The only disappointing thing was that Tony pulled out due to a sequence of crashes. In the end I got Stoney (Carl Stonehewer). I was going to Belle Vue on the Monday, and my meeting was on Thursday, and I got the call from Tony saying that he couldn't make it. I was at the bar that night with Johnno and he said, "How's it all going?" and I said, "Tony's pulled out." And Stoney was there with Johnno having a drink, and Johnno points at him and says, "Stoney will do it." He just looked at me and said, "Yeah I'll do it." The deal was, though, that I would have to go back and do his meeting, which wasn't a problem. That was pretty cool of him to do that at short notice.'

With a parade car and a personalised number plate at Swindon for his 2003 Testimonial meeting. (Les Aubrey)

Although Jason Crump scored a maximum in the qualifying races, Leigh reigned supreme in the Grand Prix-style winner-takes-all final by taking victory ahead of his old friend Jason Lyons with Joe Screen third. Having been his promoter at Arena and London, Terry Russell was one of his guests. Unwittingly, a chance remark to Russell as good as sealed his future.

'I said to him, "Look mate, I think Swindon is ready to go Elite League. It needs it, it's ready for it." I took a load of Elite League riders to that meeting, which they had been starved of, plus young kids like Antonio Lindback, and it worked really well.'

Having lost just 7 of their 28 matches, Poole finished top of the Elite League and they faced Oxford in the play-off semi-final. The Cheetahs pushed the Pirates pretty hard at Wimborne Road, eventually going down by 6 points with Leigh topping the scorers with 14 – he probably took some quiet satisfaction in being instrumental in dumping Wagstaff's Oxford out of the title race.

In a pulsating encounter with Coventry in the Elite League play-off final, Poole won the first leg at Brandon by 1 point. But then the Pirates let loose in front of 6,000 fans during the second leg with a convincing 55–35 victory to bring home their first league title since 1994 – Leigh scored a paid 13 points in the meeting.

However, they met Coventry again in the Knockout Cup Final. Fired-up for revenge, Poole struggled to see off the Bees in the first leg at their home circuit and relied heavily on the Adams/Rickardsson partnership who registered a last heat 5–1 to seal a 46–42 win. The second leg, though, lives long in Leigh's memory. On a typical, wet autumn evening, Coventry had Poole on the rack after seven races by holding a 30–12 lead, and were leading 72–58 on aggregate. With just eight races remaining, it was going to take a gigantic performance from the side to turn the result around.

'We were dead and buried, the Poole people were leaving,' Leigh recalls. 'We had won the league, and sewn that up in the play-offs against Coventry. We had a 4-point lead from the first leg and we were getting smoked. We were that far down even I thought, what's going on here? It was the end of the season and Tony was tired. Then, all of a sudden, we got into gear.'

Naturally, Poole looked to their big guns for inspiration, Adams and Rickardsson. In heat 8, Adams partnered Bjarne Pedersen for a vital 5–1. The next three races saw Tony win two and Leigh the other, but only Pedersen managed a third to bring them within 12 points on the night and 8 on aggregate. A 4–2 from Pedersen and guest Mark Loram brought them to within 6 points.

As Adams and Rickardsson lined up for heat 13 against Andreas Jonsson and Lee Richardson, the Pirates were confident of getting within 2 points overall of their rivals. And so it seemed as the two Poole stars led coming out of the second turn, only for Jonsson to storm between the pair of them in a move that *Speedway Star* described as 'pure genius'.

A chaotic penultimate race eventually saw a 5-1 for Poole's guests, Loram and Garry Stead – the latter came in for Antonio Lindback who was declared unfit to take his place in the re-run after Ryan Fisher had taken him and Billy Janniro down. This meant that Coventry required just 3 points from the final heat to win the silverware.

Out came Andreas Jonsson and Lee Richardson to meet the much-heralded Adams and Rickardsson spearhead. After all the heat victories that the Australian and the Swede had won for Poole over the season, their whole reputation rested on this final race. The tapes went up and the Poole duo hit the front, only this time when the expected attack came from Jonsson they squeezed him out along the back straight. Incredibly, Poole had come back from the dead to win the cup, and Leigh and Tony had cemented a reputation that deserves a place in Poole Speedway's Hall of Fame.

'We needed a 5-1 in the last race and Tony and I went and got it,' Leigh says proudly. 'It was amazing how we did that. I can remember finishing the race and just laughing in my helmet because of the way the meeting went about. Tony and I were going down the back straight after the race just shaking our heads with big grins. In that way, it was the weirdest meeting I've ever been involved with.'

Poole had much to celebrate and the traditional end of season dinner and dance was set to be a scene of much rejoicing and merriment. However, as Adams joined the M4 motorway, on his way to the event, his mobile phone rang and Terry Russell's name appeared on the screen.

'I had always kept in touch with Terry after the Arena days and he rang me out of the blue and said, "I just bought Swindon. We're going to run in the Elite League and I want you there next year." Which was fantastic, but I'd just had a great year at Poole so I was a bit disappointed in one way, but happy in another. As it turned out, after I'd spoken to him at my testimonial meeting he just went and bought the thing!

'Poole felt a little bit like home because I'd been there in 1989 and I'd known Matt and Middlo for a long time. I was really enjoying it and the sponsors were thick and fast down there and I had a few offers. I didn't really have time to capitalise on that, but as it turned out it was fine. I regard Swindon as my home – big time; Swindon, Leszno and Avesta I regard as my homes. I've been with Leszno for fifteen years and Avesta eight. The only time I haven't been at Swindon was when they had ridden in the Premier League or Division Two. This was the beginning of something different with Terry, and he had the Sky Sports deal.'

British Speedway has an unfortunate habit of penalising successful teams. The way the rules work usually means that after winning the league championship, that team will be broken up and some of its riders are forced to move on to pastures new. Therefore, Leigh celebrated an enjoyable and very successful season at Wimborne Road, safe in the knowledge that not only would he have a team place for 2004, but that he'd be going home.

13

Finding Kong

Considering how long it took Leigh Adams to win a Grand Prix, it was ironic that when he finished third in the World Championship in 2005, he did so without winning a single round. He won his second GP in Slovenia in 2003 – with a sweet pass on eventual champion, Nicki Pedersen – and started 2004 by taking victory in Stockholm.

'For some reason Sweden was always kind to me. I was starting to build momentum, and Stockholm was always good. I usually flew into Stockholm to get to Avesta and I had a lot of friends there. I was getting things together for the Grand Prix and felt pretty good. It was a good way to start the Grand Prix series.'

Sweden may have been kind to him, but when the 2003 Swedish Grand Prix had to be hastily rearranged because of a public sector strike that prevented access to the original venue, Stockholm's Olympic Stadium, Leigh must have felt that all his dreams had come true when they chose Avesta as the replacement. During a tough night, he qualified for the Grand Final against Ryan Sullivan, Greg Hancock and Lukas Dryml. Starting from the unfavoured outside position, he came off the first corner in second behind Sullivan but then picked up drive on the back straight and his front wheel pointed skyward. This was the opportunity that Hancock needed and he surged into the gap for second, but as they hit the pit corner Leigh crashed and brought Dryml down with him.

'I rode a normal corner and then the next minute Greg appeared out of nowhere and whipped my leg or front wheel away. The crash wasn't so bad, it was the sliding into the fence and Lukas' bike coming off the fence that was the problem. I caught that on the rebound and it hurt. I couldn't move my leg, it was a total dead leg. After I lay there for a bit, I guess the adrenalin came pumping through and I got things moving.'

Understandably feeling second-hand, and with a bike that displayed the rigours of the crash, he could only watch from third as Sullivan won with Lukas in second. A dream Grand Prix victory at his 'Swedish home' had come to a painful end. Hancock meanwhile, was decidedly unhappy with his

Australian rival, and later complained, 'I was ahead of him that's what I don't understand. I just feel Leigh made a mistake and I got penalised for it. He knows what happened.'

Adams' return to Blunsdon in 2004 certainly had a positive effect as he hit top form immediately. After their opening night was abandoned due to snow, Leigh scored 13 at Wolves before then completing five successive matches without a defeat – a sequence he repeated again in June. In the midst of that impressive run, he won the Elite League Best Pairs at Swindon with Charlie Gjedde.

The meeting was hyped up with a total prize fund reported to be £25,000. Quite often these competitions are missing some of the sport's top names, but there was little chance that the likes of Crump, Pedersen and Rickardsson

Adams and Charlie Gjedde, with whom he won the 2004 Elite League Best Pairs Championship. (Dave Fairbrother)

were going to pass up an opportunity to take the lion's share of that particular booty. Therefore, the line-up assembled was especially strong and one that was good enough to grace any Grand Prix.

However, that victory over such a quality field didn't stop the critics from attempting to devalue the triumph by pointing out that they had home advantage. A year later, Leigh won it again, with a different partner, Lee Richardson, on a different track, Peterborough, and he defeated the reigning World Champion, Jason Crump, in the final by passing him, even though second and third would have been sufficient to retain the Pairs' title. And in order to pull off that exciting manoeuvre, Leigh went to the edge and beyond.

'Peterborough is the type of track that when you're going fast you're skimming the fence. You've got to come into the corners and you've got to commit to it, if you don't, you're not going to go fast, so you've got to be in the dirt.

'When I passed Crumpie on the outside, I don't think I was in control. But I managed to come out of the corner in front of him. He said to me afterwards, on the track, "You mad bastard!" I went around him, but it was one of those occasions when you leave your brain in the tool box. There are always those occasions when you've got to stick your neck out a little bit. Carl Blomfeldt had a saying: "You've got to ride like a turtle – stick your neck out!" that's what he always told me. But I wasn't the kind of rider that would do that. If I felt in control and fast, I was happy. I was never a rider who rode out of control. If the track wouldn't allow me to go as fast as I wanted to, I would use my skill to get around it and not go over the edge to where you're out of control. When you get a shitty track, you see guys that are just on the limit, and they're just waiting for a crash – I'm not that kind of rider. I try to use my skill. If it is a shitty track, I'll try and use that to my advantage.'

Adams is regarded as one of the few top-line racers that still practices, very successfully, the art of team riding. Many believe that it's a dying art, but according to the Australian, this is more to do with the changes to the equipment rather than reluctance from the racers.

'It's just a matter of slowing the race up,' he says simply. 'It's an art that's falling away from speedway because everything is happening so quickly. It's fantastic to team ride with someone who's on the pace with you. For instance, Matej Zagar at Swindon in 2009, I had a lot of good rides with him. Heat 13, I was off the inside mostly, and I knew it was Matej coming round the outside of me – half the time I didn't even look, I could just feel that it was him coming round. It's really nice when you get a good relationship with a rider like that, it's excellent.

'With Travis McGowan I never had that at all. No disrespect to him; he was good out of the start, but his entrance speed into the corners was slow, and that was my forte – speed into the corners. It's always been my style. I was in a situation team riding with Tony Rickardsson and he generated so much speed into the corner, so if I wasn't quick, he would be right on me – I could hear him all the time. If you team ride, you've got to slow things up. If you're on the inside you're vulnerable because if the guy is not going quickly enough on the outside, which is what happened with Travis, you leave the outside free for everybody. If the outside guy doesn't commit, the other riders just go around you.

'It's getting harder and harder to team ride. In 2009 I probably did more team riding than I've ever done. I'd got myself into a lot of trouble that year too, and got passed a few times trying to help my partner by slowing down too much. I made a few mistakes and got passed by Rory Schlein and the one at Eastbourne, on the telly, when Cameron Woodward went round the lot of us. They're possibly the worst guys to pass me – two young Aussies whose dream it is to pass me!' he laughs.

Leigh came very close to winning the British Grand Prix in 2004. He faced American Greg Hancock, Lee Richardson and Jason Crump. Hancock made the start, while Adams passed Richardson and got closer and closer to the American, but ran out of laps – it proved to be his best chance to win the World Championship's showpiece event.

'I do regret not having won at Cardiff,' Leigh admits. 'I got close to Greg one time and nearly passed him on the last corner. I was third and passed Richardson and got on Greg's tail. The thing with the Grands Prix, you'd get to the stage where you just go along and get as many points as you can to become World Champion. But Cardiff was one that you went along to win, it was always very special.'

Adams left Wales sharing the lead in the championship with friend and great rival Jason Crump. But a succession of meetings where he wasn't able to transfer from the semis to the final meant that he dropped out of the reckoning and, frustratingly, finished fourth for the third consecutive year. However, he did play a small part in the destiny of that year's world crown. Crump had lost out to Nicki Pedersen the year before in dramatic circumstances when he was excluded after clashing with Rune Holta. He had been runner-up for three successive years, and although he was holding a good advantage for the final round in Hamar, Norway, the pressure and expectation was getting to him.

'He was actually sick,' Adams says. 'I just grabbed him and took him outside, he had to stop, have a chuck, and then we went for a jog – just to get his

Looking for his race partner and the opposition for Swindon in 2004. (Adams Family Archive)

mind off it and what he had to do. We've always been pretty open with each other in the GPs, and he's helped me sometimes and I've helped him. In 2007 he helped me a little bit here and there. Even at Bydgoszcz in 2009 he came up to me and said, "Come on, take me for a run, my mind is in a twist, I've got to focus on this one." It's nice to help him.

'We've always had a great relationship. It's been fierce on the track and I've always wanted to beat him, probably more than any other rider. He's tough and so consistent, the real package. Even back in Aussie, everywhere, it's like in Formula 1 they say that their first priority is to beat their team-mate and he's kind of like my team-mate, same nationality, we've raced together in the same team and always got on. Again I always wanted to beat him average-wise!'

The Adams family and the Crumps go back a long way. However, watching Crumpie take to the podium as the best rider in the world made Adams take stock.

'When Jason won the first world title it hit home; I definitely sat back and thought, man, that's what I wanted. I was pretty pig sick after Crump's first one, but you've got to use it as a positive and work harder at it!'

Therefore, in 2005 it was going to be different. Leigh has never lacked professionalism, and has always tried to surround himself with the right people to make his job of racing easier. That winter Leigh won his eighth Australian title, and a clue to his plans was seen there when tuner Carl Blomfeldt was spotted alongside him. Could Carl be the magic ingredient that Leigh needed to make a successful World Championship potion? He had been instrumental in the championship successes enjoyed by Sam Ermolenko, Billy Hamill and Tony Rickardsson.

As the European season got underway, Blomfeldt was announced as linking up with Adams for 2005. Leigh takes up the story.

'I'd been around him for years and when I was in Australia he'd come and visit. I was the guy who set Carl up with Tony because he came to me and asked what I thought about Carl. And I said, "Look he's great, he can rebuild an engine, keep on top of it, perfect." As for creating new engines

With good friend and rival, Jason Crump. (Dave Fairbrother)

and building new engines, although he could do it, that wasn't his forte. What he would do is get the parts in from wherever, build it up and go from there, and keep them maintained. Obviously he linked up with him for five or six years and they had a lot of success. Tomasz Gollob poached him from Tony and then he got him back. Then it went a bit pear-shaped and I could see what was happening, they had a big bust-up and Carl left. I think Carl had a year out and he came to Australia that year and I said, "Let's give it a go and try something." I was on the verge of hitting the rostrum in the Grand Prix, things were coming along pretty good and I'd just got a new motor home – the big red one. We spoke about it, I spoke to my mechanics and we all thought, why not? What can you lose? I had to try it, if I didn't try it I'd get to the end of my career and think that could have been the recipe that I needed. As it turned out, it wasn't my cup of tea at all.

'I don't know if it was because he was coming to the end of his career, and he'd got a bit old, and bitter and twisted, but he definitely wasn't the same Carl that I knew back in Australia,' Leigh says. 'He had a small heart bypass the year before and then a major one. I still think that affected him, and he was a diabetic, so he was on a lot of medication for that. There was something that went astray. We were touching on becoming World Champion and he had delivered the goods for Sam, Billy and Tony.'

It was an ambitious undertaking. Over January and February 2005, Leigh and Kylie decided to buy the house next door as it came on the market and appeared to be a good investment. It turned out to be perfect to house their mechanics, and also provided somewhere for Carl to set up a workshop. They had to update and equip the workshop facilities not only for Leigh's benefit, but also to take in work from other riders in order to make it financially viable.

'I was trying to buy the house and there were complications with the deeds. We were itching to get into the workshop and get that set up because we were chewing into our testing and racing time. But everything got held up, like it does. We managed to get in there but it was a huge job to put the workshop together, just the equipment alone. Carl was forever on the computer buying equipment (second-hand): milling machine, lathe, honing machines and he brought a fair bit of stuff over from America. It was a big task and I underestimated it. He'd been through it by doing the workshops with Tony and Sam. He knew what it was all about, but I certainly didn't,' Leigh says honestly.

'To make it work financially we had to bring in work from other riders and do stuff for them. And it was going good, but again, it was more work, parts, invoices, it was huge. Building the workshop was a big thing for me, but we got it together and we were up and running and we ran with it for three or four months. But the atmosphere wasn't there, and Carl wasn't the fun-loving guy that I knew and he would look down on the other mechanics.'

Kylie Adams described it as 'like having a grumpy old man around', which is far from the kind of atmosphere you experience in the Adams household. Nonetheless, everyone knuckled down and got on with the business of racing. At last, the Grand Prix organisers had dispensed with the knockout system and adopted a fairer formula that was the traditional sixteen-rider, twenty-heat format with two semi-finals and a final. Its introduction met with approval from all the competitors.

As usual Leigh's league form was scintillating, but it was in the GPs where he hoped Carl could weave his magic spell. A second place to Rickardsson at Wroclaw was a promising start, but elimination in the semi-final after joint top-scoring was a disappointment in the second round in Eskilstuna – and perhaps the first indication that the less than harmonious atmosphere generated by grumpy Carl was having a negative affect.

Things got off to the best possible start in the third round at Krsko, Slovenia, when he broke the track record, but again missed the cut in the semi and was left frustrated when Matej Zagar clamped him on the inside on the first corner. Meanwhile, Tony Rickardsson had taken his second victory and had a firm grip at the top of the leader board. The Swede won again in Cardiff, but the mood in the Adams camp was clearly becoming a problem as he finished with 7 points. Something had to change.

'The one thing that I have always asked for is a great atmosphere,' Leigh says. 'I've always wanted everyone to be happy. I've never asked my mechanics to do anything that I wouldn't do; I wouldn't ask them to drive around the world on their own because I wouldn't want to do that. So I try to be fair with them and them to be fair with me. The vibes were crap. Carl seemed to think that he was superior to the other mechanics and these guys had been with me for years, people like Broady. The results were okay I guess, but we weren't developing new engines like I wanted to and we were just grinding away with the old ones.

'We had a few hassles with my family, he didn't always tolerate the kids and we had a few problems there. The vibes were not right and I didn't enjoy it and it was a mutual agreement that we parted company. Off he went back to Canada.

'It wasn't a knee-jerk reaction, that the results were not there and it wasn't because I wasn't going to be World Champion, there was a turning point to do with my family. And my family comes first. Yes we all want to be World Champion, but when it starts interfering with the family, well, that turned the whole thing. It was a big relief from then on.'

At this point Leigh had an established team of mechanics and helpers with him in the pits during the Grands Prix who had been with him a long time. Subsequently, the equilibrium of this tight-knit group was tested but, happily, the bond was too strong to be broken by one person.

'Terry Broadbank has done every Grand Prix since that one in Italy in 1996 when I had a broken collar bone, that's pretty amazing. He's helped me all through my career, and not just as a mechanic, he's a good mate who chips in with everything, he helps cook, does the programme and is very good at stocking the fridge with beer! He's been a real backbone, not the just GPs, but he's helped out with other bits and pieces through his work – an all round good guy.

'Billy was like my brother. His name is Marcin Mroz, and the nickname, "Billy", came about because he used to help Billy Hamill at Grudziadz. I always expected quite a bit from him because he's a big lad, and he'd looked after the motor home, driven it and dealt with the financial side of that because it had a kitty, fuel card and he'd organised the ferries. Bike-wise, he's absolutely brilliant. I left it all to him and I could turn up and know that everything would be perfect.

'And then there is Mario (Mariusz Szmanda) who first came over and worked for Kasprzak and then David Ruud at Swindon. He did two years living in Sweden when he helped me, which was a big call because he was away from his wife at that time, and then we swapped things around by basing him in Poland and he drove to the meetings. That worked a lot better. He is another top guy and the last five or six years have been really good, a great atmosphere with those guys.'

With harmony restored and although the world title had gone, Leigh set about climbing up the standings. He raced, he hustled and he clawed his way up to world number three and a bronze medal.

'That was pretty good because we always hovered around fourth. Tony was so dominant that year, and I remember he went to Lonigo and didn't need to win it because he had already won the World Championship, but he smoked everybody. To finally be on the rostrum with two of my good mates, Tony and Jason, our team was happy to achieve that. I couldn't say that I enjoyed the year because it was a tough year, building the workshop, getting that set up and for all the disappointment of that not working. Maybe I expected too much, I don't know, but for me, it was the atmosphere and the hassle we had, that's where it all broke down. But we tried it, we ticked the box, and it didn't work.'

The County Ground Stadium in Exeter holds a legendary place in British Speedway. With a track measuring 396 metres, banked and lined with a steel fence, it was an intimidating place to go for visiting riders. However, the

Mariusz 'Mario' Szmanda and Marcin 'Billy' Mroz warm up Leigh's machine shortly before a Grand Prix. (Dave Fairbrother)

2005 season was to be its final year because the ground was being sold off by the rugby club to developers. Therefore, they held one last 'End of an Era' meeting. In front of a full house, sixteen riders gathered together for one last blast round the track. And on an emotional night, tinged with nostalgia that was celebrated by the arrival of ex-Exeter riders Ivan Mauger and Scott Autrey, Leigh Adams was determined to write his name into the history books.

'As a rider, I think a lot of the riders were pretty happy that it was going!' Leigh chuckles. 'The sport has got quicker and quicker and that track didn't allow for the way the bikes are now, no room for error and it was getting scary – very narrow. Back in the day it probably was a good race track, but now everything is so quick. Terry Russell had bought the promotion and he knew that it was their last year. They put a massive meeting on. Exeter never fazed me, I always enjoyed it and living down there in '89 and going every week, it meant something to me.

'I didn't top score, Lee Richardson did. There was a grand up for grabs and the other three finalists all came up and said, "Oh we've got to split it," but I said, "Nope, I'm going for it, I want to win it." The crowd was unbelievable; they could just reach out and touch you as you went down the back straight. I can remember going down the straight, over the bumps, and the crowd were right there – rock-solid and packed in. It was a nice way to end the year and it was pretty cool to win the last race at Exeter.'

He'd recovered well from a difficult first half of the season to win a bronze medal in the World Championship, and finished top of the British Elite League averages for the second year in a row. Unfortunately 2006 didn't live up to expectations. He slipped down the World Championship standings to fifth and didn't win a GP. Moreover, Jason Crump had won his second world crown.

The question of engines started to come to the fore again. The Italian-made GM had caught up with Jawa and both Rickardsson and Crump had won the world title using them. Jawa have never lacked speed, but they were proving to be problematic to set up when compared with the more forgiving GM.

'Internally, there's not much difference between them,' Leigh evaluates. 'Engine-wise, you can run the same rods, pistons and valve train, it's really the way the heads are done – the ports and camshafts, stuff like that. It's a heavier engine, probably a couple of kilos heavier and that's just through the way the castings are. Jawa has been around for many years and they've always kept the same mould, modified it and tried to reinvent new things into an old engine.

'GM started fresh. Everyone went GM for a lot of years and Jawa realised that they needed something different, and that's when Tony Rickardsson got hold of it and then everyone went Jawa. Jawa are very good on the big powerful tracks, or the big tracks where you need power and are grippy. On a track like Pardubice for the Golden Helmet, I always felt really quick. The GM tended to work better on the slicker tracks. It's just the way the engine characteristics are with the camshafts and all that.

'At the end of that year, I bought two GMs. I was still contracted to Jawa but I sneakily went around and tested them,' Leigh reveals. 'I did one meeting at the end of the year, Tony's farewell, and it just so happened that I won the meeting and won another GM – Tony's prize was a GM. I knew then that I wanted to go down the GM route. It was pretty frustrating year for me because the year before I had finished third, but I just threw so many points away through mechanical breakdowns.

'Basically, I was a factory rider for Jawa, and I was trying to help them develop new engines. Every year we'd get new engines and test them, but they just didn't feel as strong as my old ones, so I kept using the old ones that were quicker. In the end though, a racing engine doesn't last forever and I was just having non-stop mechanical failures. I blew an engine at Eskilstuna; I was leading the semi-final in Prague for the Czech Grand Prix when I stopped, and that was the final nail in the coffin that really pissed me off. That would have given me first choice in the final and gate one was working well then. After that I realised that I had to make a change and I had toyed with the idea of going with GM, but I always enjoyed the Jawa link and the relationship. I liked to help them take the engine forward, but the new stuff that we were getting just wasn't good enough. And doing a lot of meetings I just didn't have the time to test them.'

In Australia, Leigh won his ninth Australian crown riding a GM engine. Having sorted out his engines, and feeling happy with the mechanical team around him, he made one more important alteration that would help make 2007 his best season ever.

'I linked up with Neil Drew, a sports psychologist, to help me. I went to see him at the start of the year before the season got underway and just bonded with him and he was the guy I had been looking for pretty much my whole career,' he says. 'We talked, did some hypnotherapy, thrashed out a few things, and it wasn't just the mental side, there were things about how to structure your team. It's a team effort and you've got to bring them into it and make sure everyone is happy. Obviously I'm the captain of the ship and you've got to make sure that everything is good around you. Your family has got to be good and they say behind every great man there is a great woman, and I am a firm believer in that. Kylie's done an unbelievable job. Neil pointed things out to make sure that everything was okay, that there were no distractions and preparations were in place. Once that's done, you've got fewer things to think about. You've got your goals to chase and off you go.

'It was a bit of management, a bit of head work and he advised me how to get the most out of the right people. It comes back to a happy atmosphere. Like with Carl, that's a distraction, you can't be thinking about other things while you're trying to race. We had a big session together, spent all day, and I came back turbo-charged, I felt like King Kong!'

14

The Glory Road

Hans Andersen was not gracious in defeat. He called Leigh Adams an 'old man' after the Australian had passed him on the last lap to win the Swedish Grand Prix at Eskilstuna. True, he did have several years over the Dane, but more importantly he had the speed and fifteen years of World Championship experience to call upon, while in comparison Andersen's know-how had yet to be counted in double figures.

That was round three of the World Championship series and that victory had catapulted him up the standings to joint second with Greg Hancock, 15 points behind Nicki Pedersen. Nicki had started the year off like a train by winning the first two rounds and losing just one race to Matej Zagar. But in Sweden, a heavy crash earlier in the meeting had blunted his racing and he watched from fourth place as Leigh blasted by Andersen and put himself into the ring as his main challenger.

However, an early season encounter during an Eastbourne v Swindon match was an indication that 2007 was going to be about these two men.

'I've had some tough run-ins with him in the past. He's been hard, but he's settled down now and at Eastbourne we were just going for it. Earlier in that meeting I'd passed him. Then it came down to heat 13 and I was off gate one and he was off two. Neither of us was giving an inch. He went down the first time and that was deemed an unsatisfactory start. In the next one he just dropped it on me and I had no room. I hit his back wheel, it straightened me up and I went straight into the fence. I'd say that Nicki gets the most boos when he goes away from home, but he doesn't care, it's water off a duck's back. He makes that a positive.'

Pedersen's style attracts controversy. The author once asked him to describe his approach and he responded emphatically, 'I want to win.' When he won his first world title in 2003, some viewed his determined riding as bordering on being reckless. Leigh confesses that it scared him.

'He was out of control, and everyone was scared of him. There wasn't just the one occasion, like at Prague with Hancock, there were three or four and he'd just stick guys into the fence for the fun of it,' he says. 'To be fair, though, he has got a lot better and a lot more skilful. In 2007 and 2008, he could make starts from any gate – he was phenomenal. There were a few meetings when I was watching him and I'd think that he would struggle off of gate three and then bang, he'd make it work. I've got to take my hat off to him, he's become a complete rider.'

The points system in the World Championship had been modified again. In addition to the points you scored in the qualifying heats, now you collected points in the semi-finals, and the points were doubled for the final itself. When Leigh qualified for that memorable final at Cardiff – Nicki failed to transfer from the semi – the Australian closed the gap to 11 points. Then the series took a short break while the World Cup took centre stage.

On the inside of Nicki Pedersen at the Italian Grand Prix, 2007. (www.mike-patrick.com)

If Leigh was enjoying success on the world's stage, he was also experiencing good times in the league with both Swindon and Leszno. The Robins were pre-season favourites to win their first league title since 1967, while Leszno were also aiming for their first league crown for 18 years and both were riding near the summit of their respective leagues. However, racing in the Polish League is a lot different to Britain or Sweden because all sorts of gamesmanship is employed by the clubs to gain an advantage over their rivals.

Leigh explains, 'We had a meeting in Czestochowa and we tried three times to get it on. In the end the PZM (Polish Federation) said that they had to run it within the next week. They put it on a Thursday and I had the Grand Prix in Italy that weekend. We'd already arranged the normal Thursday Swindon fixture around the GP for travel reasons. I was pretty pissed off because I had just been in Poland and had got back to England. So then I had to go back to Poland and then drive to Italy and be prepared for a World Championship round.

'Greg Hancock and Nicki were riding for Czestochowa and they said to their promoter, "We're not coming on Thursday" (because they refused to ride on a Thursday before a GP), but they made us fly in. In the meantime, Nicki had flown from Sweden back into England. Ryan Sullivan had seen him at Stansted airport, and he knew that he was supposed to be riding that day. So Ryan rang his club and asked if it had been called off, but the response he got was, "no, it's still on." But we knew that Nicki was in England and Greg was still in Sweden.

'I was at the track getting ready, and the meeting was about three hours away, when Nicki rang me. I thought, that's weird, and I told him I was at the track. He said, "It's called off isn't it?" And I said, "No, it's still on." He goes, "What do you mean?" I could hear he was surprised and then he started backtracking by saying, "Oh yeah, the club's got a private jet ready for me in Luton and I'm ready to fly out." We all know that's not going to happen just like that. I just said, "'Don't bullshit me, I can tell you one thing, I'm pushing for this meeting because the whole team is here." He got caught out because Sullivan had seen him and it got around that he was in England. So he called me to cover his tracks. I put the wind up him when I said, "This meeting is going to happen, we'll race on whatever." He said, "Yes, but the track's shit," and I replied, "It doesn't matter, we'll race." In the end the referee called it off. They had it planned all along. Their promoter had told Nicki not to bother coming because they'd call it off. So I drove half-way round Europe for nothing.

'During the times when Poland held meetings only during the day and there were no night meetings, the home club could pick and choose their start time. So Wroclaw banged in a 3 o'clock start time, when they knew I was riding at Eastbourne or somewhere, and they'd figured that I couldn't make it. There was only one flight into Warsaw at that time and my club said, "Don't worry, we'll get a private plane for you." That was cool, I thought. So I turned up at Warsaw and they took me to a domestic airport. There I am expecting some sort of chartered Learjet, but I'm amazed to find myself staring at this rickety little plane, which was the plane they used to pull the gliders up with! I'm thinking, oh no, please don't. But in the end you stick the ear muffs on and you do it. Looking back you think how stupid was that? But you just want to race, don't you?

'Then when I got to the track I said to the coach there, "You guys are dickheads putting a meeting on at this time, why couldn't you put it back?" And after all that, he replied, "Oh your club should have told us, we would have put it on later!" There is so much friction and pressure, they're not shy to do these things, but then I suppose my club has been the same on occasions.'

When the Grand Prix resumed in Prague, Pedersen repeated his unbeaten performance from the opening round. Unfortunately, Leigh gave up a lot of ground to the Dane during that meeting when he finished with 8, thus leaving himself with a mountain to climb. After Nicki failed to make the final in the seventh round, Adams' determination to find the right set-up at Mallila paid off and he won. He followed that with another victory in Latvia, but with Pedersen in second, the Dane's championship lead was still a comfortable 21 points over the Australian. At Bydgoszcz, for the Polish round, Leigh failed to make the final, while Nicki finished second again – this time to local hero Tomasz Gollob – leaving the Australian to admit that, realistically, with two rounds left, his dream of a world crown was over . . . but while it was still mathematically possible, the fight was still on.

The days of a Grand Prix rider just riding in Grands Prix are way off, if they ever materialise. Therefore, racing in other competitions increases your chances of picking up a knock, and potentially damaging your World Championship hopes. And it was a fall during one of these meetings that as good as ended his wish of pulling off a miracle.

'I was racing for Swindon at Reading in a Knockout Cup semi-final. It had been re-run a couple of times, and they put it on a Friday and I was pissed off with that – so I went there with the wrong attitude. This was the return leg and they were having trouble fitting it in the fixtures. We started the meeting and things were going okay.

'Then in heat 11, Travis McGowan, who was riding for Reading then, was out in front and I was paired with Andy Moore. I thought, I'll just let Travis go, that's fine, and Andy was on the outside and I was on the inside – we

Holding off the challenge of Poland's Tomasz Gollob while on his way to victory in the Latvian Grand Prix. (www.mike-patrick.com)

were just covering second and third. Back then Travis had a few crashes and wasn't that confident – I believe that he was still injured and didn't have the strength to hold on. I also think he was on a bit of a mission - he got in front of Leigh Adams!

'Coming off the fourth bend he went in too wide, picked up grip and rode into the fence. At that moment, I looked around to see where Andy was, so I didn't really see him crash. The next minute there were bodies and bikes laying on the track in front of me. Andy had hit Travis' bike, which came across and caught my right arm. I nearly got away with it, but that tore me off the back of my bike and it was big crash. Krzysztof Buczkowski was the guy behind me and everyone was saying what a good job he did by avoiding us. Well I wasn't too bothered about that because I was in enough pain.

'As soon as I got up, I knew straight away that I had pulled my shoulder out. The first aid people tried to put it back in but it wasn't going to go because it was out pretty good. And I was getting pissed off with them because they were telling me to grab bags, pull this and pull that to try and get it back in, and it wasn't happening. So I said to Rosco (Alun Rossiter, team manager), "Take me back to Swindon." He got me a driver to take me to the hospital, and it's just down the road from my home, so Kylie met me there. They had to X-ray it, and then they drugged me up to put it back in.'

Understandably, Kylie remembers the sequence in more detail. 'It wasn't amusing at the time, but it is now,' she says. 'They gave him something intravenous that relaxed him so much that he almost went to sleep for just a few minutes while they manoeuvred his shoulder back into its rightful place! Once it was all done and X-rayed again to make sure, we had to keep nudging and talking to him to keep him awake so that we could take him home!'

The crash occurred just over a week before the penultimate Grand Prix. Unfortunately for Leigh, Pedersen clinched the championship in that round in Slovenia by winning it. However, with one round remaining, Adams was now assured of silver.

'It came exactly at the wrong time,' Adams says of his injury. 'I had two more rounds to go in the GPs. I pretty much knew it was over in Bydgoszcz; it was going to take a miracle from there wasn't it? But you never know. So we went to Krsko and I did okay. We put a bit of pressure on him when I came out and passed him in the first race. But I wasn't fit. I was pissed off because the track was good and everything looked good, but I knew that I couldn't do my best. It was frustrating.'

His injury also came just as his clubs were gearing up for the league championship play-offs. He missed Swindon's semi-final clash with Peterborough, but he still played the captain's role by helping out in the pits. Damian Balinski rode his bikes in that meeting and the side did enough to get through to the final. They met Coventry in the play-off final and won the first leg by 6 points at Blunsdon. The Robins were under no illusions as to how difficult it was going to be to defend that lead at Brandon, though, and their problems started on the parade.

'It was so funny,' Leigh grins. 'It was a wet, shitty night and I did a practice start down the back straight. Sebastian Ulamek was in front of me and he did a practice start too. I put my head down, did a start, came boring down to the bend and there was Ulamek standing on the track . . . without his bike

... and I thought that was even weirder,' he laughs. 'I went back into the pits and the next minute they start to wheel his bike in, well you couldn't wheel it in, they had a broom handle through the front wheel because it was bent up. He'd done a practice start on the back straight, but his throttle jammed open and he had to bail out. His bike had cleared the safety fence and landed on the dog track. It wasn't the ideal circumstances to start the night. Then he went out in heat 1 and set the fastest time of the night and we got a 5–1! But it went downhill from there, and he didn't score another point!'

It's been a characteristic of Ulamek's career that he's always lacked consistency. However, on the surface, he appears professional and committed; but there's a temperamental side to him.

'Seb Ulamek was a funny one, and always wanted heat 15 when the going was good, but didn't want it if it was a last-heat decider,' Leigh recalls. 'If he did get heat 15 he always wanted the best gate. I'm pretty casual that way, and share heat 15s around. If it comes down to a last-heat decider, I'll take the worst gate because that's my job, as captain, and that's what I feel justifies my job as number one. But he was so passionate about it and he spat his dummy a few times when he didn't get his own way. That's not good for team spirit. So we used to take the piss out of Seb a little bit. I know he was the same in Sweden and always wanted everything his own way.'

Coventry took control in heat 4 with a 5–1 and never looked back, eventually winning 59–34 and breaking Swindon's hearts in the process. Team manager Alun Rossiter was gutted and described the performance as 'disappointing – everything went wrong.'

'It was heartbreaking to lose and it was hard work. Tomasz Chrzanowski had been there earlier that year and got 18 points or something and you sit back and think, hmmm. And Ulamek used to ride for Coventry and he helped them win the league two years before. That was awful for me because I put a lot into it, and it was the first real chance that Swindon have had of winning the league for many years. I wasn't 100 per cent fit, I did okay, but we were beaten by a better team who were a rock-solid outfit.'

Leigh did all he could to assist new signing Balinski, who was also a team-mate at Leszno, but, as he reveals, 'He never enjoyed it. I had to twist his arm that hard you wouldn't believe it. He's always been in a comfort zone wherever he's been. He's always has his van and a mechanic, hates travelling, hates flying, so I when I asked him to join Swindon he said, "No chance." In the end, to get him to ride, I had to supply bikes for him, my mechanic from Poland had to fly with him to help him get there and then mechanic for him. He was living like a rock star, he had everything – he had it made. I've always put everything into my team, whatever it takes to win. I've probably tried too hard by lending engines – especially when it came down to the end of the year.'

Leszno had also waited a long time for a league championship medal and they faced Torun in their play-off final. Torun's team included Australian rival Ryan Sullivan, GP star Wieslaw Jagus and Matej Zagar. A massive 23,000 people watched Leszno win the first leg 49–41 with Balinski top-scoring with 13 points, while Leigh netted 10. Although hampered in the second leg by an injury to Jaroslaw Hampel, Leszno utilised the rider replacement facility to good affect to pull-off a 2-point victory and win the Polish Extra League Championship.

'That was definitely one of the highlights of my career,' he says with some satisfaction. 'To win for Leszno was unbelievable. We got close one year with second and we were always a top club. We brought in Hampel and the team just gelled. I have never seen an atmosphere like it. That was the biggest crowd I have seen there – even for a Grand Prix. Torun hadn't been beaten at home all year and we won there. And then, Irek, my translator, said, "We've got to go back to Leszno because we've got a presentation tonight!" It was a night meeting and we had to jump in our vans and drive all the way back there. Outside the stadium they set up big screens so people could watch it, and a massive big stage. At 12.30 or 1 in the morning, there were still 5,000 people there – it was amazing. 2007 was a really good year in Poland and I finished near the top of the averages. I was solid everywhere. To do it for Leszno was a dream come true.'

The MD of Leszno, Irek Igielski, agrees that it was a dream fulfilled for Leigh. 'His involvement with Leszno Speedway is fundamental. I can remember when he got onto the stage, he was holding the huge trophy with the gold medal in his teeth, he was so pleased with that trophy and I know it was one of his dreams to win the gold medal with the Leszno club. He did it and he was so pleased about it,' he says.

'For the past fifteen years he's been the best rider every single year and he was one you could always count on. He never complained about having three races in a row, a tactical ride, and was good for team spirit. I know there are a lot of Leszno riders who look up to him and try to learn more from him.'

In October 2007, Leigh's contribution to the Leszno Speedway club and the success he helped bring to the town was recognised when he was presented with an Honourable Citizen of Leszno award. Furthermore, on 26 January 2008, Mildura Rural City Council granted him a 'Key to the City' in recognition of his outstanding achievements in sport. He admits that it doesn't really have any materialistic meaning, but he is proud to have received such acknowledgment in both countries.

Looking back, Leigh believes that he hit his peak form in 2007. There were many things that came together for him that year. The input from Neil Drew was valuable, but the switch to GM engines made a big difference.

'I bought eight new engines and started again, and had a lot of testing to do. It was interesting, I loved it, I was like a kid with new toys because I was trying stuff non-stop. I can remember saying to Gary Patchett (Swindon co-promoter) that I was going GM and he said, "A change is as good as a rest." I can always remember that, and that's what it was, it was like a new lease of life for me.'

'It was like a new lease of life for me.'

Inspired by finishing runner-up in the World Championship, Adams was feeling confident about mounting another attack on the sport's ultimate prize. However, the shoulder injury he received as a result of that 'stupid crash' did give him some cause for concern.

'I thought I'd come back the next year stronger,' he says, 'and having got so close to the world title, I got the taste for it. I really went away and put in a lot of training and took a year off from Australia to let my shoulder heal. I got a specialist to look at it, who was the same guy, Dr Andrew Saies, who worked on my wrist back in '91. He's a great guy, a great orthopaedic surgeon and he'd been watching me on telly. He said, "Look, if you were younger I would operate, because the younger you are the muscle form hasn't built up properly, and that's when they can drop out. But now you're older you've got a lot more strength there." He did say if he operated on me he'd want me out for four months without riding a bike, and I didn't have the time for that. But him telling me that I would be fine was more for my own peace of mind.'

The road to World Championship glory is a hard one; no two seasons are the same. On your journey you'll pass the wreckage of broken dreams that's left by some who have gone before you, and you can expect to experience a full gamut of emotions during your quest for glory. In fact, the road is a maze, and no sat-nav in the world is ever going to be able direct you down the right route to take your place among the greats. It's discovered by a combination of experience, determination, talent and luck.

Over the next two years, Leigh Adams would have many of these experiences. The first two Grands Prix of 2008 illustrated perfectly the highs and lows of racing at the top level. During the first round at Krsko he scored 5 points in a meeting that was marred by wet weather. Every rider wants a good start to their world title campaign, and that was not it. But the next GP was at Leszno. Here he threw himself back into the hunt with a memorable victory.

'I wasn't that dominant through the meeting,' Leigh acknowledges. 'It was tough but I got things organised and set-up during the meeting. It was really slick, very unusual for Leszno because it's always pretty grippy and still is now. That was probably the highlight of the year.'

The next three GPs, on temporary one-off circuits, certainly weren't highlights, but for very different reasons. Gothenburg's Ullevi Stadium was dropped from the calendar in 2003 after an embarrassing postponement due to poor track preparation. There were some who felt that the 2008 meeting should have gone the same way because the marathon meeting resembled a demolition derby as the ruts and holes in the surface caused horrendous crashes. Leigh didn't enjoy the event one bit.

'I hated every minute of it, there were guys falling off everywhere,' he says. 'Gothenburg was dropped for a couple of years and it was the new, revived Gothenburg. But you had to run the ruts to be fast, and AJ (Andreas Jonsson) and Gollob had a crash right at the end of the straight. I was watching all these guys crashing and I thought this is not good. I was against both Rune Holta and Freddie Lindgren in the semi and Lindgren passed me on the inside and Holta on the outside. I wasn't committed to it, I didn't like running ruts because, mainly, they can shoot you everywhere and you're not in control. Lindgren was the only one that could ride the ruts and be safe that night. You carried a lot of speed down the straights there. You could drop off a fair bit of speed because the corners were quite tight, but the size of the place . . . it wasn't like a big circle where you could keep going and build up momentum. I didn't enjoy it at all.'

He left Gothenburg with 9 points, which put him fourth overall with 34 points, and trailed the leader, Pedersen, by 15. Unfortunately, after the Danish round in Copenhagen, he slipped down to fifth by adding just 8 to his total. That meant he travelled to Cardiff requiring a good result: a victory would be ideal, but a final appearance was almost a necessity.

Arguably, the track surface at Cardiff that year was the worst it had ever been. There were so many crashes caused by the inconsistent surface that afterwards Jason Crump called for the organisers to 'sort it out' because it was becoming dangerous. The first indication that it wasn't going to be Leigh's night was the result in heat 5. Adams and American Greg Hancock were involved in a photo finish at the chequered flag. While most people couldn't separate the two riders, the referee, Marek Wojaczek, gave the victory to Hancock when a dead heat seemed inevitable. Although disappointed with that verdict, it was a minor irritation for Adams and he got on with the business of racing.

Following his first four rides he had amassed a steady 7 points and he faced Rune Holta, Andreas Jonsson and Nicki Pedersen in his last qualifying race. Two points was considered to be enough to get through to the semi-final, and it would have been a big upset if he didn't make it. But no-one reckoned on the Polish referee, Wojaczek. The race only got as far as the first bend when it was stopped after Pedersen had slid off following the slightest of knocks from Adams. With the Australian on the inside, Nicki tried to get across from the outside and failed to complete the move. Furthermore, with the track full of ruts on the inside and being in front, Adams had the right to choose his line. Therefore, it was a clear-cut decision: first bend bunching, all four back. Not according to the ref who, to the amazement of the 40,000-plus audience and thousands more watching it on TV, excluded Leigh Adams.

'I was just shocked, basically. I came back into the pits and was giving my mechanics orders to prepare for the re-run, like, "Come on, let's go," and Tommy Cox was looking at the monitor and he goes, "You're excluded." I looked and said, "Nah, that's wrong, don't worry about that, let's go." And he said, "No, no, you're excluded, that's your colour. Look, they're showing the lights, you're excluded." I couldn't believe it, but what do you do? I fought my case with the referee, I spoke to him, but he was Polish anyway so I couldn't have a good one-on-one with him.

'Something must have gone wrong with his brain that night because he made the same stupid decision in the semi-final with Bjarne, when Nicki did exactly the same thing and he excluded Bjarne. That's what you call "your year" – you get kissed on the dick!

'I felt Nicki hit me because when you come into the corner, you want to get your back out but you can't, because he's there. It probably shot me past the corner a little bit. He milked it though, and he never said anything to me; it didn't bother him, he had the points in the bag.'

Kylie Adams also found it disappointing and hard to believe. 'I didn't think for one minute that Leigh would be out of the re-run, but when that became a reality, I was dumbfounded. It made me wonder whether it was all worth it. Leigh made his point heard at the time and afterwards, but sadly, nothing was going to change what happened.'

'It was one of those ones – do you laugh or cry?' says Leigh philosophically. 'You've got to laugh about it, but looking at the bigger picture I was chasing World Championship points and I needed a good one to get back up there.'

Leigh certainly didn't find anything to laugh about, and he was so incensed and upset by the decision that the normally affable Australian swore at the referee and it was captured on live TV. Wojaczek's handling of the meeting was universally criticised and he was removed from the list of GP referees. That didn't help Adams, whose World Championship hopes were as good as buried. He remained fifth, but was now 31 points adrift of championship leader, Pedersen. The Dane tightened his grip on the lead when he won the next round.

However, Leigh returned to form when he rode brilliantly at Mallila to win the Scandinavian GP by defeating Hans Andersen, and the two main protagonists Pedersen and Crump.

'That was my one hundredth Grand Prix,' he recalls. 'In Sweden they're always pretty good race tracks. Other than Lezsno, Mallila is my favourite GP track. Even when it rains they can still do things with it, and sometimes it can be better because working on it produces more dirt from the moisture. It was one that I always loved and it's out in the woods.'

Leigh is widely regarded as one of the most professional riders in the world. However, the goings-on at the final round at Gelsenkirchen, Germany, made him feel unprofessional. Another temporary surface was installed and the venue had a roof, so the chances of it getting called off due to the wet weather were nigh on impossible – or so we thought. Shockingly, it was postponed! The material had got so wet where it was stored that they couldn't dry it out and, embarrassingly, the GP organisers had to call it off. To make matters worse, the Super Prix was going to be concluded that night with a US$200,000 prize fund up for grabs.

'When we got there we knew they were in trouble, but we thought they'd sort it out,' he says. 'There had been times when we arrived at a GP and they had to cancel practice, but you'd come back the next day and it's sorted. Well, we came back the next day and it was worse.

'I don't know how he did it, but Ole Olsen managed to convince us; Nicki, Crumpie and myself, to go out and practice. But we couldn't turn and just cruised around. There were ruts in the track and they said, "Okay, come back tomorrow." We came back but it was worse still. That was when the penny dropped and we knew it really was in trouble. I still couldn't believe that they'd called it off because they had a bloody roof overhead and I remember thinking, it can't be. The surface was laid on concrete, so it couldn't drain anywhere and they just kept trying to get some air through the stadium and in the end they rotary-hoed the track to try and get air into it – that only made it worse. But it was so unbelievably wet, it was like clay, it just kept moving and it wouldn't settle.

Discussing track conditions with Nicki Pedersen. (Dave Fairbrother)

'I felt as though it degraded our sport,' Leigh sighs. 'You just get on with it and move on, but I felt unprofessional and felt as though it wasn't right. It was disappointing because BSI had put a lot of work in and IMG had come in that year. Since then I've seen a lot worse in other sports and it was one of those things that the organisers didn't think would happen – the impossible was made possible.'

However, there was still a final Grand Prix to be run to determine the finishing order. Therefore, as Gelsenkirchen was mainly a football stadium, an alternative venue had to be found. The choice of Bydgoszcz was not a popular one among the riders because not only had they been there a few weeks before, but it was also Tomasz Gollob's own backyard. And by virtue of his win in Copenhagen he was one of the qualifiers for the big money Super Prix final.

'I thought it was a farce,' Leigh says angrily. 'They said that it was the only track that could organise a GP in such a short space of time – what a load of crap! My thought was Wroclaw, they'd lost the GP that year, they had the facilities, perfect track, they had the manpower and it would have been a bit more neutral for everybody. It made a mockery of the Super Prix!'

Adams' own preparation for what was now called the Final Grand Prix, was far less ambitious than his normal routine. His decision to downsize his operation was influenced by the fact that he was due to ride at Torun in Poland the day after the rearranged GP.

'For the first time ever I flew in Saturday morning and didn't do practice, and sure enough, I qualified.'

'I was pretty pissed off with the GP at this time, I was stuck in sixth and I couldn't go up and I couldn't go down. For the first time ever I flew in Saturday morning and didn't do practice, and sure enough I qualified for my first final at Bydgoszcz. Normally I'd have the motor home, but I just went there with two mechanics, two bikes, a skeleton crew, a small Vito van and I made the final. It just proves that practice being an advantage is a bit of myth really.'

After the problems of laying temporary tracks at Gothenburg, Cardiff and the disaster at Gelsenkirchen, there were some who began to wonder if it was time to ditch the showpiece stadiums and revert to proper race tracks which, in turn, would hopefully produce better racing. With typical Aussie frankness, Leigh sums it up, 'How can you put it, you've got great stadiums with shit tracks, and shit stadiums with great tracks. My theory: redevelop the shit stadiums. But they want a showpiece – we'll have to see what happens.

'I don't know which way Benfield and IMG are headed,' he ponders, 'but I don't want to knock them because they've done a lot of good for the sport and done a lot of good for myself. I've made myself some money with the way in which the Grands Prix have turned out with television, it's gone to another level and we can go out and get our sponsors and give them value for money. I'd love to see some proper race tracks, though.'

If the World Championship was a bit of a disappointment for the Australian, then the achievements of his club, Swindon, were a pleasant surprise because at the beginning of the season they were written off as probable wooden spoonists. He led a young team to the play-offs that included Troy Batchelor, James Wright, Mad Korneliussen and, later, the highly-rated Croatian teenager, Jurica Pavlic.

In the semi-final they drew an away tie at Lakeside and the Robins were confident of pulling off a win because they had won there earlier that year when, during his first ever visit to the track, Pavlic shook British speedway by registering a 21-point maximum. Unfortunately for Swindon, Lakeside prepared the track so slick that it resembled a bowling alley, which meant that making fast starts would be paramount. Although Leigh top-scored with 14, they lost the match 56–33 and it was a frustrating experience. Troy Batchelor in particular registered his annoyance over the surface by being a bit over-zealous when he returned to the pits.

'Troy came speeding into the pits, put his bike on the side stand and wiped out Cookie (Jon Cook, Lakeside team manager)! He jumped up and started pushing Troy, so I jumped in and started pushing Cookie!' Leigh laughs. 'Then they all jumped in and started pulling us off each other. Troy was in the wrong, but I was just protecting my guy. I think it was more frustration than anything. We had a pretty good year because everyone wrote us off, and it helped me knocking around with the young kids. They all needed to be pointed in the right direction and shown what to do. I remember at the start of the year thinking that it was going to be hard work, but they all adapted pretty well.'

Leigh took the decision to rest during the Aussie season of 2007/08, but for the following campaign he decided to return to action and reclaim his Australian title – what would be a record tenth championship. He didn't just win a tenth title, nor rewrite the record books, he burned his name into the history books with a sizzling performance that saw him win all three rounds and also win every single race! There was no dispute about who the champion was.

'I didn't really make out that I wanted my tenth Aussie title, I don't race for records, although it's obviously a nice record to have. I wanted to go back racing again because I've always enjoyed my racing at home. I had a goal to win every race, not to be beaten and the competition was getting better and better – that was pretty cool to be able to do that. It was a nice way to set up the year.'

There were some doubts about whether or not he would enter the Grand Prix again. However, he felt that he had some unfinished business and maybe, just maybe, lady luck would shine a light on him this time. 'I had a lot of decisions that went against me in 2008, it just didn't go my way. I felt a bit hard done by and that's why I came back in 2009 – to give it another go.'

15

One Last Time Around the World

I t was freezing cold in Bydgoszcz in October 2009. Everyone was searching for big coats and woolly hats to insulate themselves against the very low temperatures. With minutes to go before the start of the last GP of the season, even Leigh Adams was seen sporting a furry trapper-style hat instead of his now familiar Owen Bros cap. Always the professional, it wasn't quite as important to wear the cap this time because he had announced his retirement from the Grand Prix during practice the day before.

Few were surprised after the very disappointing World Championship campaign that he'd endured. It started off reasonably well with a fourth place in Prague behind the sensational Russian Emil Sayfutdinov, Freddie Lindgren, and his long-time rival, Jason Crump. And with Leszno next on the agenda it looked promising.

However, at Leszno he had 6 points from his first three rides and required 2 more points to make the semi-finals, but then disaster struck.

'I was chasing Kenneth Bjerre when I hit a rut and I crashed into him and that put me out. It was really disappointing and every year we've really struggled to have a good start to the season, but we had a constructive start in Prague, so leading on from that it should have been fantastic. I was drawn at number one, but it was so slick you wouldn't believe it. And they kept watering the track, it was just a nightmare. I caught the water truck every race too so I'd come out to a freshly watered track – it was awful. It was one of the most depressing nights. That was kind of the start of where it all went wrong.'

A trio of temporary tracks followed and he scored 3 points in Gothenburg and then 6 in Copenhagen and told journalists that the championship had gone – 'it's over,' he said. That was followed by a nightmare in Cardiff where he finished with 3 again.

'Cardiff was rock bottom,' Adams says. 'I had mum and dad there and the results just weren't coming. I felt as though I rode okay at Cardiff, but I just couldn't make any starts and always had trouble with the big, deep ruts. It's just a bit of a flaw in my style that I tend to sit up when I hit big ruts, and I get the bike on the back wheel and just lose forward momentum. I've always struggled there, although I've managed to get by, but this time I just couldn't do it. That was really bad.'

As the GP concluded with the traditional fireworks display, Leigh sat in his motor home with his wife and was totally gutted by his performance. It was, perhaps, his lowest point for many years. He even wondered if he should 'pull the pin' on the Grand Prix there and then. After all, he had never been in it to make up the numbers. Predictably the response from his wife was an emphatic 'no'. While that thought was a knee-jerk reaction to a very upsetting night, one thing that Leigh isn't, is a quitter.

However, it was equally disappointing to lose the World Cup. During a rain-delayed and rain-affected final at Leigh's Polish track Leszno, it came down to a last-heat decider between Australia and Poland. The final heat saw Adams, the Leszno track specialist, versus Tomasz Gollob, Poland's hero. Gollob, though, had struggled and borrowed machinery from Krzysztof Kasprzak. However, Tomasz rediscovered his touch and out-gated Leigh and won a dramatic finale.

'I tend not to remember the ones we don't win,' Leigh jokes. 'If it had been held anywhere else, it would have been called off. The riders didn't want to ride after that downpour, but all the team managers went into a jury meeting with Ole Olsen, then all of sudden the Poles said, "No we gotta ride." I had no influence at all, even though Leszno was my home track. The promoters were only doing what the jury president wanted.

'I still believe, if it hadn't rained, we would have won because we were on top of the track and the Poles weren't. After the rain they scraped most of the dirt away and it played into their hands. It was devastating to lose and we wanted to win it badly. Gollob had done nothing all day, 3 points, then he jumped on Kasprzak's 'superbike' and he just smoked me. I tried to stick with him but he was gone. By that stage there was one big dirt line, where they'd pushed the mud out to the dirt, if you got in that you had no chance.'

When he scored 11 points in Daugavpils, Latvia, it seemed that he had turned the corner in the GPs, but although his performances were better than at the temporary venues this wasn't the Leigh Adams who was near the top of the British Elite League averages and leading Swindon to another play-off appearance.

'I knew it was going to be my last year and I don't know if that was playing on my mind or what,' Leigh muses. 'I got into this mindset that, if I had a bad one, ah, it doesn't matter, I don't need those points for next year. I've had a bad one and I don't need that to stay in the top eight. I was thinking negatively and I really believe that's why I ended up eleventh.'

He also believed that the effort wasn't going into the track preparation like it had been – 'they've either been slick or wet,' he said. In fact, the entertainment on track had been spoilt by the 'follow-my-leader' style of preparation but, hopefully, with a new race director, Tony Olsson, that will change.

Before his final GP in Bydgoszcz, Adams helped guide the Swindon Robins to the play-offs. With a team that included Matej Zagar and Simon Stead they defeated Coventry over two legs in the play-off semi-final. Their opponents in the final were the in-form Wolverhampton team, but ahead of that meeting Adams had an opportunity to add a title to his name that, until this point, had always eluded the Mildurian – the Elite League Riders' Championship at Brandon Stadium, Coventry.

His 12 points from the qualifying races put him in the semi-final from which he qualified to the Grand Final. He met the up-and-coming Australian Chris Holder, the league's top man, Freddie Lindgren and home hero Chris Harris.

'Deep down I wanted to win the thing because I had never won it. I had the last pick of gates and I was left with gate one, which was like the booby prize because no-one had done anything from that gate – you were really going to struggle to make the start because the others were pretty dominant. Chris Holder was off gate two and I was off one.

'Chris made the start on me, which I expected, but I just ran the kerb, literally, while the others went to the outside trying to stop each other and chase the dirt. The next thing I know is that I'm coming off the corner in front! I thought, this is good, and then you've got to close the door, go straight to the fence, close anybody coming down the straight

> **'Deep down I wanted to win the thing because I had never won it.'**

because you get such a good run coming off the corner. So I shut the door, and I won the race pretty easily because those two, Holder and Harris, were trying to pass each other. It was definitely nice to win it, to put that in the resumé.'

Confident, and inspired by that victory, the Swindon team travelled to Monmore Green for the first leg of the Elite League play-off final. However, Swindon were disappointing and they lost to Wolves, 54–38. Unusually, Leigh failed to win a race in his 8-point tally, and such was his disappointment that on the way back he hardly spoke. In the return, Swindon won 52–41, but Wolves did enough to break Swindon's hearts again.

'We had a really good team, possibly a lot better team than 2007. 2007 was strong, but we had our little flaws there, the Poles were always good at home but not very good away. I definitely felt as though we had the team to do the job. We ran solidly all the way through and we finished top. For some reason, though, we tapered off towards the end, and Wolves just picked up momentum and their last month was solid. I think everybody thought we were going to do it – it was very disappointing. It was one of the lows of the year and I felt as though I had let the team down in the first leg. I certainly didn't do the job that I should have – I was gutted!'

Even the influence of four-times World Champion Barry Briggs couldn't bring the title to Wiltshire, but his input in the pits did help and it would also play an interesting role in Leigh's last GP in Bydgoszcz.

'I was in the car and I got a phone call from Briggo and he said, "I'm coming down on Monday, do you mind if I come in and have a talk with the boys because I think, from what I can see, you're all just riding, you're riding around doing your thing and you're not racing, you're not putting that little bit extra in. Do you mind if I come into the pits?" And I said, "No, love to have you in there." So he came into the pits, typical Briggo, no bullshit, straight down the line, a few jokes, told us that we were cruising and what was needed. And we came out pretty strong, and we could hold our hand up and say that we went down fighting, we didn't roll over.

'I saw him at Bydgoszcz during practice and I said, "Thanks for doing that, that was really cool," and he said, "No problem." Then before the meeting I was walking around and he said, "Hey, what's the go tonight, do you need a hand?" And I said, "Yeah, come in," because I just like his style, so he linked up with me that night.

'I'd made a mistake against Gollob. I came off gate two, made a start over him but I didn't drop it enough and he just put his wheel over the kerb and passed me. I came in and Briggo said, "Right, that's your one mistake for the night, park that and get on with it." I said, "I made the start, I thought I had that covered." And he said, "Obviously you didn't because he was able to come up on the inside of you. Don't worry about it, that's your mistake for the night, you're allowed to make one, let's just get on with the rest of the meeting." Great approach.

'I knew it was my last one and it was a good vibe. The whole team was just enjoying themselves and we nearly won the thing. I got a big run on Sebastian Ulamek and then came up on the inside of Nicki Pedersen, but he

Leigh dispensed with his trademark Owen Bros cap for this trapper-style, furry hat for his final Grand Prix in Poland. (www.mike-patrick.com)

just stopped me in my tracks. If I had pushed it we would have both ended up in a big heap. It was right at the end of the straight, he turned left and stopped me; again, a crap track, everyone was just queuing up waiting for someone to make a mistake. It was a great result and a nice way to bow out of the World Championship. Randy was there, Kylie and the kids and it was good for the team because they'd put in a lot of work. It was the end of an era, and I had a smile on my face – I was quite proud of that.

'Regardless of the results, even if I had become World Champion, I was going to bail out. Kylie and I spoke about it at the start of the year and we agreed that it was the right time. I honestly believe that. We put everything into 2007, had a good year, but that was followed by a disappointing year.

Barry Briggs in the pits with Leigh during his last Grand Prix. Could Briggo have been the missing link to win the World Championship? We'll never know. (www.mike-patrick.com)

We thought I couldn't bail out like that so let's try again and see what we can do, still chasing the ultimate goal, to be World Champion.'

It will be an endless debate for speedway historians and enthusiasts: why someone as talented and professional as Leigh Adams didn't win the ultimate prize?

'I wasn't hard enough, that was one of the big things,' Leigh responds. 'I wasn't an aggressive rider and you needed to step it up another 10 per cent in the Grands Prix. I honestly believe it was because I wasn't hard enough. I put everything into it. I trained as hard, if not harder than anyone else. 2007 was my best and most consistent year, and that second place was the big one for me. Maybe if it wasn't going to happen then it was never going to happen. The next year I finished sixth, and then I thought, give it one more year, but it never materialised. I'm not bitter about it, I had great times in the Grand Prix, I won eight Grands Prix and I am not going to sit back in my chair and ponder about the ifs and buts and all that, I can't be like that. I wasn't good enough, it's as simple as that.'

Naturally, his parents are very proud of their son's achievements and, while they're disappointed for Leigh that he didn't win the world crown, they're proud that he's one of the best riders in the world.

John Adams reflects, 'When you get around the circle of speedway, people say he's one of the best riders in the world not to have won a World Championship. To me that's good. He's going to go home with enough funds to do what he wants to do, whether he won a World Championship or not. We'd love it, don't get me wrong, it would have been the icing on the cake, but the cake still tastes good without the icing.'

Privately, Leigh had told the author that he didn't want to be racing a speedway bike in his forties, and in early February he announced that the 2010 season was to be his last. With his children growing up and education playing such an essential role, now seemed to be the right time to start winding down his career.

He has no firm plans at present, but without a busy racing schedule he will have more time to fulfil some of the other motorcycle ambitions that he has.

'There are a couple of big enduros in Australia that I'd like to do,' Leigh says. 'There is one up in Alice Springs called "The Finke Desert Race" and it's probably the toughest desert race in Australia and some of my mates do it. There is also one in Mildura. They've always been things that I'd miss and I always enjoyed my dirt bikes. I'd like to go back, get fit and go pretty hard, not go there to make up the numbers, not that I'm going to go there and win it, but I want to put my best into it and do the best I can. So things like that I've always missed. I've always had to sacrifice something and go back to England.

'I'd like to go back home and retire, but I don't think I can because I can't sit still. I'm always doing something, I'm always busy – I'm pretty hyper!'

Although Adams has experienced a lot of success, he's put something back into Australian Speedway and he runs training schools when he goes home. And that's something he'd like to develop further.

'I do a two-day one when I do junior speedway on a Saturday and senior speedway on a Sunday. They're always well-attended. I enjoy them and the kids are the best. You've got to get them early because if they've got any

Skilful and silky smooth, the style of Leigh Adams. (Adams Family Archive)

bad habits you can knock it out of them. When they do get into seniors they really struggle to get rid of their bad habits, so you've got to correct them at grass roots level. That's a thing I'd like to do, try to set up an academy and it can only help!

From the Nowingi Salt Flats to the glamorous World Championship surroundings of the Millennium Stadium, Jason Lyons has ridden against and alongside his boyhood friend. At close hand he's watched the man they call 'The Book' or 'The Armchair Thriller' regularly show his back wheel to the best of his era, and baffle them with his speed and ability.

'He's one of the hardest riders to beat because he's so tidy and fast. He's not hard to beat because he's a dirty rider, but he is hard to beat because he is so bloody fast. It doesn't matter what the track is like, he makes it look smooth. He frustrates everybody because when you go to a rough track, Leigh is the sort of person you can go up to on that particular day, even if you're riding on the opposite team, you can go up to him and say, "What gearing have you got on, or how the bloody hell are you riding this place," and he'll suggest something. You'll still struggle to beat him though!

During the 2009/10 close season, Leigh Adams rode a Suzuki GSXR600 around the Phillip Island track during a Suzuki track day. He reached a speed of over 158mph, but then modestly said that once he got with the more experienced riders around the circuit, he 'ran out of talent.' That is something that he will never ever be accused of by anyone in speedway racing.

Major Honours

World Championship Record:

WORLD FINAL:

| 1993 | 4 pts | 15 th |

GRAND PRIX:

1996	28 pts	15 th
1997	42 pts	10 th
1998	51 pts	11 th
1999	67 pts	7 th
2000	65 pts	6 th
2001	69 pts	5 th
2002	127 pts	4 th
2003	126 pts	4 th
2004	131 pts	4 th
2005	107 pts	3 rd
2006	106 pts	5 th
2007	153 pts	2 nd
2008	125 pts	6 th
2009	81 pts	11 th

Grand Prix Appearances: 115
Grand Prix Finals: 20
Grand Prix victories: 8
Scandinavian Grand Prix Champion: 2002, 2007, 2008
Swedish Grand Prix Champion: 2004, 2007
Slovenian Grand Prix Champion: 2003

European Grand Prix Champion: 2008
Latvian Grand Prix Champion: 2007

Grand Prix Challenge Champion: 1995 & 1998
Grand Prix Challenge runner-up: 1996
Grand Prix Challenge, third place: 1997

International Honours:

World Under-21 Champion: 1992
World Cup Champion: 2001 & 2002
World Cup Silver Medallist: 2003 & 2009
World Cup Bronze Medallist: 2007
World Team Champion: 1999
World Pairs Silver Medallist (with Todd Wiltshire): 1990
Czech Golden Helmet Champion: 1999, 2000, 2001 & 2004
Commonwealth Champion: 1993
International Speedway Masters Series Champion: 1997, 1998, 2000, 2001

National Honours:

Australian Champion: 1992, 1993, 1994, 1998, 2000, 2002, 2003, 2005,
    2006 & 2009
Australian Under-21 Champion: 1988, 1990, 1991 & 1992
Australian Long Track Champion: 1992, 2000
Australian Best Pairs Champion (with Jason Lyons): 1992
Australian Junior Champion (Under-16): 1986
Australian Under-16 Pairs Champion (with Jason Lyons): 1986
Victorian State Champion: 1989, 1990, 1991, 1992, 1994 & 1995

Club Honours:

BRITAIN:
Poole 1989; Swindon 1990–92; Arena-Essex 1993–95; London 1996;
    Swindon 1997–98; King's Lynn 1999–2000; Oxford 2001–02; Poole 2003;
    Swindon 2004–10

Elite League Champion (Poole) 2003
Elite League Champion (Oxford) 2001
Elite League runner-up (Swindon) 2007 & 2009
National League Champion (Poole) 1989
Knockout Cup Champion (Poole) 2003
Knockout Cup Champion (King's Lynn) 2000
British League Cup Champion (Poole) 2003
Elite League Shield Champion (Swindon) 2008
Elite League Riders' Champion, 2009
Elite League Best Pairs Champion (with Lee Richardson) 2005
Elite League Best Pairs Champion (with Charlie Gjedde) 2004

POLAND:
Lublin 1991–92; Wroclaw 1993; Lublin 1994–95; Leszno 1996–2010

Extra League Champion (Unia Leszno) 2007
Extra League Silver Medallist (Unia Leszno) 2002 & 2008

SWEDEN:
Vetlanda 1994–95; Indianerna (Kumla) 1997–99; Masarna-Avesta 2000–08;
  Lejonen (Gislaved) 2009–10

Elite League Champion (Masarna-Avesta) 2000
Elite League runner-up (Masarna-Avesta) 2001

Bibliography

Books

Bamford, Robert (ed.), *Speedway Yearbook 2004*, Tempus Publishing, Stroud, 2005

Bamford, Robert & Shailes, Glynn, *The History of the World Speedway Championship*, Tempus Publishing, 2002

Domhnullach, Alasdair, *Speedway: An Introduction to the World of Oval Racing*, Empire Features, 1992

Loader, Tony, *Loader's Speedway Annual 1990*

Loader, Tony, *Loader's Speedway Annual 1991*

Loader, Tony, *Loader's Speedway Annual 1992*

Oakes, Peter (ed.), *Speedway Star Almanac*, Pinegen Limited, 2006

Oakes, Peter (ed.), *Speedway Yearbook 1990*, Front Page Books, 1990

Oakes, Peter (ed.), *Speedway Yearbook 1991*, Front Page Books, 1991

Oakes, Peter (ed.), *Speedway Yearbook 1993*, Front Page Books, 1993

Oakes, Peter & Rowe, David (eds), *World Speedway Yearbook 2009*, Peter Oakes Management, 2009

Periodicals

Speedway Star
Speedway Mail International
5-One Magazine